TOURING IN WINE COUNTRY
NORTHWEST ITALY

MITCHELL BEAZLEY

TOURING IN WINE COUNTRY
NORTHWEST ITALY

MAUREEN ASHLEY MW

SERIES EDITOR
HUGH JOHNSON

Contents

Touring in Wine Country Northwest Italy
published by Mitchell Beazley,
part of Reed Consumer Books Limited,
Michelin House, 81 Fulham Road,
London SW3 6RB
and Auckland, Melbourne, Singapore
and Toronto

First published in 1997
© Reed International Books Limited
1997
Text copyright © Maureen Ashley 1997
Maps copyright © Reed International
Books Limited 1997
All rights reserved

ISBN 1 85732 864 7

Editor: Lucy Bridgers
Senior Art Editor: Paul Drayson
Commissioning Editor: Sue Jamieson
Executive Art Editor: Fiona Knowles
Design: Watermark Communications
Picture Research: Claire Gouldstone
Index: Angie Hipkin
Gazetteer: Sally Chorley
Production: Christina Quigley
Cartography: Map Creation Limited

Typeset in Bembo and Gill Sans
Origination by Mandarin Offset,
Singapore
Produced by Mandarin Offset
Printed and bound in Hong Kong

Foreword

Wine, more than anything else that we eat and drink, is resonant with the sense of place. Wines are formed by the ecology of their region, their soils and climates – but what shapes their character is a broader amalgam. The whole culture of region and country, all the cross-currents of history that form its taste and individuality, determine the kind of wine its people are accustomed to.

All these factors, from the geology underlying the land, the summer rain and spring frost, to the ruling dynasties of centuries ago, form part of the elusive concept of *terroir*. The richer the region and the longer its fields have been profitably cultivated the more they stamp their personality on their produce. Why are the world's most valuable wines those from vineyards with the longest consistent records? Because every generation, every decision by their owners, has contributed to their unique qualities. (This is not to say they cannot be mishandled to produce poor wine, but that their potential is the sum of their past and present.)

You can, of course, understand wine without being aware of its origin and roots. It would be underestimating our ancestors to say that because they may never have seen a vineyard they could not appreciate and memorize its character. But we are in the happy position of being able to trace our wine directly back to the trellises, cellars and families that shaped it. It is a journey anyone can make. We can eat the food that they eat with it: become as it were honorary members of the community and culture that forms it.

No wonder wine tourism is growing exponentially. Once you have discovered the hospitality of wine growers, their desire to share (amazingly, often with their rivals too) and the way the wine community spans the globe in friendly collaboration you will want to explore it all.

Few regions are so tightly-defined, so homogenous, as the Alpine foothills of northwest Italy. Yet few, with so small a compass, produce a wider range of wines from such a small palette of grapes.

Piedmont feels, to the visitor, not so much at the foot of the mountains as a range of considerable hills locked in the embrace of encircling peaks. In spring and autumn a belvedere in Piedmont reveals an almost complete circle of snowy crags on the horizon.

These are the conditions, on the face of it, that produce an isolated culture with its own norms and customs. Piedmont can certainly show you buildings, customs, dishes and wines, forms of speech and dress you will find nowhere else.

But at the same time northwest Italy is crossed by some of Europe's most ancient and vital routes. Turin has the strategic position of the city before the Alpine passes, while Genoa on the coast is both a great port and the principal city of the tortuous coast road from Italy to France.

What comes as a surprise, in a region which produces some of Italy's most famous (and among reds most expensive) wines, is that they are a relatively recent invention. Noble names such as Barolo and Barbaresco seem to have the resonance of ancient history. In reality they took shape only in the latter half of the 19th century – and in their modern, luxurious forms they have scarcely existed more than 20 years. New kinds of wine, indeed, are still being devised to take advantage of grapes unknown elsewhere growing in the peculiar climate of the Alpine enclave.

One thing that does not change about Piedmont is its devotion to food. Meals are longer here, with more different dishes, than anywhere else in Italy. And the foggy autumn, when the uniquely pungent white truffles appear as if by magic, is a time of gastronomic pilgrimage from around the world.

Hugh Johnson

Northwest Italy

Picture-book images of Italy rarely include the northwest, so its glories are poorly known. This makes the discovery of its wonderful, diverse countryside and quiet villages even more exciting. From first touching Italian soil in the Aosta Valley, an amazingly beautiful landscape opens up which cannot fail to enthral.

Aosta gives way to the dreamy plains and rolling hills of Piedmont, the heartland of the northwest and the region where much of this guide is concentrated. For, from the most powerful of long-lived reds to the lightest, most delicate white, Piedmont's wines are numerous, varied and justifiably renowned. To the south are electrifying passes through the steep, high Apennine chain and the arresting splendours of the luminous Ligurian coast. While in the east, the gentle foothills of the Oltrepò Pavese, overlooking the lumbering Po River, bring the northwest to a tranquil end beside the plains of Lombardy.

The most rewarding times to travel are spring and autumn. Spring brings a riot of flowers, green, sprouting vines and fresh, bright days. Vineyard colours are magnificent in autumn, also the season of truffles and numerous festivals, not to mention the grape harvest. Summer is good for those who like the heat and appreciate long days, meals outside and fabulous sunsets. Winter, though, is risky. The lowish lands around the River Po and its tributaries, including much of central Piedmont, suffer frequent fogs. It can be wonderfully evocative walking under colonnades enveloped in a misty solitude and silence. However, unless you have few limits on your time, it can be restricting.

As well as vistas and wines there are numerous things to see and do: remarkable churches, villas and castles; intriguing craftworkers; artisanal producers of cheese or salami; magnificent, complex sundials adorning walls and much more.

Left *The diversity of the northwest's landscapes, here near Barolo, is reflected in an abundance of different foods and wines.*

Above *Nebbiolo, the finicky but supremely rewarding grape variety responsible for the northwest's greatest wines.*

Northwest Italy

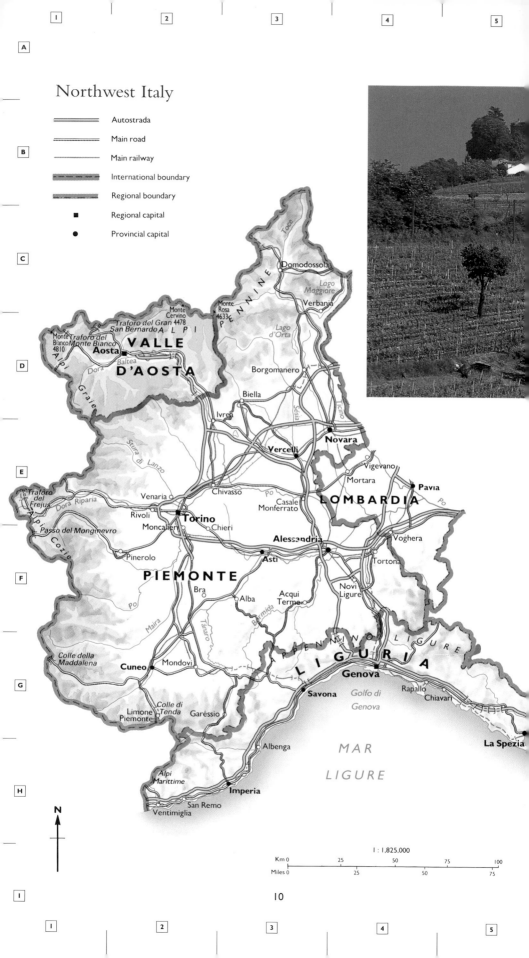

Autostrada

Main road

Main railway

International boundary

Regional boundary

■ Regional capital

● Provincial capital

Domodossola

Lago Maggiore

Toce

Verbania

A L P I

Monte Cervino 4478

Traforo del Gran San Bernardo

Monte Rosa 4633

P E N N I N E

Lago d'Orta

Monte Bianco 4810

Traforo del Monte Bianco

VALLE

Aosta

Baltea

Dora

D'AOSTA

Alpi

Graie

Borgomanero

Biella

Sésia

Ticino

Ivrea

Novara

Stura di Lanzo

Dora Riparia

Vercelli

Vigevano

Mortara

LOMBARDIA

Traforo del Frejus

Venaria

Chivasso

Po

Casale Monferrato

Pavia

Alpi Cozie

Passo del Monginevro

Rivoli

Torino

Moncalieri

Chieri

Alessandria

Voghera

Pinerolo

Asti

Tortona

Po

PIEMONTE

Bra

Alba

Acqui Terme

Novi Ligure

Maira

Tanaro

Bormida

A P P E N N I N O *L I G U R E*

Colle della Maddalena

Cuneo

Mondovi

LIGURIA

Genova

Rapallo

Chiavari

Colle di Tenda

Garèssio

Savona

Golfo di Genova

Limone Piemonte

La Spezia

Albenga

MAR

Alpi Marittime

LIGURE

Imperia

San Remo

Ventimiglia

N

1 : 1,825,000

Km 0   25   50   75   100

Miles 0   25   50   75

The few large towns are surprisingly uncluttered and characterful, the small villages harbour a multiplicity of delights. In short, touring in northwest Italy will be a revelation.

Above A patchwork of small vineyards, with different cultivation methods, interspersed with other crops. This is a frequent sight in the northwest, and seen here at Montemagno (near Asti), which is renowned for the quality of its Barbera.

THE ENOTECHE REGIONALI

You won't have to travel too far to find an *enoteca*. The word, which means 'wine collection', is interpreted broadly: wine shops, wine shops offering tastings, wine bars, even some *trattorie* serving wine by the glass may be included. Piedmont also has several semi-official, regional *enoteche*, sited in spacious, impressive surroundings, displaying wines from the immediate locality. There are good tasting facilities (usually free), and visitors with a real interest in wines will get serious attention. Some communes have a local *bottega* too – similar but with a reduced range and facilities. All are listed in the appropriate sections of this book.

TRAVELLING AROUND

The northwest is easy to navigate if you stick to the state (SS) and provincial (SP) roads. Others have an alarming tendency to finish in a dead end. Signposting is reliable throughout, although signs are often sited right at junctions, giving hardly any warning. There is also a good chain of motorways (AS for *autostrada*: signs in green). If planning to use them a lot, buy a toll debit, or Viacard. Otherwise, avoid the Viacard and residents' credit system lanes, or else you'll create a jam and make people very irate.

Part of the fun of travelling through vine country is identifying the most important vineyards (*crus*) and checking their aspect. So take a compass. It will also help you identify landmarks on the horizon. Pack a torch too: it is quite common in Italy for the electricity to be cut during storms.

Visiting estates

There is no barrier to visiting estates in northwest Italy. Most estates are small and family run and almost without fail producers are wonderfully hospitable and really enjoy receiving visitors and talking about their work. But, at the risk of sounding nannyish, it is important to remember that it is their work, not a hobby and, with the best will in the world, they can't always drop everything to give you an hour or so of their time. A few estates are happy for you to drop by on the off-chance; a goodly number insist that you book first by telephone; and in both cases this is noted in the information given on individual producers. The rest, however, strongly welcome a telephone call to advise them you will be visiting – if only to save them the embarrassment of not being able to offer you the level of hospitality they would like, or maybe so they can, for example, get their neighbour's daughter in to act as interpreter. So, always telephone first – you'll get a far better reception if you do and you won't waste time trying to find producers who are working in vineyards several kilometres away. NB The foreign languages spoken on wine estates have been given in abbreviated form after the telephone number.

Some estates, reasonably enough, restrict visits to working hours, roughly between 8.00 or 8.30 to 6.00 or 6.30 Monday to Saturday, with a sacred two hours or so reserved for lunch. If you do want to visit late or on a Sunday, choose an estate where 'working hours only' isn't stipulated in the text and ask gently. If there is the slightest

Below *Young vines hardening in the winter sun of Canale, in the sandy hills of the Roero district.*

Right *Street art in Neive, one of the three communes in the Barbaresco zone.*

hesitation by the producer, back off immediately: it probably means he prefers not to see you then but is too generous to say so.

You may find few people around on either side of the first weekend of April, the period of Italy's most important wine fair, while January and August are common holiday months. Harvest time (mid–September until the end of October) is the most exciting but producers are very hard-pressed and may have less time for you.

If arranging appointments from home before leaving (the code for Italy is 0039), it's safer to reconfirm once you are in the area. But it is not necessary to give vast amounts of notice. A day or so is ideal; even half an hour may well be enough. You'll notice while travelling around that few estates are signposted, especially the smaller ones, which may consist of no more than an average-sized house, so it is wise to set off with clear instructions.

Once you have arrived most producers will show you round the cellar, explaining how they make their wines, age them, bottle them and so on. Surprisingly few, however, will think to show you the vineyards. If you want to see them, ask. Nearly all estates will let you taste their wines. A few charge for this (these are noted in the text) but most are happy to open a bottle or two for free. There is no obligation to buy wine, but do so out of courtesy, especially if the producer has given lots of his time and/or opened lots of bottles.

There is no better way to get to know the wines of an area than to meet the people who make them and no better way to get the most out of an area than through talking with those who live there. Both are strong reasons for visiting estates. But the most important is that it is great fun. So don't be put off: you will have tremendous memories of some fabulous encounters.

AGRITURISMO

Agriturismo (or agritourism) started as a way of giving townies an idea of what working country life was all about, now it is just a pleasant, comparatively inexpensive way of staying in the Italian countryside. You rent a simply furnished apartment (usually; a few offer rooms in villas) on a farming estate and are left to your own devices. If meals are provided, they will usually be predominantly from foodstuffs grown on the estates. Agritourism can be a delightful way of resolving the accommodation problem, combining the peace of country life with the independence of having your own apartment. However, despite firm regional controls on what must be offered, standards vary widely, from the impeccable to the thrown together – and the best are booked up fast.

There are plenty of agritourism enterprises in the wine areas of northwest Italy. There are relatively few, however, actually on wine estates. Lists of this type of accommodation are kept by all the tourist offices (for their province only) and should also be available at all the chambers of commerce.

Above *Wine villages and wine routes, enticing either way, particularly here in the Alba zone.*

Viticulture

There are vineyards of all shapes and sizes in the northwest: from pocket handkerchief-sized plots to vast expanses; from thick, old, poorly-productive stumps of plants, to slim, vigorous new growth; from widely spaced vines to the densest of plantations; from low-trained bushes to high-trained pergolas; and from the neatest of lovingly tended patches to rather casually grown parcels. There are as many reasons for these variations as the differences are numerous but local traditions, the grape variety and the value of the crop are all important factors. In general, though, vineyards are small, often uneconomically so. Comparatively few producers own enough vineyard to supply all their needs – and even if they do it may well be scattered around in a number of small plots. Several lease vineyard or possibly buy grapes from local, trustworthy growers to make up the shortfall.

Growing grapes on a good site is paramount in this area of Italy where the weather can be variable, where there is a notable difference in temperature between sunny and shady spots and where the innumerable hills give an infinite variety of aspects and exposures. All cultivation of any worth will be on hills – across the slope if it is not too steep or on terraces, a method used far more extensively in the past. The sunnier sites are the finest: the Piedmontese dialect word *sorì*, meaning (roughly) sun-bathed, is often prefixed to the vineyard name of those that are so blessed. The additional exposure of sites across the crest of a hill is also prized; once again these are described in Piedmontese dialect, by the word *bricco*. The finest sites, the *crus*, are often obvious, even to the casual observer. The vines are trained low, often quite close together, stretched across wires on a grid formation of great accuracy, and neatly cultivated into perfectly tidy shapes.

These days the tendency is to increase the density of planting as, despite the increased costs and intensity of labour, most believe that quality benefits greatly. There is also a consensus that, for many of the grape varieties, the best training method is guyot, where the trunk is kept as a short stump and one or two canes are trained horizontally from it to provide the fruiting shoots of the year's growth. One of those shoots then becomes the following year's cane. Pruning, done during the vine's winter rest period, not only reforms these shapes but, vitally, restricts growth. Wine laws specify a maximum yield but the best growers aim for even lower maxima, sometimes even lopping burgeoning bunches to concentrate quality in those remaining.

The vine's growth restarts in early spring. Buds at this point are susceptible to frost damage although harm is not irreparable. A patch of warm weather will see shoots spurting remarkably quickly and growers not consistently active in neatening or tying growth to wires may be left

Above It's vital to pick grapes into small containers so they are not crushed and split before arriving at the cellars.

Below *A large bunch of Nebbiolo grapes, for making Barolo. Top producers pinch out any imperfect berries before crushing the bunches.*

Below *The delicate Moscato grape glistens gold and translucent when ripe and, in good hands, produces an enticingly scented, grapey wine.*

with a mass of tangle. The vine flowers in late spring/early summer. This is a period where fine weather is crucial to ensure a full pollination and avoid malformed or partially formed berries – an annual concern. Vine flowers are not particularly attractive, nor perfumed, however. During the growing season some growers leave the grasses that spring up around the vines to fix the topsoil, others plough them in for humus, a few expunge them with herbicides. As the bunches form, growers usually trim some foliage to give better light- and sun-exposure. Grapes develop their colour in the month before full ripeness. A spot of rain at this point to flesh them out, especially if the summer has been hot and dry, is a help. The harvest itself, which lasts from early September to late October, the whites ripening earlier, needs to be dry. Wet weather creates dilution, rot and terminally depressed producers.

GRAPE VARIETIES

The grape variety used will affect the flavour of a wine as much as the variation in taste between a Granny Smith and a Golden Delicious apple, say. The northwest is blessed with a large number of grape varieties, both red and white and most wines are made from single varieties, without blending, so the character of the grape clearly determines the character of the wine. The features of each are described as they are encountered along the wine routes. Producers are, in general, strongly convinced of the high quality of their grape varieties and proud of their characteristics. That, however, does not stop them experimenting and the international varieties Cabernet Sauvignon, Chardonnay, Sauvignon Blanc and so on crop up in a number of wines, sometimes in intriguing blends with the native grapes.

Winemaking

RED WINE

The colour in red wines comes from grape skins, as do tannins and other flavouring elements that give red wine its particular properties. Therefore the grapes are first crushed, to bring skins and juice (called must) into contact and they then ferment together. Temperature has to be carefully controlled: too low and there's poor extraction from the skins; too high and the wine picks up baked, 'off' flavours. The skins, being light, tend to rise to the surface and various techniques are employed to keep them immersed in the vat so they macerate fully and (just as important) are not attacked by bacteria. Once enough extraction has occurred the juice is separated from the skins and fermentation finishes without them. The skins are pressed to release the remaining juice and some of this press wine may be added to the main batch. Each producer (or his consultant) decides the best temperature for the particular crop, how long to leave the juice on the skins and whether to add in some press wine – and judgements will differ from year to year. If a blended wine is being made, the varieties are usually fermented separately, as they tend to ripen at different times, and are combined later. Occasionally they are mixed at the beginning.

After fermenting, some reds go into oak casks for a while. The traditional casks, called *botti*, are large (holding 25 hectolitres or more), made from Slavonian oak (occasionally chestnut) and are used for many years, maybe even a century. These soften the wines, round them out and help them to mature without adding an overtly oaky character – the wines have enough flavour already. Recently, however, there has been an increasing trend to use *barriques*, small (225 or 500 litres), new or practically new barrels of

French oak, for part or all of the maturation period. It has changed wine styles dramatically. Some now regard *barriques* as *de rigueur*; others can't stand them – it's a matter of taste.

Reds may be fined, to draw out substances that could cause cloudiness later on, and might be filtered. Once bottled, they are usually left for a few months at least to settle before being released for sale.

WHITE WINE

The freshness and fruitiness of white wines comes from the pulp of the grape, hence bunches will be pressed immediately to separate the skins from the juice and only the latter fermented. Occasionally, though, winemakers will leave the skins with the juice for just a few hours and at a very low temperature, for a firmer, fleshier style of wine. In either event the skin-free must is clarified, either by leaving it to settle at a low temperature or by centrifuging, so that what ferments is clean and gunge-free. White juice is more delicate than red and fermentation temperatures are kept lower, typically by about 10°C. As white wine is rather sensitive to oxygen, air will be excluded as much as possible throughout, some cellars having highly sophisticated techniques to prevent any air contact whatsoever.

White wines are also mainly kept in inert containers. Stainless steel are most popular although older cellars will have vitreous-lined cement. Occasionally *barriques* are used and, if so, most producers prefer both to ferment the wine and mature it in them.

Nearly all whites are fined and most are cold stabilized (chilled right down to precipitate out crystals of tartrate, a natural wine constituent which, inconveniently, becomes insoluble when the temperature drops) and filtered. Some sulphur dioxide is also added at one or more stages of the winemaking and at bottling, to deactivate any stray bacteria or yeast problems and prevent the wine from oxidizing. It is a necessary evil which is undetectable and harmless if added lightly. If there is too much it may give a 'morning after' head where your temples seem held in a vice-like grip. (Reds usually have much less.)

Whites may be sold as early as six months after the harvest, maybe even sooner. Italians love drinking white wine very young and even the top growers find it hard to resist their customers' pleas for wines ever earlier in the season.

ROSATO WINE

Pink wine is made from red grapes, macerated on the skins for just long enough to give the requisite pink colour. From then on winemaking continues as for white wine.

SPARKLING WINE

Most sparkling wine is made by adding yeast and sugar to a dry wine and letting it re-ferment, trapping the carbon dioxide bubbles that are formed. Piedmont's famed Asti Spumante is different. For details *see* page 84.

Above *Gaja's cellars in Barbaresco exemplify the investment needed for fine wine production: temperature controlled stainless steel vats and long-seasoned barriques of finely grained, new French oak.*

Left *A moment of intense concentration at Cantina Bava to ensure only healthy grapes are conveyed to the crusher.*

Wine classification

WINE LAW

There is absolutely no need to understand Italy's wine classification system to understand the wines of the northwest, but it may help to have a bit of background, especially if meeting producers or shopping for wine.

Most of the wines you will encounter will be DOC (*Denominazione di Origine Controllata*) or DOCG (the G standing for *e Garantita*). These are the offical categories for wines whose production is controlled, along with the less tightly regulated IGT (*Indicazione Geografica Tipica*). Anything else is simple table wine (*vino da tavola*). The *denominazione* (denomination) rules principally concern genuineness of style and origin. Hence, each DOC regulation lays down growing area boundaries, grape varieties, minimum ageing requirements and so on, together with maximum yields, minimum alcohol and other analytical data. DOCG criteria are somewhat tighter than DOC but when they were created, entire zones were 'promoted' from DOC, not just the best areas or wines within them.

The DOC system dates from the early 1960s but in 1992 a major revision took place, whose effects are very slowly changing nomenclature, vineyard structure and thinking. The main development is that sub-zones and smaller areas, even single vineyards can be recognized and gain their own DOC or DOCG, with increasingly severe production constraints the smaller the area. In addition, innovative wines, usually from non-traditional grape varieties, which had simply remained outside the system are now being drawn into it. Another change particularly affects the northwest where, traditionally, many wines have been named by grape variety followed by provenance: Grignolino d'Asti, say, or Nebbiolo d'Alba. Following EU guidelines geographic names are now taking precedence over varieties. So, for example, a wine previously called Arneis delle Langhe becomes instead Langhe Arneis.

DISTRIBUTION OF WINE STYLES

In most parts of Italy the denominated zones are usually more or less discrete: disregarding the nesting of sub-zones and smaller areas and the occasional choice of denomination based on qualitative distinctions, any piece of wineland is likely to be the domain of one or at most two distinct DOC(G)s. The northwest or, more precisely, its central region of Piedmont is different. Across most of the wine production area several grape varieties are grown and as wines are generally named by the grape name as well as geographically it is more usual for there to be several overlapping DOC(G)s in force.

For example, the small village of Alice Bel Colle in the province of Alessandria is denominated for five varieties: Dolcetto d'Acqui, Brachetto d'Acqui, Barbera d'Asti,

Above *Tying down the canes which will produce the following year's growth is a lengthy but important task.*

Top *Winter fog gives the Langhe vineyards a melancholic, reflective air. The Italian for fog is* nebbia*, hence the name of the Nebbiolo variety.*

Moscato d'Asti, Cortese dell'Alto Monferrato. The geographical part of the name is sometimes the province, for example 'Asti', although, as can be seen from the instance above, the DOC(G) border may not tally with that of the province itself. Alternatively, the areas may comprise territories that straddle provinces, for example, Alto Monferrato; parts of provinces, Alba, say or Acqui; or communes, for instance Casorzo d'Asti or Chieri, although once more the DOC area is unlikely to tally with the administrative one. Even where wines are named purely geographically, for example, Gavi, Barolo, Lessona, these are hardly ever the sole denominations covering the district.

If it all sounds terribly confusing and a glance at the map on pages 82–3 does nothing to alleviate matters then, for now, simply ignore the whole thing. For each locality has only one or two varieties that are of prime importance and each section of the book concentrates just on these, enabling you to get to know the grapes, their styles and their domains as you come across them. And after covering a couple of the itineraries and tasting a handful of wines it will all start to fall into place.

Food and eating out

EATING OUT

Eating out in northwest Italy is a joy. Unless you happen to be in a particularly touristy area (the coast, say, or the lakes), pop into any *trattoria*, especially one where people are eating alone and you're likely to eat well, maybe much better than you could have imagined. There may not be a brilliant wine list, nor even staff who know what's what in the wine world but the chances are you won't drink badly. And even though prices have been rising inexorably in this prosperous part of Italy over the past few years, you can still have a really good meal without it costing a fortune.

In some places, though, there is no written menu, and waiters tend to recite the choices at break-neck speed. They will repeat, slower, if asked and will normally make every attempt to help you to understand – they want you to pick dishes you will like, after all. If there is an offer to choose for you, accept; you'll probably get whatever is best and freshest that day. In any event, choosing is often a much more collaborative procedure in Italy. In fact, eating out is far less formal in general. Even in the smartest places it can seem like eating in an acquaintance's home and everyone is genuinely keen that you really enjoy your meal. Dress up or down as much as you like too, no one worries much. And children are expected to join in the feast.

It is always wise to book first. Apart from avoiding turning up at a restaurant already full or closed for holidays (there's no pattern to this), alerting the staff to your foreign status can get you a special welcome.

A TYPICAL MEAL

There is no such thing as a typical northwest Italian meal. How could there be, when territory ranges from mountain pasture to coastal bay, where the staple may be pasta or rice and the principal fat lard, butter or olive oil? Throughout the book, therefore, traditional, local foodstuffs and specialist dishes are described, area by area. However, the most widespread diet is that of central Piedmont, the heart of the northwest. Here, a meal typically begins by a nibble of real *grissini*. These are long (maybe half a metre), crusty and a world away from the pre-packed, commercial types.

The unique aspect of eating in Piedmont – and a trap for the unwary – is the number of *antipasti* (starters) served. A minimum of three or four is normal, five or six is quite common and the more important the meal (or the restaurant) so the number grows. Salami are usually included, as are various vegetable-based dishes and this is the area where cooks show their inventiveness. The next course, the *primo*, the pasta (or rice) course, has two leading specialities. *Agnolotti dal plin* are small, squarish meat-stuffed ravioli, closed with a pincer that lightly squeezes them, usually served with *ragù* (meat sauce) or butter and sage. *Tajarin* are

very thin taglietelle, homemade from egg pasta (sometimes using the yolk only) and dangerously moreish.

At the main course, the *secondo*, meat is to the fore. *Brasato al barolo* is a rich, succulent braise of beef, cooked in Barolo; other specialities are *bollito misto*, a huge array of boiled meats, served with various relishes and *fritto misto*, a remarkably filling plateful of various deep fried, largish morsels, savoury and sweet. Sausage, lamb, chicken, sweetbreads, courgettes, mushrooms, peaches, almond biscuits, may all be included. In restaurants it may need ordering in advance. Other important dishes are *vitello tonnato*, a summer dish of cold roast veal, covered with a creamy tuna sauce and *bagna cauda* (or *caoda*). This winter warmer may be a starter, main course or entire meal. Vast quantities of raw vegetables are served and each participant picks and dips them in his own powerfully flavoured 'bath' of olive oil, garlic and anchovy, kept warm by a small spirit lamp. It is best in large groups with lots of time and loads of alcohol.

In autumn mushrooms are used extensively, as are white truffles (*see* page 53). Otherwise, use of vegetables is variable but always seasonal. There are good local cheeses, while leading desserts are the extremely indulgent *panna cotta*, crème caramel made with pure cream and *Bonet* (or *Bunet*), a chocolate-rich custard pudding. Piedmont has good nuts too, especially chestnuts and hazelnuts.

FOOD SHOPPING

Italians still prefer buying foods at small, specialist shops and most shop daily. So, although there are plenty of (increasingly popular) supermarkets, few have the range and quality you might find at home. But every town has its butcher, cheese shop and *salumeria* (for cured meats, salami, prosciutto etc) and bread is widely available. Fruit and vegetable shops are abundant too, while the larger towns have daily markets, most mornings only and much frequented. There are also plenty of small 'convenience stores'. In short, unless you insist on shopping during early afternoons, when shopholders are eating or sleeping, buying what you need for picnics or self-catering could hardly be easier.

Top left *Gnocchi, made from potato flour, a typical dish of Liguria, enlivened with* basilico (basil) *and cheese shavings.*
Far left *Antipasti don't have to be complicated: some olives and olive paste, a large plate of anchovies, good butter (and crusty bread) make a regal starter.*

Near left *The bright colours of peppers, a Piedmont speciality, abound in markets and greengrocers in summer months.*

Rice

The foodstuff most vital to northwest Italy is not, as you might think, the white truffle. Nor is it Liguria's abundant production of olive oil. It is rice, rice for risotto, that wonderful, creamy, filling dish that absorbs and combines so well with numerous other flavours – especially those of the truffle. Travel around northern Piedmont, east from Ivrea and Turin across the Po Valley flatlands of Vercelli and Novara provinces, and you will see mile after mile of paddy fields, neatly carved into largish, rectangular plots, each bordered by a small canal. These run into larger canals, which themselves flow out into one of the major canals that drain the area. The water can course through the larger canals at quite a lick and its passage has to be well controlled. In fact, the whole system is well controlled, a remarkable tribute to the cooperative venture that runs the industry.

There are two main types of rice, Japonica, which has a short grain and, with starches mainly on the inside, is quite

Above *Green shoots of rice growing in flooded paddy fields in the heart of the cultivation zone, near Vercelli.*

Left *Perfectly cooked grains of well-flavoured rice, a good few shavings of white truffle: there is little to match a good risotto.*

absorbent but whose structure is not very resistant to cooking, and Indica, with a longer grain and more starches on the outside, which is more resistant but less absorbent. Japonica was originally the type planted in Italy but for a good risotto the rice has to be both resistant and absorbent. It also needs starch on the outside of the grain as well as on the inside so the risotto can become good and creamy and the grains hold together. So today's rice has developed from various Japonica-Indica crosses.

There are many rice varieties and each cook swears that one or another is patently superior. *Arborio* is probably the best known outside Italy but *Vialone Nano* and especially *Carnaroli* are regarded even more highly. Regardless of variety, rice comes in different qualities, mainly depending on the grain size: length, appearance and shape. Very roughly, the longer the better. *Originario* is the smallest and roundest and is usually used for soups; *semifino* and, one stage up, *fino* are of middling quality and tend to be used for puddings and similar. The quality for risotto has to be the best, *superfino*.

Rice seed is planted around April and the fields are immediately flooded so that it can germinate: the water is warmer than the air. Lower-growing plants have now been developed to reduce the wind damage that can decimate the crop. Harvesting is in September or October. The rice must first be dried – the slower the better. Then the cereal is separated from its husk. At that stage the grains are graded: any green (showing unripeness) or misshapen ones are removed and the rest are sorted by thickness. Some is packed at this stage to be sold as wholegrain rice (*riso integrale*), the rest is shelled and sold as refined rice (*riso raffinato*) – the whiter the better. All the processes have been mechanized to a greater or lesser extent, yet, rather as with wine, the lesser the mechanization and the more old-fashioned and labour intensive the methods used, the better the end product. The best cooks who really care always search out the few remaining artisanal producers.

Surprisingly, rice does not keep all that well and can pick up germs, although the vacuum packs now on the market have diminished the problem. To delay its decline, rice should be kept in the dark and those who know always buy the smallest quantity possible, replenishing as and when required, rather than keeping stocks. In any event it is safe to regard its lifespan as no more than one year and throw out all stocks in winter when the store-cupboard rice will have come from the previous harvest and the new crop will be on sale. Doing a winter clearout of the larder, of all starches, dried pulses and so on is part of good Italian housekeeping — maybe on New Year's Eve?

As for cooking risotto, don't worry about stirring continually — just give the dish a jolly good stir every couple of minutes. Time it by bite, rather than by the clock, and don't wash the rice beforehand, you'll remove the starch that holds it all together. But for a really good risotto, try one while in Piedmont.

How to use this guide

Above Barbaresco's evocative signs mean you can't miss spotting the commune's most prized crus.

You may have purely a passing curiosity in the wine of northwest Italy, it may be just one of several reasons for making a trip to the area or it could be your main motive. Whichever the case, this book will enable you to find the best, most captivating vineyard scenery and the most interesting producers as well as shedding light on the hows and whys of the wines produced in each locality.

While travelling in the northwest you can hardly fail to come across vines and local wines. Yet trying to find the road to get a closer view of the vineyards without being diverted off in the wrong direction or ending up in a muddy ditch can be extremely irritating; as can not knowing where to buy decent wine or which restaurants will provide both good food and good wine. This book will remove these frustrations. It leads you through all the region's wine producing areas, in a series of picturesque routes that have been carefully planned to show the vineyards at their best, both close to and panoramically. It also points out the most important *crus*, the prestige vineyard sites of greatest renown. The routes are generally fairly short, on average lasting a couple of hours at a leisurely pace and ignoring stops, but may take just half an hour or occasionally a whole day.

If wine is simply an adjunct to a more general tour, just pick any route that coincides with where you happen to be. Otherwise, one will lead on to the next, taking you on a complete round trip from northwest Italy's breathtaking Alps to its magnificent coastal riviera and back. The starting point is the Mont Blanc tunnel, by the French border, but the tour can be picked up at any point, whether arriving by air at Turin (page 41), Genoa (page 97), Milan Malpensa (page 139) or Milan Linate (page 119), or by car taking a different border crossing. The itineraries give suggestions for those wanting to plunge in even deeper or cut out bits; they are anything but rigid.

Additionally, at every stage, background information on the wines of the zones you are travelling through is given. Each section can stand alone but will also build up into the full picture – enough to make you a wine buff but not a wine bore.

WINE PRODUCERS

Thumbnail sketches of local wine producers form an important part of the book. Those that are included have been chosen mainly for the quality of their wines but also for their welcome to visitors. They are listed by their location, even if they make wines from elsewhere. If you want to visit any – and it will put everything in a new light if you do – make sure you read pages 12–13 first.

RESTAURANTS

There are suggestions for eating out from the smartest restaurant to the simplest *trattoria*, many with tables outdoors in summer (or air conditioning), and all featuring good wines, whether they offer just a few choices, a huge list or just rather good house wine.

FOOD AND WINE SHOPS

The better food shops are listed too, for those self-catering, planning picnics or wanting something intriguing to take home, and naturally the *enoteche* – places to buy and sometimes taste wine – are highlighted.

HOTELS

The most convenient stopping-off places along the route are indicated, together with some recommendations for comfortable, friendly hotels in which to stay. A few agritourism apartments (*see* page 13) are listed too.

PLACES OF INTEREST AND SPECIAL EVENTS

The most interesting cultural and historical sites in northwest Italy are pinpointed, as are any festivals and celebrations with a wine or food interest.

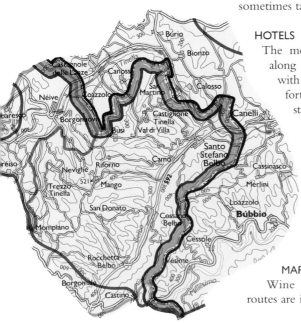

MAPS

Wine maps illustrating the described routes are included in the relevant sections.

Aosta and Northwest Piedmont

Of all the ways to arrive in Italy, none is more thrilling than to emerge from the gloom of the Mont Blanc tunnel into the sparkling brightness of the Aosta Valley and to start a rapid descent, sensing the whole country opening out before you. It is tempting to stay on the *autostrada*, to hasten arrival in Piedmont, tempting, but a mistake. Practically all the *autostrada* in the upper Aosta Valley, the part between the border and Aosta town, runs through tunnels, depriving you of some magnificent views; the alternative, the *statale* is generally a good, straightish road; also, vitally, the Valle d'Aosta boasts some remarkable vineyards, which would be a great pity to miss.

The first vineyards of Piedmont form the tiny area of Carema with wines from the famed Nebbiolo grape. The strangeness of the cultivation system cannot fail to surprise and the intensity of labour required to form its steep terraces, held by dry stone walls, and tall columnar supports cannot fail to impress. The Canavese begins as soon as Carema ends and there is a sudden change in wine styles, from generally assertive reds to elegant whites, with some soft sweet versions. The area marks the sudden opening out of the river valley and heralds a sweep down to Turin. Of all Italy's major cities Turin is probably the least well known and, as such, its best kept secret. Anyone imagining it as a mainly industrial place is in for a huge surprise.

After Turin, you may wonder why you should travel east towards Chieri instead of straight down to the hills of the Roero. Chieri, after all, is no great shakes: a small, busy, industrial town, set in a rather uninspiring plain. But some surprises are in store. Not just unusual grape varieties, not just unexpecedtly fine countryside but more...

Left *Ancient towers and lush trees contrast vividly with the stark Alpine peaks of the upper Aosta Valley.*

Above *The low-trained vineyards of Morgex are almost lost in a mass of spring flowers.*

Valle d'Aosta

THE WINES

Vines in the Aosta Valley grow in discrete plots, with many vine-free areas. In order to ripen in the harsh conditions of the narrow, steep-sided high valley (many vineyards at well over 500 metres), most are on tiny, precipitous terraces and all are on southeast- or south-facing slopes. This means, in practice, that nearly all are sited on the left bank of the river – the Dora Baltea (which flows into the Po at Turin). If you are travelling through the area in early morning or late afternoon it is all too apparent how vineyards cluster in the patches where most sun penetrates, avoiding the long shadows of the towering mountains.

Cold as it may be in winter, the valley attracts considerable heat during the day in summer (which nevertheless dissipates overnight) and the speed of the Dora Baltea's flow discourages the build-up of cloud. Nevertheless, viticulture is at best marginal here and many of the wines are intriguing rather than mind-blowing, despite the superhuman efforts of the growers to combat all that nature throws at them. The vast majority of wines are made by cooperatives:

Below Bright winter days and clear air makes the upper Aosta Valley a skier's paradise.

Valle d'Aosta

═══════	Autostrada
▬▬▬▬▬	Main road
─────	Main railway
▬▬▬▬▬	International boundary
▬▬▬▬▬	Regional boundary
■	Regional capital
─────	DOC boundary
	Wine route

VALLE D' AOSTA SUB ZONES

1 MORGEX ET LA SALLE
2 ENFER D' ARVIER
3 TORRETTE
4 NUS
5 CHAMBAVE
6 ARNAD-MONTJOVET
7 DONNAZ

Left *The vineyards of Carema, on the edge of Piedmont, are close to the lowest point of Aosta Valley.*

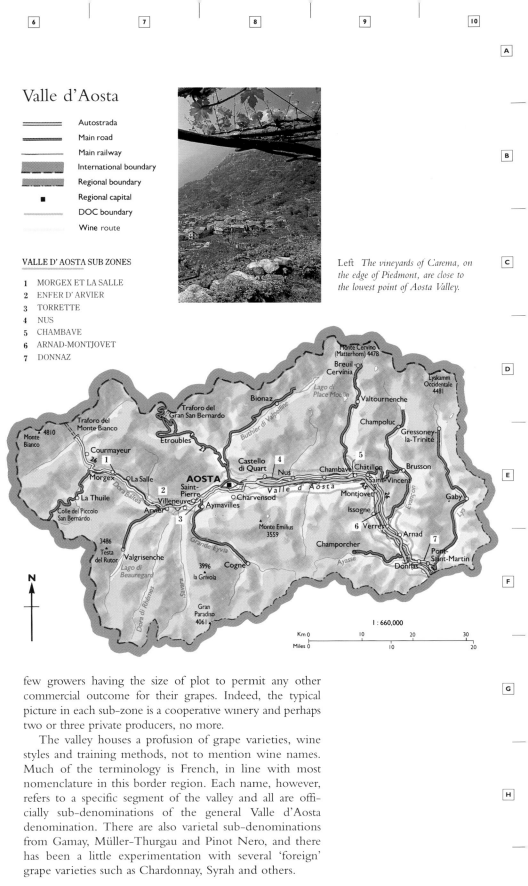

few growers having the size of plot to permit any other commercial outcome for their grapes. Indeed, the typical picture in each sub-zone is a cooperative winery and perhaps two or three private producers, no more.

The valley houses a profusion of grape varieties, wine styles and training methods, not to mention wine names. Much of the terminology is French, in line with most nomenclature in this border region. Each name, however, refers to a specific segment of the valley and all are offi-cially sub-denominations of the general Valle d'Aosta denomination. There are also varietal sub-denominations from Gamay, Müller-Thurgau and Pinot Nero, and there has been a little experimentation with several 'foreign' grape varieties such as Chardonnay, Syrah and others.

Right *The stark majesty of the Alps forms a breathtaking backdrop to Aosta's sparse vineyards.*

VALLE D'AOSTA

RECOMMENDED PRODUCERS

Les Crêtes
Aymavilles
Tel: 0165 902274; E. F.
Go-ahead estate creating great excitement. Les Crêtes hill the focal point. Wines are Torrette and a range of varietals. Must book; good tasting room but pay for tastings, unless significent purchase made.
Owned by:
Costantino Charrère
Aymavilles
Tel: 0165 902135
Shares cellars and visiting arrangements with Les Crêtes but still has ancient cellar and old mill. One of Aosta's leading lights.
Institut Agricole Régional
Aosta
Tel: 0165 553304
This important research centre and school markets results of its work on exalting the typicity of local varieties, plus a few others raising interest.
Ezio Voyat
Chambave
Tel: 0166 46139; F.
Tiny production, organic principles, much research into own vineyards; individualistic wines created by hard graft and traditional ideas. Must book; pay for tastings. Agritourism.

For a general idea of the various wine styles try the following coops, who control most production. All are open for tastings, but booking is essential.

Cave du Vin Blanc de Morgex et de La Salle
Morgex; *Tel: 0165 800331*
Co-Enfer
Arvier (Enfer d'Arvier)
Tel: 0165 99238
Cave des Onze Communes
Aymavilles (Torrette)
Tel: 0165 902912
Cooperativa La Crotta di Vegneron
Chambave; *Tel: 0166 46670*
Cooperativa Agricola La Kiuva
Arnad (Arnad-Montjovet)
Tel: 0125 966351
Caves Cooperatives de Donnas
Donnas; *Tel: 0125 807096*

THE VINEYARDS

All the major vineyard areas can be seen from the *statale* that leads to Aosta town and on to Turin. In the lower Aosta Valley the *autostrada* will also provide some views, if only from a distance. Any of the detours from the *statale* described below are therefore optional, but definitely recommended for a real appreciation of the region and its diversity. The entire route, taking in all the detours could be completed in half a day, although if possible, it is better to allow more time.

From the border, pass through the ski resort of Courmayeur and then continue to twist down for a little over five minutes. Suddenly a band of vineyards appears on the left: the beginning of the zone Blanc de Morgex et de La Salle (white wines from Blanc de Morgex grapes). A short distance further on, just past a pair of petrol stations (IP and Agip), turn right at the signpost Morgex, and curve back under the *statale* towards the vineyards. Turn right again (towards Villair), leading to a T-junction. First turn left, to get a really good close-up view of the vineyards and their characteristic, but unusual low pergola training. Then turn back to head through the viticultural heart of the two communes, Morgex and La Salle.

Just before reaching the first village, at a spot marked by a signpost on the wall on the left, turn right along the Strada Pineta. Turn left at the bottom of the descent, towards La Salle and through Thovex. At the next T-junction, head right, signed 'capoluogo' (main town), back down to the *statale*. Next turn left to Villaret and continue on the road to this village. The route is dotted with green, hooded water sprays. These provide much-needed summer moisture not only for the vineyards but also for the Valdostana cattle pastures. At Villaret (five to 10 minutes later) follow the signs to Aosta to return to the *statale*.

After less than five minutes the next vineyard zone appears, the tiny Enfer d'Arvier, which makes a red wine mainly from Petit Rouge grapes. There are a few tiny vine patches on old terraces but most is in one distinct plot, of more modern appearance, planted across a steep slope. Sadly, there's no closer access for cars but walkers and cyclists can use a footpath (entrance by the Hotel Ruitor).

At Villeneuve, a minute or so further on, Enfer d'Arvier gives way to Torrette, also planting the Petit Rouge variety. Just off the main road is a major sales point for Fontina, the soft, creamy cheese produced exclusively in the Valle d'Aosta, and other local agricultural products. Torrette is also one of the centres of apple production.

Just prior to Saint-Pierre, turn left at the crossroads pass Cofruits – another cooperative sales point for fruit and vegetables, turn left again, then right; from here are the first really good views across the valley. At the next sign towards Aosta (to the right), fork left instead, curving up the hill to the left. If on two feet or two wheels, you can head down to the right into the vineyards. Cars must continue upwards for the vines. Go through La Croix and at the T-junction turn right. Pass the next crossroads and then follow the Aosta signs into the best part of Torrette, towards Sarre. Some vines are *alberello* trained, others *guyot*, reflecting different philosophies and planting epochs. The road is narrow and twisty but has excellent views and soon reaches the railway. Keeping left leads into Aosta, through more hillside vineyard. Of more importance at this point, however, is the Torrette cultivation area across the river.

ENOTECHE

Enoteca La Cave
Via Festaz 53, Aosta
Well laid-out wine shop with good range from Aosta plus a decent selection from rest of Italy and abroad.

Enogastronomia Cavallo Bianco
Via Croix du Ville 25, Aosta
Plenty of local wines and smart labels from elsewhere. Good delicatessen.

FOOD SPECIALITIES

Fontina cheese
Soft, ripe, creamy cheese produced only in the Valle d'Aosta from local cattle breeds; numerous sales points. Most controlled by a cooperative.

Apples
Especially the Renetta variety and, to a lesser extent, the Martin Sec pear.

Honey
From bees feeding on alpine flora.

Lard
Marinated in brine with herbs, especially from around Arnad.

Mocetta
Prosciutto, traditionally from chamois, now more commonly from beef.

Pane Nero
Rye bread, often used in soups.

Caffè Valdostano
Coffee mixed with lemon or orange peel, *grappa* and sugar.

EATING OUT

Café du Bourg
Arvier, Via Lostan 12
Tel: 0165 99094; closed Thurs.
More an *enoteca* with food. Wide range of Aosta wines plus top bottles from other regions, good distillates. Snacks from 5pm, full meals, from short menu of local specialities later. Must book. Open late. Cash only but not costly.

Hostellerie de la Pomme Couronnée
Aymavilles
An oddity to try for fun: meals based entirely on dishes using apples for accompaniment, seasoning, saucing etc.

La Brasserie de l'Hostellerie du Cheval Blanc
Aosta, Rue Clavalité 20
Tel: 0165 239140
Simple, tasty local dishes, well priced, serious wine selection, served in richly comfortable surroundings. Also luxury hotel.

Left In the Valle d'Aosta it seems amazing that vines can flourish in the proximity of such Alpine conditions.

Right *The Gran Paradiso nature reserve in southern Aosta, a vast area of unspoilt Alpine beauty offering an oasis of calm.*

Taverna da Nando
Aosta, Via de Tillier 41
Tel: 0165 44455; closed Mon.
Inexpensive spot, centrally located, with glorious and good value wine list plus a vast choice of *grappe*. Mainly local dishes, but several from other regions.

Bar-Pasticceria Boch
Aosta, Via de Tillier 2
For tip-top coffee, accompanied by walnut tart. Ice-cream good too.

Casale
St-Christophe, Loc Condemine 1
Tel: 0165 541402; closed Mon.
Traditional, rustic dishes. Short wine list concentrating on top Aosta wines. Mid-priced but good value.

Batezar
St-Vincent, Via Marconi 1
Tel: 0166 513164; closed Wed.
Very costly, very smart. Refined, classic dishes and broad Italo-French wine list. Eves only, except weekends.

Chez Pierre
Verres, Via Martorey 43
Tel: 0125 929376; closed Tues.
Solid fare with plenty of flavour. Tasting menu available. Specialities – cheeses and trout. Wines from Aosta and Piedmont. Tables outdoors.

Osteria della Società Cooperativa
Hône, Via Colliard 77
Tel: 0125 80341; closed Mon.
Large choice of Aosta and Piedmontese dishes, carefully prepared to be full of flavour. Shortish wine list, based on strictly local Arnad and Erbaluce. Great value but cash only.

HOTELS

Brenva
Courmayeur, Fraz Entreves 14
Tel: 0165 869780; fax: 0165 869726
Warm, welcoming and, unlike most in Courmayeur, open nearly all year.

Milleluci
Aosta, Loc Rappoz 15
Tel: 0165 235278; fax: 0165 235284
Small, delightful, spacious rooms.

Cross the railway line, follow the road right, passing the imposing castle of Sarre. Head right towards the traffic lights, there turning left, over the river, signposted Cogne and Aymavilles. Go through the village and sweep leftwards round a U–shaped bend (at Gressan), passing to the left the cellars of Les Crêtes, the Valle d'Aosta's biggest private producer. The large vineyard up in the hills to the left is Les Tulles; most are far more fragmented. At this point the production zone is signed along the road. Head towards the conical, vine-covered hill to the right. This is Les Crêtes, the vineyard belonging to the eponymous estate and one causing great excitement in the area for the quality and novelty (new vine varieties) of its products. The building atop the hill is being developed as a tasting area. Just before the hill, divert right to see the majestic castle of Aymavilles with, just in front, the valley's largest wine cooperative structure. Turning back, either pass behind the hill (on unmade road) or in front of it (better road but less impressive views) before crossing back over the River Dora Baltea through Gressan to Aosta town.

At Aosta, return to the *statale* following the signposts to Torino (Turin). Practically all the vineyards up in the hills behind the town belong to the Institut Agricole Régional (regional agricultural institute). Just past the merge point of

Left *Sturdy old vines in Morgex are trained this low to combat the harsh climate – they seem to have been cultivated by dwarfs.*

AGRITOURISM

Les Ecureuils
St-Pierre, Fraz Homené-
Ste-Marguerite; *Tel: 0165 903831*
In the hills behind Sarre. Top meals served, also open to non-residents in winter. Goat's cheese a speciality. Cash only.

Lo Dzerby
Arnad, Fraz Machaby
Tel: 0125 966067
Accessible only by foot (10–15 minutes), hidden in the woods behind Arnad. Wine from estate's own production. Good lard. Meals served too; must book. Cash only.

FOOD SHOPPING

Con Pro Val
Villeneuve, Fraz Trepont 16
All from Aosta coops, including wine, cheese and honey.

Pain de Coucou
St-Pierre
For all typical Aosta produce, food, wine and craftwork too.

Latteria Gerard Lale
Aosta, Via De Sales 14
Good matured Fontina.

Macelleria Bertolin Peaquin
Arnad, Strada Statale 6
For Aosta salumi, notably *mocetta* and the famed Arnad lard.

PLACES OF INTEREST

Aosta is well known for its ski slopes. There is also the Gran Paradiso nature reserve, a vast area of alpine parkland with areas suitable for hill walkers, hill climbers, skiers, windsurfers, as well as the less energetic.

the *statale* (which bypasses the town) with the main road east from Aosta, turn left at the traffic lights towards Croix Noire and Saint-Cristophe. Follow the road right (signed Gerardin), passing vines on the left. This is the cross-over area between Torrette and Nus, which produces red wine from the local grape variety Vien di Nus and white and *passito* from Pinot Grigio, sometimes, oddly, called Malvoisie. It is also a zone of the three local varietals (Gamay, Müller-Thurgau and Pinot Grigio). At the next major block of signs, turn left up into the hills, but keep the hotel you will see to your right. Next turn right (direction Coutatepaz) and follow this high road through the tightly packed, low-trained vines, some *spalliera*, some *alberello*. At the first T-junction turn right, then left at the next towards Quart and, weather permitting, there should be a glorious view over the Dora Baltea. This cut-through comes to an end at what is practically a T-junction, with a block of signs on the wall to the left. Turn hard right and wiggle back down onto the *statale*.

From here, there is little to be gained by turning off the *statale*. Any decent road that exists merely leads up into the mountains and there is no choice but to turn back down again. Anyway, from here the *statale* passes as close to most of the vineyards as anyone could wish. After a few minutes

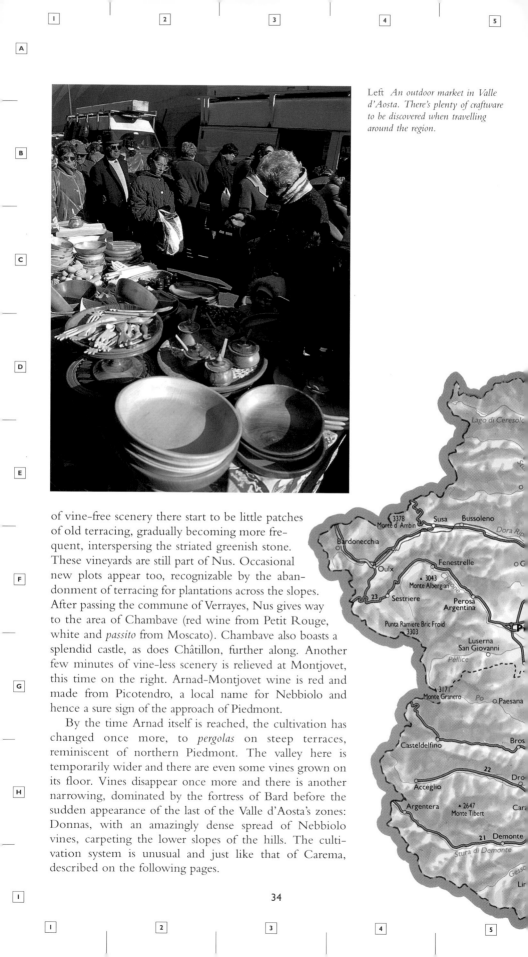

Left *An outdoor market in Valle d'Aosta. There's plenty of craftware to be discovered when travelling around the region.*

of vine-free scenery there start to be little patches of old terracing, gradually becoming more frequent, interspersing the striated greenish stone. These vineyards are still part of Nus. Occasional new plots appear too, recognizable by the abandonment of terracing for plantations across the slopes. After passing the commune of Verrayes, Nus gives way to the area of Chambave (red wine from Petit Rouge, white and *passito* from Moscato). Chambave also boasts a splendid castle, as does Châtillon, further along. Another few minutes of vine-less scenery is relieved at Montjovet, this time on the right. Arnad-Montjovet wine is red and made from Picotendro, a local name for Nebbiolo and hence a sure sign of the approach of Piedmont.

By the time Arnad itself is reached, the cultivation has changed once more, to *pergolas* on steep terraces, reminiscent of northern Piedmont. The valley here is temporarily wider and there are even some vines grown on its floor. Vines disappear once more and there is another narrowing, dominated by the fortress of Bard before the sudden appearance of the last of the Valle d'Aosta's zones: Donnas, with an amazingly dense spread of Nebbiolo vines, carpeting the lower slopes of the hills. The cultivation system is unusual and just like that of Carema, described on the following pages.

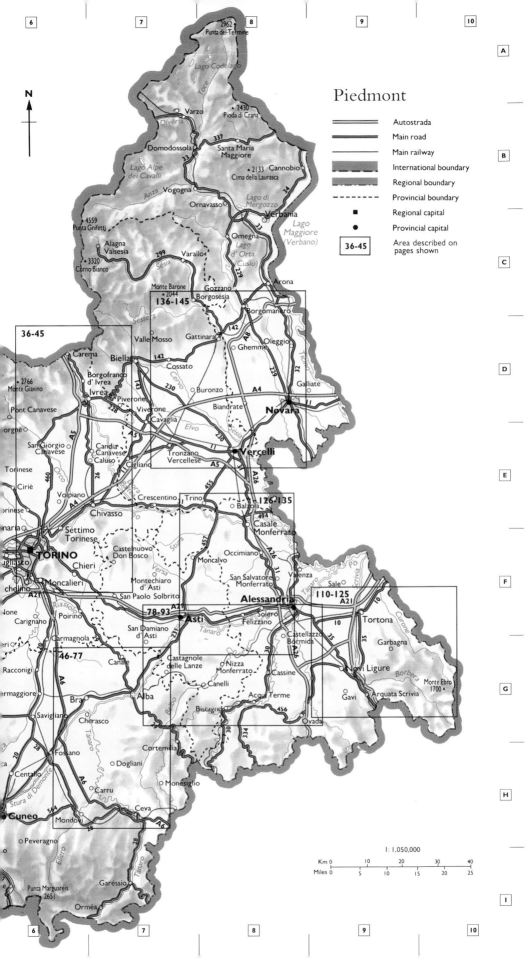

Carema and the Canavese

CAREMA

RECOMMENDED PRODUCERS

Luigi Ferrando e Figli
Tel: 0125 641176; E. F.
Carema's leading light. Ferrando has worked hard with local growers to preserve the traditions of the area and at the same time to improve viticultural practices. 'Standard' Carema, aged four years, has white label. Special selection, best years only, known as Black Label. Cellars in Carema and Ivrea. Also produces Erbaluce di Caluso, including *cru* Cariola and Le Campore, produced for estate Gabriele e Fiamenghi; Solativo, late harvest Erbaluce, lightly sweet; Caluso Passito (for Boratto); sparkling Erbaluce; *grappe* of Carema and Erbaluce.

ENOTECA

Luigi Ferrando e Figli
Ivrea, Corso Cavour 9
Ferrando also runs a well-stocked *enoteca* in Ivrea with shop design unaltered since 1929.

THE CANAVESE

RECOMMENDED PRODUCERS

Luigi Ferrando e Figli
See above.
Colombaio di Candia
Candia Canavese
Tel: 0125 641176; E. F.
Produces crisp, smoky Erbaluce of good richness. Must book.
Orsolani
San Giorgio Canavese
Tel: 0124 32386; E.
Good and improving wines. Vineyards in San Giorgio and Caluso itself. A small part of the Erbaluce is oak-fermented, Caluso Passito is given five years' ageing: both branded 'La Rustia'. Classic method sparkling from Erbalulce, freshly fruity. Also tiny Barbera vineyard at Agliano d'Asti. Must book.

FOOD SPECIALITIES

The Canavese is famous for the quality and quantity of its mushrooms.

EATING OUT

La Panoramica
Loranzè, Via San Rocco 7
Tel: 0125 669966; closed Sat lunch, Sun eve.

CAREMA

Pont Saint-Martin marks the southernmost point of the Valle d'Aosta. Just past the village Piedmont begins. It is a matter of seconds before a slim fork in the road appears, with Ivrea marked to the right and Carema to the left. Follow left onto a rather narrow road. (A couple of the first few doors on the right lead to the old cellars of Luigi Ferrando.) Once past a *trattoria* and then a bar with a telephone sign hanging outside, turn left and a yellow sign leading to another *trattoria* confirms you have picked the right road. This leads straight up into the vineyards and winds up as far as an electricity pylon, beyond which the road is private in one direction (and can be closed off at any time) and lacks turning places in the other. Having explored on foot, turn round and head back down. There are fabulous views down onto the pergolas carpeting the hillside in green, and the town of Ivrea along the valley with the Dora Baltea snaking through. On the descent, just past a bend to the right is a parking bay (or passing place) on the right. From just behind here a footpath leads back up (almost parallel with the river) through the hills. After a minute of energetic walking a tiny chapel suddenly appears, perfect for gentle contemplation, with calm views over the valley.

Once back down at ground level, turn left onto the road you left (towards Ivrea). The vine-covered hill stays on the left for a couple of minutes, then just as the intersection for the motorway appears, the density diminishes. This is all there is of the tiny zone of Carema. Any vineyards from now on belong to the Canavese (*see* over).

THE WINES

The vineyards were planted by the Romans and the terraces carved out from the crumbling hillside to maximize the vines' chances of ripening. There are still frequent landslips and erosion of any section not carefully maintained. The supports, made of stone and held together by a cement-like mixture, are hollow, perhaps intended to retain heat and

Left *The sturdy, hollow, stone supports give Carema's vineyards a sense of solidity and stability.* Bottom left *Carema's unusual, high-trained vineyards carpet the hillside above the village.*

Top notch place. Mix of classic and innovative dishes, served in elegant surroundings. Choice of tasting menus. Very good cheeses. Good wine list, with inexpensive as well as grand wines, local and foreign, all well priced. Food good value too. Seats outside.

La Trattoria
Ivrea, Via Aosta 47
Tel: 0125 48998; closed Sun
Bright, cheery place with closely packed tables. Menu based on simple, traditional dishes with daily additions of trendier fare. Short but well-balanced wine list. Fair pricing.

Casa Vicina
Borgofranco d'Ivrea, Via Palma 146/a, Fraz. Ivozio
Tel: 0125 752180; closed Wed.
Family-run, long-standing place. Can eat outside on terrace with good views. Traditional Piedmontese dishes, prepared with skill. Tasting menu. Home made ice-cream. Full list of local and Piedmontese wines, some from rest of Italy and abroad. Fairly costly but fair value.

La Pergola
Scarmagno, Via Montalenghe 59
Tel: 0125 739760; closed Mon.
Carefully prepared traditional foods in peaceful, comfortable surroundings. Two tasting menus, both well worth while, depending on your appetite. Meals based entirely on mushrooms available (not in winter). Fritto Misto Piemontese available if booked in advance. Huge wine list, many served by the glass, plus good list of distillates. Not costly.

La Luna
San Giorgio Canavese,
Piazza Ippolito San Giorgio 12
Tel: 0124 32184; closed Mon.
Forget the uninspiring surroundings, enjoy the good value, satisfying, traditional foods with frequently changing menus based on seasonal availability. Short wine list, based on Erbaluce and Piedmontese reds. Lunch only, except weekends. Cash only.

Gardenia
Caluso, Corso Torino 9
Tel: 011 9832249; closed Thur, Fri lunch.
Short menu, based on traditional dishes but given a lighter touch, served in a renovated farmhouse. Not too costly. Broad range of local and Piedmontese wines. Seats outside. Amex and Diners cards only.

warm the vines. Yet many replacement supports are the more normal wooden stakes and the vines don't ripen significantly less. Wood was probably far more valuable for heating and other purposes two millennia ago. Yet stones were (and still are) plentiful, as the river bed reveals.

The grapes are all Nebbiolo, here at the northern limits of its growth area. A funnel effect, formed by the sudden opening out of the Aosta Valley, and the swift movement of the river combine to help keep clouds at bay, just increasing the amount of sunlight enough to allow the grapes to ripen. The resulting wine is a softer, more gentle version of the muscular wine produced in Nebbiolo's heartland around Alba. Nevertheless, Carema still has the characteristic tannin and acidity which permit it to age well.

ANOTHER SURPRISE

Stay on the *statale* for Ivrea and just after passing Settimo Vittone you enter the commune of Borgofranco d'Ivrea. Watch for a sign on the left pointing to 'Balmetti di Quinto'. Take this road and pass through what looks like a ghost town, comprising small, two-storey buildings. They are, in fact, cellars (locally called *balmetti*). The ground floor houses cellars kept at a steady 8°C all year round by the particular air currents in the zone. Above are rooms used only for parties or other celebrations – with wine on tap, of course. Finally turn left back onto the *statale* towards Ivrea.

Castello di Pavone
Pavone Canavese
See Places of Interest.

HOTELS

The area's hotels serve mainly
Olivetti clients and tend to be
priced accordingly:

La Serra
Ivrea, Corso Carlo Botta 30
Tel: 0125 44341; fax: 0125 49313.
Central Ivrea's sole decent hotel.
4* level.
Sirio
Lake Sirio
Tel: 0125 424247; fax: 0125 48980.
Mid-range, comfortable; tranquil
views over lake.
La Villa
San Bernardo
Tel: 0125 631696; fax: 0125 631950.
Small, simple and comparatively
inexpensive.
Castello di Pavone
(See Places of Interest)
Rooms and suites available
from early 1997.

AGRITOURISM

For information contact Assessorato
Agricoltura, Attività Economiche e
Lavoro, Via Lagrange 2, Turin.
Tel: 011 57561.

FOOD SHOPPING

Pasticceria Balla
Ivrea, Via Gozzano 2
Go for the classic *Torta Novecento*
Pasticceria Strobbia
Ivrea, Corso Botta 30
Try the speciality *Polenta d'Ivrea.*
Pasticceria Brustia
Ivrea, Corso Vercelli 33
For chocolate!
Salumificio Avenatti
Feletto
A little out of the way but a great
place for stocking up on salami,
prosciutto and various other
carnivorous delicacies.

PLACES OF INTEREST

The fascination of the Canavese lies
mainly in the number and quality of
its castles:

Castello di Montalto Dora
Impressive to look at but remains
closed.
Castello di Masino
Completely restored, contains tomb
of Italy's first king, Arduino
(9th-century); large park. Open
to public. For guided tour book:
0125 778100.

THE CANAVESE

The area forms a large circle around Ivrea, which lies towards the north of the zone. The vines are on south-facing slopes of the low hills that form the rim of the area. The hills are, in fact, formed from the terminal moraine of the Alpine glacier that is now the Aosta Valley, and from one or two laterals. It would be possible to follow these gentle uplands right round in a large circuit but as there is little variation it is probably more interesting to cut across the zone, in a short tour taking a little over an hour.

THE WINES

The Canavese is known principally for the white Erbaluce grape and the two wines made from it, Erbaluce di Caluso and Caluso Passito. Caluso is only one of the 38 communes of the Canavese but the one to have given its name to the wines. Erbaluce di Caluso combines high acidity with a rich, floral centre which, when made with care, results in a refreshing, stimulating wine, best with food, even, for example, rich salami. Poorly made examples are thin and sharp. The acidity can give a beautiful lift to the sweet *passito* version and occasional examples can have extraordinary longevity. There are also some semi-sweet wines made in a lighter style from partially *passito* grapes and one or two experimental dry wines. Other wines (red as well as white) made in the area are called simply Canavese, a new denomination, yet to make a serious impact but accounting for about half the total production.

THE VINEYARDS

From Borgofranco d'Ivrea (*see* previous page), pass the commune and castle of Montalto Dora. Then fork off left (following signs to Biella) to skirt Lake Sirio, where folk from Ivrea often go for their *passegiata*. After the lake follow signs back to Ivrea. You could go into the town at this point or, bypassing it for now, start following signs for Vercelli. You find yourself on a swift, straight road – the Ivrea–Vercelli *statale* – which shortly skirts the most important patch of vineyard. Follow the road for several minutes until it passes Lake Viverone, the largest lake of the area, and a good spot for getting right into the vineyards on the unmade roads to the left. Then turn back and turn left off the *statale* at the traffic lights to Azeglio.

From Azeglio follow signs for the Castello di Masino, one of the area's most impressive castles. It is definitely worth seeing, not least for the startling views across the entire Canavese. From the castle, go back down to Caravino and from there head towards Perosa, via Strambino, Scarmagno and part of the road to Castellamonte which takes you across the valley, crossing successively the river, the railway line and the *autostrada*, to the west flank of the zone.

From Perosa, follow signs to Parella. The Castello di Parella is more château than castle. After crossing the river bed and immediately after passing under a main road turn

Above *As well as an abundance of Alpine cheeses, don't ignore the sausages.*

Left *Plaques marking the first day of the grape harvest in the Canavese, which varies between end September and end October.*

Castello di Parella
and **Castello di Loranzè**
For visiting hours contact Ivrea tourist office, Corso Vercelli 1.
Tel: 0125 618131.

Castello di Pavone
Tel: 0125 672111
Fully restored, no expense spared, to replicate ancient castle life but with all mod cons. Includes magnificent decorated wooden ceiling acquired after competition with the Louvre. Has well-patronized restaurant with well-presented, upmarket food. Sadly visits available to restaurant guests only.

SPECIAL EVENTS

Carnival
Completely takes over Ivrea for the 10 days prior to Lent. Various celebrations, parades and high jinx, including an orange fight!

left, and it appears straight ahead, with the Castello di Loranzè above. At the Castello di Parella is a T-junction. Turn left (to 'Centro') and up a narrow road with vines on the right. At the following crossroads go right under a large arch and up on a cobbled road to the vineyard surrounding the Castello di Loranzè, one of the area's best. It produces a tiny amount of top class wine, all of which is consumed in the adjacent restaurant. After circling the complex, head back down to Ivrea. This is best done by crossing over the first road signposted to the town via Colleretto Giacosa and then taking the second road in, with views of the Castello di Pavone (right) on the way.

IVREA

Ivrea is completely dominated by Olivetti. The company is the major source of employment here and, before the recent recession, brought considerable wealth. Ivrea is small and easily negotiated as a one way system circles the old town. The centre is well worth investigating, but Ivrea is not particularly well off for restaurants; the townsfolk prefer to hire private rooms in one of the castles for meals out.

Turin

TURIN

ENOTECHE

Turin has all too few of the wine bar type of *enoteca* but possibly two dozen wine shops. These are among the more interesting:

Antica Enoteca del Borgo
Via Monferrato 4
Wine shop and bar. Good range, Italian and foreign. Light snacks. Popular for aperitifs.

Il Vinaio di Vada Via Cibrario 38
Excellent range. Mainly Piedmontese (especially Barolo) but also Italian and foreign plus whiskies and cognacs. Small selection of food specialities. Have a look too at the large collection of antique bottles.

Casa Del Barolo
Via Andrea Doria 7
Pays particular attention to the wines of small, often lesser known producers. Will also send wine to your friends and loved ones.

La Petite Cave Corse de Gaspari 2
Excellent selection. Also spirits and tempting food goodies.

Gabri 2 Corso Raffaello 6
Good range from Italy and abroad including champagne. Also distillates and some inviting food products.

Bruno Milano Via Artisti 26
For a comprehensive range from most regions of Italy, plus champagnes, whiskies etc.

Ostu Via Cristoforo Colombo 63
Wine bar/*trattoria*. Go for a bite and a glass, or a meal and a bottle. Great choice of wines, from simple to grand and a great atmosphere.

Rabezzana
Via San Francesco d'Assisi 23/c
As well as a fair, broad-based range, the Rabezzana family sells wine from their estate in San Desiderio d'Asti. Advice given on wine selection and wine and food matching.

Refettorio Via dei Mille 23/d
Wine bar. Weekly choice of 20 wines plus more by bottle. Snacks throughout day, also full lunches.

Vicenzo Nebiolo
Via Priocca 10; closed Sun.
Rough and ready wine bar serving substantial sandwiches for the market crowd at Porta Palazzo plus own carafe wine (very cheap) or a small selection of bottles. Pay cash.

Right Turin's easily-accessed walks along the Po — here by the Vittorio Emanuele I bridge — bring an oasis of peace in the heart of the city. Centre-right is the Capucins Mount.

GETTING THERE

From Ivrea and the Canavese Turin beckons, so head south, either on the *autostrada* or the *statale*, which passes through Caluso itself. For a detour to see more of the Canavese's castles before approaching the city, leave Ivrea towards Castellamonte, then branch across to Aglié, on to San Giorgio Canavese, through Caluso and across to Mazzè, before returning to one of the main routes south.

THE CITY

Turin is probably Italy's best kept secret. It is spacious, well-planned and easy to navigate. The streets are wide and airy, not overly noisy and are fringed by well cared for buildings, rarely more than a few storeys high. The central streets have long sweeps of porticoes giving extra depth and removing any garish shop fronts from the perspective, giving an even, balanced, ordered aspect. They protect from sun and rain too. There are also many triumphantly large squares, each with a character of its own.

By night central Turin's appearance changes dramatically, becoming bright and glitzy. Above the porticoes are numerous, vertical neon signs; cheerful without becoming brash, bringing splashes of colour, while streets are well lit and many of the important buildings and statues are floodlit.

The city is fringed to the north and east by rivers. To the north passes the *torrente* Stura di Lanzo, although roughly parallel to it and firmly within town is the River Dora Riparia. In the east it is the Po, which flows regally in a northerly direction. The Torinese have made a positive feature of the river bank of the Po, with broad walks along much of its length.

Immediately beyond the Po is a rapid incline, a bank of hills that provides a natural barrier to the city's expansion. The elevation houses some rather smart accommodation but Turin's smartest residences, villas in spacious grounds, home to the seriously wealthy, are on the back side of the hills, some with fabulous views over Piedmont and the Alps.

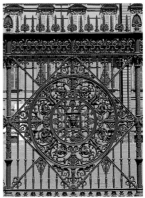

Left *Many of Turin's squares sport imposing statues. This warrior in Piazza San Carlo is Emanuele Filiberto, Duke of Savoy.*
Above *Detail of gate to the Royal Palace.*

CAFFE

Among the best are Baratti in Piazza Castello, Bar Torino in Piazza San Carlo, Platti Caffè in Corso Vittorio Emanuele II.

EATING OUT

Antiche Sere Via Cenischia 9
Tel: 011 3854347; closed Sun.
In an old residential area. Prettily countryfied. Eat outside, under a pergola, in summer. Friendly and attentive service. Menu mainly Piedmontese, with Lombard influences, changing daily. Good desserts. Short wine list well selected. Not expensive. Cash only. Eves only.

Dai Saletta Via Belfiore 37
Tel: 011 6687876; closed Sun.
Very popular spot. Simple, good and robust local dishes served in a welcoming atmosphere. Short but good wine list, house wine good too. Cash only. Inexpensive.

Al Gatto Nero Corso Turati 14
Tel: 011 590414; closed Sun.
For a change: Tuscan cuisine. Good, broad wine list. Quite expensive.

Il Brandé Via Massena 5
Tel: 011 537279; closed Sun, Mon.
Near station, much frequented. Excellent traditional menu or, for a change, selection of fondues, in hot, aromatized wine. Good wine selection. Cash only. Eves only.

Monferrato Via Monferrato 6
Tel: 011 8190661; closed Sat, Sun.
Long-standing and busy restaurant, picturesquely sited by the Po overlooking Piazza Veneto. Excellent, absolutely traditional, mainly local dishes. Very well chosen wines, a browser's delight. Very fairly priced.

As a counterpoint, just east of the station is a cheerfully scruffy area, home to artisans and the odd ageing hippy.

Add to its natural refinement and style the wealth of historical and cultural splendours, and it becomes increasingly puzzling why Turin is not one of Italy's major magnets for visitors. It may be partly that the Torinese do not relish the idea of their city being trampled by hoards of tourists and it would be hard to blame them. So those who do visit can enjoy freedom from tourist tat and can relish being treated as a guest in town rather than just another foreigner.

FOOD AND DRINK IN TURIN

Turin is not generally regarded as a gastronomic city, although it has its fair share of good restaurants and innumerable wonderfully tempting food shops. Its *tour de force*, however, is its *caffè*. These coffee bars are a central facet of social life. You can down a quick espresso or cappuccino or sit and chat quietly and at length over a drink, a snack or a pastry or two. Many are large, in period style and surpremely elegant. Some are renowned for their *pasticceria*; others for their savoury snacks, others simply for the quality

Montecarlo
Via San Francesco da Paola 37
Tel: 011 8126966; closed Sat lunch, Sun.
Smart fish (mainly) restaurant. Wines
mostly white and from outside
Piedmont. Quite expensive; dress up.

Neuv Caval d'Brons
Piazza San Carlo 157
Tel: 011 5627483; closed Sun.
Very central. High class, high quality
restaurant spread over three small,
highly elegant dining rooms. Choice
of tasting menus: fish, vegetarian or
Piedmontese; all prepared to highest
levels of taste and flavour. Extensive
wine list. Quietly attentive service.
A superb experience. Costly but
justifiably so.

Porticciolo Via Barletta 58
Tel: 011 321601; closed Sat lunch, Sun.
Good fish and sea food, well chosen
wines to accompany. Mid-priced.

Porto di Savona
Piazza Vittorio Veneto 2
Tel: 011 8173500;
closed Mon, Tue lunch.
Good value, inexpensive *locale*,
much frequented by regulars, serving
strictly Piedmontese fare. Small but
decent wine list. Cash only.

Spada Reale
Via Principe Amedeo 53
Tel: 011 832835; closed Sun.
Very popular restaurant near Piazza
Veneto. Unusual, inventive dishes
and long, broad based wine list.
Open late. Not costly.

Tre Galline Via Bellezia 37
Tel: 011 4366553;
closed Mon lunch, Sun.
Long standing restaurant in old city
centre. Mainly traditional dishes with
some innovations. Two tasting menus,
but wine list is real draw – long, mainly
Piedmontese. Wines reasonably priced.

of the coffee (or these days tea, which is very chic) and the
general ambience. The main factor, though, is the grace and
refinement of the surroundings and the service.

There is a central fruit and vegetable market, Porta
Palazzo, by Piazza della Repubblica. It is bustling and lively
and offering everything in abundance and, therefore, a
must to visit. But for shopping, it is far better to wander a
short way out of centre into more residential areas where
there are many daily open-air markets – at these Torinese
stock up on all manner of goods. Most are along the central
reservations bisecting many of the wide streets, providing
convenient space without cluttering up the pavements.
Corso Svizzera, for example, in the northwest of town, is a
case in point. Yet demand is such that it can sustain a further
market in Corso Racconigi, a few hundred metres away.

Unlike most cities, food shops are not huddled together
in bursts. Yet walk along any shopping street and you will
soon pass some specialist food outlet: clean, neat and with
the sort of window display that is manifestly design-
conscious Italian. Keep walking and you will come across
another and another so that, before long, you will have
seen the full range of any normal high street. One thing
rarely seen in Turin, though, is vermouth. Despite its historical links with the city, most of the major vermouth
companies have moved away from Turin, mainly to Canelli.

THE SIGHTS

There is no shortage of things to see in Turin, although not
so much that you are kept running from museum to art
gallery without time simply to enjoy the city around you.
The main draw is the museum of Egyptology, in Via
Accademia delle Scienze – one of the greatest collections
in the world. Within the Accademia is also the museum of
antiquities and the Subauda art gallery. They are located
just beside the most exciting and stirring walk in Turin:

Two of Turin's most exciting squares:
Above *One end of the long, lively*
Piazza Vittorio Veneto.
Right *The magnificent Piazza*

San Carlo, with its elegant
porticoes and the twin churches of
Santa Cristina (centre-left) and
San Carlo (centre-right).

north from the central station along Via Roma and through Piazza Carlo Felice, Piazza San Carlo (the best of all) and Piazza Castello (with the stunning Madama palace), coming out by the Royal Palace and into its pleasant gardens. The other major museum is along the Po, in a more southern area of fairly modern, showcase buildings, the museum of the motor car; this is, after all, the city of Fiat.

The emblem of the city is the Mole Antonelliana, a folly with a tall, metal spire, built in the mid–19th century. Frustratingly though, despite its height, it generally remains hidden and suddenly glimpsing it from up close can be quite a shock. More peaceful is the view over the Po from Piazza Vittorio Veneto, onto the piazza of Gran Madre di Dio, with, behind it, the Gran Madre church. Up in the hills behind is the Cappucins Mount, while further along the river to the right is the Valentino park, with two remarkable fountains, one rather specially lit at night. In the park is the French Renaissance style Valentino castle and an oddity, a 19th-century reconstruction of the medieval quarter.

Throughout the city the influence of the House of Savoy, pride in Turin's importance during the Italian unification of the 1860s, and a notable monarchist attitude are evident.

LEAVING TURIN

Leaving Turin is straightforward; it is simplest to take the *autostrada* from the south of town or the *statale* to reach Chieri, the starting place for the next route. There are, however, more scenic ways out of the city: so scenic that they are marked out as visitor itineraries. They all go over Turin's eastern hill range. The best known and one of the most beautiful is via the Superga basilica which, at 670 metres, gives surperb views, from Monviso to Monte Rosa. There are several others, all shown in clear diagrammatic form at the departure point by the Ponte Margherita over the Po. The only problem will be choosing which to take.

HOTELS

Turin has a vast wealth of hotel accommodation, much of it as elegant as the city itself. Finding a good room without paying exaggerated city prices is, however, less easy. Try among the following:

Amedeus e Teatro
Via Principe Amedeo 41 bis
Tel: 011 8174951; fax: 011 8174953.
Attractive, recently refurbished, air conditioning, garage.
Giotto Via Giotto 27
Tel. 011 6637172, fax. 011 6637173.
Quiet, modern, welcoming. Bright rooms with good bathrooms. Some have cooking facilities. Good value.
Lancaster Corso Turati 8
Tel: 011 5681982; fax: 011 5683019.
Quiet. Attractive, well furnished rooms and bathrooms. Unmodernised rooms for lower prices. Garage.
Le Petit Hotel
Via San Francesco d'Assisi 21
Tel: 011 5612626; fax: 011 5622807.
In old centre. In refurbished 19th-century building. Try for top floor with views over city rooftops. Garage.
Liberty Via Pietro Micca 15
Tel: 011 5628801; fax: 011 5628163.
Quite central. Attractive, old fashioned, *fin de siecle* hotel. Parking.
Montevecchio
Via Montevecchio 13
Tel: 011 5620023; fax: 011 5623047.
Simple 2*. Clean and welcoming. Modern, functional rooms. Garage.
Roma e Rocca Cavour
Piazza Carlo Felice 60
Tel: 011 5612772; fax: 011 5628137.
Central, long-standing. Rooms in various styles, most overlooking gardens. Garage.

The edges of the heartland: Freisa and Malvasia

THE EDGES OF THE HEARTLAND

WINE PRODUCERS

Cascina Gilli
Castelnuovo Don Bosco
Tel: 011 9876984; E. F.
Situated in a two hundred-year old
building close to the Abbazia di
Vezzolano. Owner Giovanni Vergnano
is determined to improve quality levels
throughout zone, notably the local
clone of Malvasia. No visits Suns.

Bava
Cocconato
Tel: 0141 907083; E. F.
Large, dynamic company producing
over 30 different wines under the
names Bava, Casa Brina and, for
sparkling wine, Cocchi. Roberto Bava
is a music lover, classical, jazz and
more, and describes wines in terms
of pieces of music. Several styles of
Barbera d'Asti, led by the *barrique*-aged
Stradivario. Also an important
producer of Malvasia and of Malvaxia,
a *passito* version. Must book for visits
outside normal working hours.
Tutored tastings also available, for a
fee. Advice given on local attractions.

Martini & Rossi
Pessione
Tel: 011 94191; E. F. S.
Such an important, well-known
company that it is almost superfluous
to give details. Apart from the
famous vermouth, there is an
important production of Asti
Spumante and good quality, dry
sparkling wine. The museum is a
'must' (see next page). Must book.

FOOD SHOPPING

Excellent food products available in
Cocconato. Bava will advise where.

EATING OUT

Trattoria del Freisa
Moncucco Torinese
Tel: 011 9874765; closed Tue, Wed.
Traditional, easy-going, rural *trattoria.*
The usual long series of antipasti,
followed by strictly classic fare. Good
selection of local wines. Cash only.
Eves only, except weekends.

*Right A dog sniffing out truffles
in a, necessarily, secret location in
Northwest Italy.*

THE WINES

The rather joyless town of Chieri gives its name to Freisa di Chieri, a wine produced, in theory, in a large ring around the town. The area reaches Turin to the west, the *autostrada* to the south and similar distances north and east but, in practice, there is hardly any wine produced at all: it needs no more than a glance to see that, apart from the hills ringing Turin, this is not wine country. Most Freisa is produced a little further east, just past Castelnuovo Don Bosco, and is denominated Freisa d'Asti. Freisa is a strange red variety, appreciated locally but sometimes served to outsiders almost as a bet: will they latch on to it or turn their noses up? It is light in colour and weight, but with firm acidity, a lean edge and a haunting, raspberry-like fruitiness. It was often made fairly sweet but now is more usually dry and, most frequently, a touch *frizzante*, although it might occasionally be still or even fully sparkling. Although this is its heartland, vines are scattered throughout both Asti province and the area of Alba, where it comes under the denomination Langhe.

This is also the area of Malvasia di Castelnuovo Don Bosco, a wine of great renown but another with very small production; there are only seven or eight producers in total and of these most grow Malvasia as a sideline. The Malvasia grown round Castelnuovo Don Bosco is from the red version of the grape, here from a local clone known as Malvasia di Schierano. The wines may be red but are more often *rosato*, with a little or more fizz. They are sweet or at least sweetish, powerfully perfumed and roundly flavoured. Malvasia is also grown around Casorzo d'Asti (*see* page 132).

THE VINEYARDS

This route is quite short, only taking a couple of hours, even with a number of stops. (*See* Asti map page 82.) It also covers a sliver of Barbera country, an important segment but one inconvenient to reach from elsewhere. From Chieri, take the road past Andezeno and Mombello to

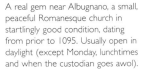

Left *The Romanesque Abbazia di Vezzolano* (see *Places of Interest*). Below *Spring in the vineyards near Castelnuovo Don Bosco*.

arrive at Castelnuovo Don Bosco. If you do spot any vines along the way they are rare Freisa di Chieri sightings. Apart from the historical and architectural lure of Castelnuovo it is also worth going up to the old centre for the beautiful views of its vineyard area offered on the way back down. Leave Castelnuovo, continuing on the same road on which you came in, the Via Monferrato, signed to Asti. The road runs under a couple of tunnels and through a heavily wooded road (a wood is *bosco* in Italian). Just past the turn-off to Passerano you pass out of the Malvasia di Castelnuovo Don Bosco zone without having seen any vineyards along the road. Don't worry; you will.

Continue towards Asti until, just a few minutes later, you turn left to Piovà Massaia. From Piovà, follow signs to Cocconato, approaching this village on a tiny road, marked on only the largest scale maps. It snakes through a gentle, upland area of softly rounded hills, where Barbera d'Asti (or del Monferrato) is the main wine but Freisa d'Asti is also produced. At first, vineyard is quite sparse but as Cocconato gets closer the density increases significantly. If you are travelling in late autumn, you can pick out Freisa by its yellow leaves compared with Barbera's red foliage.

Cocconato is another hilltop town. The old centre is narrow, cobbled and best explored on foot: don't miss the splendid old sun dial at Casa Brina. From Cocconato, the road down to Moransengo leads to the Bava estate. Otherwise, descend on the Turin road, through mixed vineyard and woods, turning right at the bottom (signed Casalborgone), then, after about five minutes, left to Albugnano. At this point you cross back into the Malvasia di Castelnuovo Don Bosco zone and begin to rise. Suddenly, once at the top, a view opens up which is just magnificent.

From Albugnano, return to Castelnuovo Don Bosco (following signs), this time through the heart of Malvasia (and Freisa) country. Once back at Castelnuovo, head towards Buttigliera, passing signs to Colle Don Bosco. From Buttigliera, it is a quick dash across the plain to Riva, fully named Riva presso Chieri, with good views back to the right of Turin's hills, then on to Pessione, where Martini and Rossi have their cellars and a stunning museum.

PLACES OF INTEREST

Abbazia di Vezzolano
A real gem near Albugnano, a small, peaceful Romanesque church in startlingly good condition, dating from prior to 1095. Usually open in daylight (except Monday, lunchtimes and when the custodian goes awol).

Other Romanesque churches are dotted around Asti province, producers will advise on those closest to their estates.

Castelnuovo Don Bosco
This small town atop a very steep hill is well worth exploring. Well preserved and sympathetically restored centre. Inextricably linked with the 'new' saint, the 19th-century Don Giovanni Bosco.

Colle Don Bosco
Don Bosco had the then ground-breaking idea of creating a sort of 'Boystown' for orphan children. His works have been commemorated by a huge, grandiose sanctuary, college and 'temple'.

Conbipel Leather Factory Shop
Cocconato, Strada Banchieri 1
For excellent leather-wear at knock-down prices.

The Martini Museum
Tel: 011 94191.
This museum of winemaking and its history will astound. Beautifully exhibited in 16 themed rooms, including many Egyptian, Etruscan, Greek and Roman finds in excellent condition. Not to be missed. Entrance is free. Open 9.00–12.00 and 14.00–17.00 every day except Mon. If in a group, must pre-book.

Alba

Alba is an officially non-existent geographic entity which acts as a sub-province of Cuneo, where vines dominate and wines have worldwide renown. Its axis is the Tanaro river. North of the Tanaro is the Roero (or Roeri hills), the southern hill ranges are the Langhe (or Langa, in the singular). The Langhe are home to the top areas of Barbaresco and Barolo, which cover the lower reaches, close to the Tanaro. There is also the gloriously beautiful Alta Langa (High Langa), further south.

In Alba, king pin is Nebbiolo. The grape needs savvy to cultivate and is picked late; often still ripening when late season fog (*nebbia*) starts to descend. Its wines, with their high tannin and acidity, can seem harsh and astringent but their multi-faceted aromas, the subtleties of their flavours and the compexity of the best wines, not to mention the longevity of many, make them world beaters.

Star-status wines are also made from Dolcetto and Barbera. Dolcetto is early ripening and produces firm but joyously fruited wines, lower in acidity than most Piedmontese reds, usually drunk fairly young and ideal when something big and heavy is just too much. It is easy to spot by its red-veined leaves. Barbera has a magnificent swathe of acidity, cutting through its cranberry-like fruit, making it the perfect foil for rich food. It ripens mid-season. Less widespread red varieties include Freisa, Grignolino and the rare Pelaverga, while white are led by the refined Arneis, with the floral Favorita and the ubiquitous Moscato.

Throughout the area the importance of site is paramount. Prized hillsides give single-vineyard wines, or *crus*, while wines from particular plots on these hillsides will be further distinguished, the plot being called Vigna.

Note: in Italian 'Barolo' (or 'Barbaresco') refers to the village or commune, 'il Barolo' the wine.

Left *The incomparable colours of vineyards in autumn brighten a misty day near Barbaresco.*

Above *High quality peppers for sale in the market in the town of Alba, famed for its truffles.*

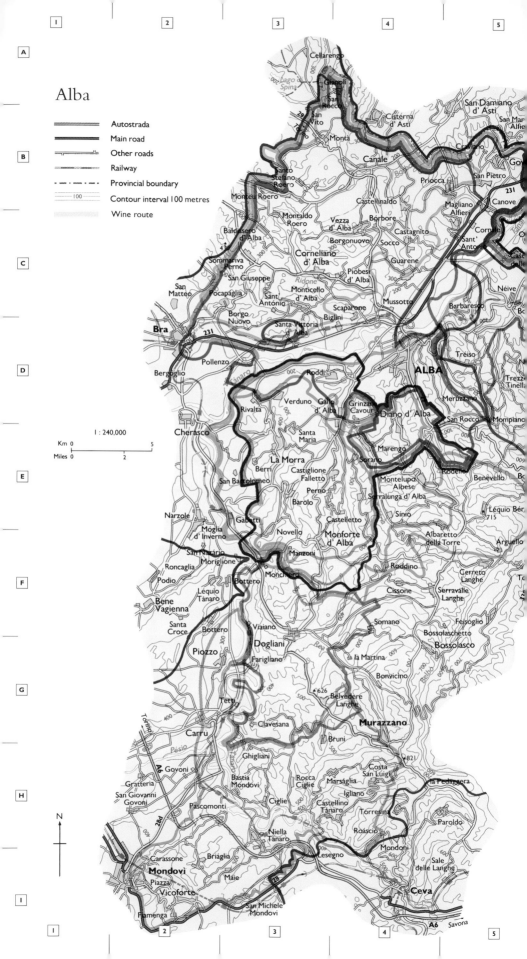

Alba

≡≡≡	Autostrada
▬▬▬	Main road
⊢⊣	Other roads
▦▦▦	Railway
─·─·─	Provincial boundary
100	Contour interval 100 metres
	Wine route

1 : 240,000

Km 0   5
Miles 0   2

N

Cellarengo
Lago di Spina
Ginoli
San Rocco
San Vito
Monta
San Damiano d'Asti
San Mar
Alfie
Cisterna d'Asti
Canale
Cravino
Govo
Santo Stefano Roero
Priocca
San Pietro
231
Monteu Roero
Castellinaldo
Magliano Alfieri
Canove
Montaldo Roero
Vezza d'Alba
Borbore
Sant'Antoni
Cornel
Baldissero d'Alba
Borgonuovo
Castagnito
Cast
delle
Corneliano d'Alba
Socco
Guarene
430
Sommariva Perno
San Giuseppe
Monticello d'Alba
Piobesi d'Alba
Néive
San Matteo
Pocapaglia
Sant'Antonio
Scaparone
Mussotto
Barbaresco
Bo
Bra
231
Borgo Nuovo
Santa Vittoria d'Alba
Biglini
300
Ridone
Treiso
Pollenzo
Roddi
ALBA
Trezz
Tinell
Bergoglio
Verduno
Gallo d'Alba
Grinzan
Cavour
Meruzzano
Rivalta
Diano d'Alba
San Rocco
Mompiano
Cherasco
Santa Maria
Marengo
Rodello
La Morra
Berri
Castiglione Falletto
Sorano
Montelupo Albese
Benévello
San Bartolomeo
Perno
Serralunga d'Alba
Léquio Bér
715
Narzole
Gabotti
Barolo
Castelletto
Sinio
Moglia d'Inverno
Novello
Monforte d'Alba
Albaretto della Torre
Arguello
San Nazario
Moriglione
Manzoni
Roddino
Cerreto Langhe
Roncaglia
Bottero
Monchiero
Cissone
Serravalle Langhe
Podio
Feisóglio
Léquio Tanaro
Somano
Bossolaschetto
Bene Vagienna
Viaiano
la Martina
Bossolasco
Santa Croce
Bottero
Dogliani
Bonvicino
Piozzo
Farigliano
Belvedere Langhe
Tetti
626
Carru
Clavesana
Murazzano
Bruni
Ghigliani
Costa San Luigi
la Pedaggera
Goyoni
Bastia Mondovi
Rocca Ciglie
Marságlia
Gratteria
Igliano
Paroldo
San Giovanni Govoni
Ciglie
Castellino Tanaro
Torresin
Pascomonti
Roáscio
Niella Tanaro
Mondoni
Sale delle Langhe
Carassone
Briáglia
Lesegno
Mondovi
Piazza
Maie
Ceva
Vicoforte
28
San Michele Mondovi
Fiamenga
A6
Savona

	Boundary of Barbera d' Alba DOC
	Boundary of Dolcetto d' Alba DOC
	Boundary of Nebbiolo d' Alba DOC
	Boundary of Dolcetto di Diano d' Alba DOC
	Boundary of Dolcetto di Dogliano DOC
	Boundary of Dolcetto della Langhe Monregalesi DOC
	Boundary of Moscato d' Asti Spumante DOC
	Boundary of Barola DOC
	Boundary of Barbaresco DOC
	Boundary of Roero DOC
	Boundary of Monferrato DOC
	Boundary of Langhe DOC
	Boundary of Verduno DOC

The Roero

The Roero covers a small area in Alba, bounded to the south and east by the River Tanaro, to the north by the provincial boundary and to the west (roughly inside a line from Bra to Cellarengo) by the disappearance of suitable slopes. The old Turin-Alba *statale* cuts through the middle: a slim valley with hills reaching 300–350 metres, rising up on either side. The prettier slopes are to the east, the western side is wilder and more rugged. This tour, progressing generally from north to south, loops across both sides to give a broadly comprehensive view of the zone. Two hours should be sufficient to do it all justice.

THE WINES

Red Roero is made from Alba's leading grape, Nebbiolo. It is lighter and fruitier in style than the Nebbiolo reds of the Langhe further south, mainly because the Roero hills are less high and the soils sandier, but also partly because a tiny percentage of white Arneis is meant to be used alongside the Nebbiolo. Roero is also the heartland of Nebbiolo d'Alba (100 percent Nebbiolo), generally weightier than Roero and gentler than Barolo. Those Roero producers who make both wines tend to make their Roero for early drinking and the Nebbiolo d'Alba for ageing a little longer.

White Arneis is also produced on its own, in Roero Arneis. This variety became quite fashionable in Piedmont as growers gloried in a native grape that, with coaxing, produced a refined, lightly perfumed, dry white wine with ageing potential. Encouraging results have also been achieved with Arneis in the Langhe but most remain convinced that it does best north of the Tanaro. The other white grape of note is Favorita. It provokes mixed reactions, however. Some really enjoy its light, perfumed, easy-drinking, floral style; others regard it as slight and forgettable.

Roero also lies within the area of Barbera d'Alba and a small outcrop of the Asti DOCG area surrounds the village of Santa Vittoria d'Alba, in the south of the zone.

Above *Countryside near Canale in the Roero. Canale, the main town of the district, is the base for several of the Roero's wine estates.*

*Above Canale's church and this
quiet village's meeting place.
Right The high climb to
Castellinaldo is rewarded by a
remarkable panorama.*

ROERO

RECOMMENDED PRODUCERS

Malvirà
Canale, Loc Canova
Tel: 0173 978145; E. F.
Medium sized, high quality estate,
mainly white wine production.
Three crus of Roero Arneis.

Angelo Negro e Figli
Monteu Roero, Fraz S Anna
Tel: 0173 90252; E.
Excellently sited vineyards and great
believers in the quality of Arneis.
Visits working hours only.

Carlo Deltetto
Canale
Tel: 0173 979383; E. F.
Finely-tuned, fresh, attractive wines,
particularly whites, from this family-
run estate. Must book.

Cantine Ascheri Giacomo
Bra
Tel: 0172 432021.
Just outside the Roero zone. Large,
family-run company, making wines
from several sites in Alba. Well
typed, lighter and softer than most.

Antiche Cantine F Cinzano
Tel: 0172 477111; E. F. G.
Sta Vittoria d'Alba
As well as vermouths, an important
producer of Asti and dry sparklers.
Book a week prior: visit includes the
fine, old cellars, vermouth production
and a glass museum.

ENOTECHE

Bottega del Vino
Castellinaldo

THE VINEYARDS

From Pessione (*see* page 45 and Asti map page 82) cross the
railway line and head southward to Poirino. From there
follow the *statale* to Villanova d'Asti and on towards San
Damiano. About ten minutes from Villanova, follow signs
right to Cisterna. This leads onto a narrow, but fairly straight
road through woodland. Cisterna marks the boundary
between Alba and the province of Asti and, once through
the village, descending to Canale, vineyards gradually spread
from over to the left to surround the road and good views of
the rather angular hills become more frequent.

Canale, reached after about five minutes, is the Roero's
main centre. It is the only town worthy of the name in the
zone and houses several of its major producers. On entering the town go right, through the old centre, following
the sign to Carmagnola then fork left to Monteu Roero.
This leads firstly along a valley with brilliant views of vines
in a series of amphitheatres across the hills, then up to
Monteu itself, for panoramic views and an impressive castle.
Next, curl back down but instead of heading back to
Canale, turn left at the first junction to Santo Stefano Roero.
This goes right through the most rugged part of the zone
with big, dumpy hills, intensively planted with vineyard.
You may optionally detour up to Santo Stefano itself – it
has little that can't be found elsewhere – before returning
to Canale. The circuit takes roughly 20 minutes.

Next, leave in the other direction, towards Asti. Shortly
after, turn right onto an unmade road to Castellinaldo.

Osteria Murivecchi
Bra, Via Piumati 19
Run from the old cellars of the
Ascheri wine family. Simple, homely
food and over 40 Piedmontese wines.

FOOD SPECIALITIES

Baked ham
Speciality of Canale. Sold by Federico
Faccenda, Via Roma 113, and Nino
Damonte, Piazza Trento e Trieste 75.
Peach market – Canale

EATING OUT

Centro
Priocca, Via Umberto 5
Tel: 0173 616112; closed Tues.
Easy-going restaurant, strictly local
fare including less commonly found
dishes. Wine list, knowledgeably put
together. Good value.
La Cantinetta
Castagnito, Via Roma 24
Tel: 0173 213388; closed Mon eves, Tue.
Warm, friendly place. Dishes given a
light hand. Tasting menu (excellent
value). Broad range of wines.
La Pergola
Vezza d'Alba, Loc Borgonuovo
Piazza San Carlo 1
Tel: 0173 65178; closed Mon.
Small, smart restaurant led by
its extraordinarily comprehensive
Piedmontese wine list. Very good
value. Seats outside.
Le Clivie
Piobesi d'Alba, Via Canoreto 1
Tel: 0173 619261; closed Mon, Sun pm.
In 19th-century villa: elegant, not too
costly. Classically-based dishes. Wines
mainly Piedmontese. Also hotel.
Al Castello
Sta Vittoria d'Alba, Via Cagna 4
Tel: 0172 478147; closed Wed.
Dishes evolved from Piedmont-
Ligurian roots. Wines, local and
from further afield. Seats outside –
with a view. Also hotel.
Osteria Boccondivino
Bra, Via Mendicit Istruita 14
Tel: 0172 425674; closed Sun.
Popular, friendly *locale*. Centre of the
'Slow Food' organization, so not the
spot for a hurried snack. Huge wine
list, wine-food recommendations.

PLACES OF INTEREST

**Museum of historical peasant
skills: trade, crafts and arts**
Cisterna d'Asti
Cinzano Museum
Tel: 0172 477356
Adjacent to the cellars. Fascinating
collection of glass and glasswear;
'must see'. Entrance is free. Open
9.00–12.00 each day except Tues,
Thur. Groups must pre-book.

More dense vineyard sights abound as the road twists up.
Castellinaldo glories in a fabulous castle and is also the
starting point of a short round tour of this prettier eastern
edge. Head towards Magliano Alfieri but before reaching it
(this village lies just outside the zone), fork left to glorious
Priocca, and back round to Castellinaldo. Before rising into
the town centre, turn left onto Via V Emanuele, which
leads towards Vezza d'Alba (signpost on wall to your right).
Continue down to the Alba–Canale *statale*. Turn left onto
the *statale* and head for Piobesi d'Alba, thence to Corneliano.

Corneliano d'Alba is a long, narrow village, fine for a
short leg-stretch or quick coffee but glorified by a superb
medieval tower that looms over the place. Follow signs for
Bra until, after a couple of minutes, there is a left turn to
Monticello. This also boasts a serious castle. Next, turn
right to Santa Vittoria, the southern limit of the zone.
These last few minutes of the tour take you up through
softer, prettier countryside. At Santa Vittoria go right up to
the castle at the top (Via Castello) where there's also a small
shop for wine and local food produce. From the castle walls
there are commanding views over the Tanaro River and the
first glimpse of the Langhe hills on the other side. Then
twist back down to the Tanaro Valley, either on the steepest
road (direction Alba) or on a shallower descent (direction
Bra). From the latter, a left turn to Alba at the valley floor
goes past the huge Cinzano establishment and its glass
museum; if the 'direct' road down is taken, divert right
briefly to Cinzano before turning back to reach Alba.

The town of Alba

RECOMMENDED PRODUCERS

Pio Cesare
Tel: 0173 440386; E. F.
Once one of the Langhe's most traditional estates, now a breeze of innovation is prompting changes. Receives only those with a serious interest in wine. Must book.

Ceretto
Tel: 0173 282582; E. F.
Highly regarded, stylistic wines, modern, elegant. Main wines all from single vineyards. Must book; visits only weekday working hours.

Alfredo Prunotto
Tel: 0173 363717; E.
Expect a gradual but continuous change in these well-typed wines from the estate's new owners, the Tuscan giant Antinori. Must book.

Poderi Colla
Tel: 0173 290148; E. F.
Three estates grouped together and based at San Rocco Seno d'Elvio. Also a small museum. Organically-inclined, careful cultivation on well-exposed sites. Must book.

Mauro Sebaste
Tel: 0173 262148; E. F.
Young estate. Grapes selected from various zones of Barolo (reds) and Roero (white), vinified in up-to-date cellars, just past Gallo d'Alba.

ENOTECHE

There are two great drinking spots at:
Fuori Orario Corso Torino 4 and
Osteria Lalibera Via Pertinace 24/a.

Above and right *Displays of civic pride in Alba during the truffle festival.*
Far right *The ugly misshapen tuber that creates all the fuss: the white truffle.*

The thought of reaching the town of Alba has terrific appeal. The idea of being right at the focal point of the production of Piedmont's most famous wines gives the place a lure that elevates it almost to a wine lover's place of pilgrimage. Touring Piedmont without setting foot in Alba would be unthinkable; it is, to all intents, as important a wine town as, for example, Beaune. The reality is more prosaic. Alba is certainly a major wine centre, it has certainly given its name to a plethora of fine wines, without doubt it links the zones of Barolo and Barbaresco and is but a stone's throw from either; but Alba does not live just for wine. Its main wealth comes from Miroglio, a hugely important textiles concern, which has a number of factories around the town, and from the local Ferrero chocolate company.

Alba itself is rather small, squashed into the narrow strip between the River Tanaro and the Langhe hills, with little space for other than a tiny old centre surrounded by a cluster of modern but smart residences. Approaching from north of the river, from the Roero (or Asti), there is little more than a sense of increasing population density and light industry until, suddenly, the river is crossed and, before blinking, you are in central Alba. From the Langhe hills, the approach is even more dramatic with Alba's towers below seeming close enough to touch.

Most of Alba's very smart shops straddle one narrow street, Via Vittorio Emanuele II, which runs out of the

central square, Piazza Savona. Several shops sell wine and more offer various types of often costly, edible goodies, not to mention truffles when in season (*see* below), as well as related products, truffle oil, pâté, cream, paste etc, throughout the year. The street is even more crowded on Saturdays when market stalls fill its centre. At the other end of Vittorio Emanuele, some of Alba's famous towers draw eyes steadily upwards. Apart from these and the nobility of the Duomo San Lorenzo, Alba's magnetism quickly palls.

TRUFFLES

Alba is recognized as the home of the prized white truffle, or *tartufo bianco*. This magnificent tuber is far superior to the black French version and is the subject of as much myth and blind adoration as factual discussion. It is in full season from October to December, when a Saturday market in Via Vittorio Emanuele leaves the street perfumed with its heady aromas for hours afterwards. Be aware, though, that Alba is the centre of the commercial gloss, rather than the true trade. Many of Alba's truffle sellers buy their wares at the main daily market in Asti. There are also many with no qualms about selling lesser-quality *tartufi bianchi* from outside Piedmont or indulging in even more heinous swindles.

There is, as yet, no reliable way of cultivating white truffles although experiments are continuing. *Tartufi bianchi* grow in the roots of trees, mainly oak and poplar, and are sniffed out by specially trained dogs. Most Piedmontese know roughly where the truffle areas are (mainly in the north of the region) but few know exactly where. Precise locations remain a heavily guarded secret; hunters set out at dawn to avoid being seen and followed to the best sites.

The white truffle is a knobbly, misshapen thing. Its great attribute is its pungent perfume. Hence *tartufi* are not cooked but shaved over dishes. If possible, try with risotto or scrambled eggs – foods which absorb and highlight the aromas. Truffles are sold by weight, and prices are mind-boggling. Just a few shavings over a dish can more than double its price. The fresher the tuber the better, as with time the aromas fade. To take one home, it is best packed in uncooked rice, but tissue paper and newsprint can be used.

Enoteca Fracchia e Berchialla
Via Vernazza 9
Most enthralling of Alba's wine shops. Cool tasting rooms downstairs.

FOOD SPECIALITIES

White Truffles See main text. Leading outlets are: Tartufi Ponzio, Via Vittorio Emanuele 26; Tartufi Morra, Piazza Pertinace 2. Both also sell truffle products.
Torrone Tooth-breakingly delicious toffee-like substance with added roast hazelnuts.
Nutella Hardly high gastronomy but a chocolate-hazelnut spread popular throught Italy, produced by Alba's chocolate company, Ferrero.

EATING OUT

Osteria dell'Arco Piazza Savona 5
Tel: 0173 363974; closed Sun.
Alba's leading *locale*. Temperature controlled wine dispenser, with Piedmont's best. Excellent value tasting menu and special lunch menus for those with less time.
Caffè Umberto Enoclub
Piazza Savona 4
Tel: 0173 441397; closed Mon lunch.
Pass Alba's youth and go downstairs to an old cellar with tables. Huge wine list; traditional food, local and well flavoured. Not costly.
Osteria Italia
Fraz San Rocco Seno d'Elvio 8
Tel: 0173 441547; closed Wed.
For a glass of wine and a snack or a full meal (inexpensive) from a short menu. Mainly youngish crowd. Largish wine list, mainly local.
Porta San Martino Via Einaudi 5
Tel: 0173 362335; closed Mon.
Smart. Local dishes with a refined hand. Good, wide wine list, mainly Piedmontese. Surprisingly good value.

HOTELS

Hotel Savona Via Roma 1
Tel: 0173 440440; fax: 0173 364312.
Centrally located, decent standard, pleasant enough but not exceptional.
Motel Alba Corso Asti 5
Tel: 0173 363251; fax: 0173 362990.
Just outside centre. Better than usual motel standard. Swimming pool. A new, and higher standard hotel, **I Castelli**, should be open in 1997.

SPECIAL EVENTS

Truffle fair October.
Wine fair Easter.
Donkey Palio October: parody of Asti's more serious event (see page 80). Pokes fun at 13th-century siege of Alba (by Asti).

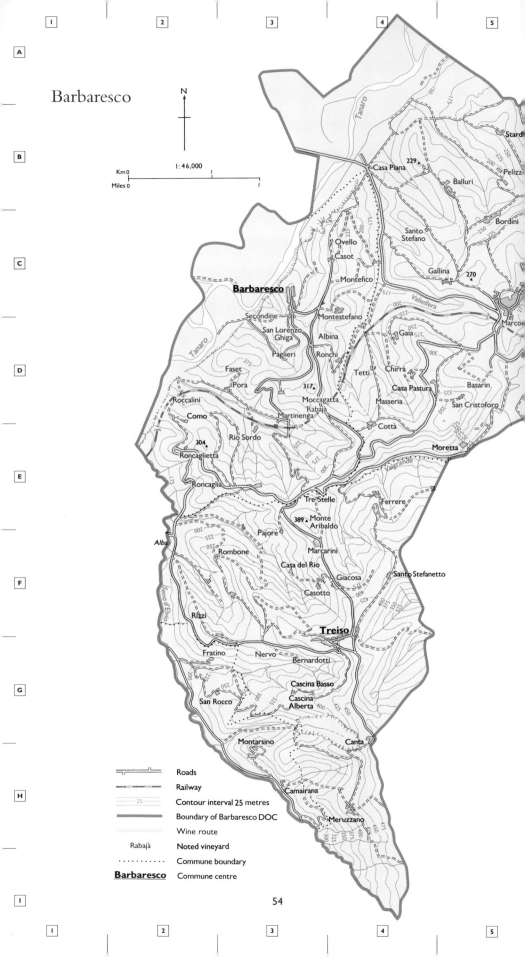

Barbaresco

N

1 : 46,000

Km 0
Miles 0

Tanaro

Stard

Casa Piana   229

Pelizz

Balluri

Bordini

Ovello
Casot

Santo
Stefano

Gallina   270

Montefico

Marco

Barbaresco

Secondine

Montestefano

Valsellera

San Lorenzo
Ghiga

Albina

Gaia

Paglieri

Ronchi

Faset

Tetti

Chirra

Pora

317

Casa Pastura

Basarin

Roccalini

Moccagatta
Rabaja

Masseria

San Cristoforo

Como

Martinenga

Rio Sordo

Cottà

304

Moretta

Roncaglietta

Roncaglia

Valgrande

Tre Stelle

Ferrere

Alba

389   Monte
Aribaldo

Pajore

Marcarini

Rombone

Casa del Rio

Santo Stefanetto

Seno d'Elvio

Giacosa

Rizzi

Casotto

Treiso

Fratino

Nervo

Bernardotti

Cascina Basso

San Rocco

Cascina
Alberta

Montarsino

Canta

Camairana

Meruzzano

	Roads
	Railway
25	Contour interval 25 metres
	Boundary of Barbaresco DOC
	Wine route
Rabajà	Noted vineyard
··········	Commune boundary
Barbaresco	Commune centre

Barbaresco

THE WINES

Barbaresco producers must be pretty fed up with being considered a Barolo add-on. It is quite common for people to refer to 'Barolo' but actually to mean both wines. Yet there is no sense of the second class about Barbaresco. The wines, exclusively from Nebbiolo, may come from lower slopes than their neighbour but this aids ripening, a factor assisted by the closeness of the Tanaro Valley (from the Alba-Asti road, running along the valley, you can see Barbaresco's westernmost slopes) which makes the climate a little warmer and drier. There may well be a little more clay in the calcareous–marl soil but this does not detract from quality. Barbaresco wines may, legally, only need one year in wood, compared with Barolo's two, yet this is a huge advantage, giving producers freedom to use increased bottle ageing instead. The wines may be a tad less muscular and aggressive than their better-known neighbour but they doubly repay any loss with enhanced refinement and finesse.

There is no difference in aesthetic appeal, either; the views may come and go with the curves of the hills, rather than being ever-present, but that makes the impact of their beauty even more powerful.

No, the real difference between Barolo and Barbaresco is that the latter is much smaller, producing a third of Barolo's output, and with estates usually smaller too. In addition, many Barolo producers also make Barbaresco. As these larger estates have been the ones to bring both wines to our notice it is hardly surprising that they have given prominence to their 'home' product. Certainly, there is more consistency of quality with Barbaresco and fewer duff estates.

As usual in Alba, Nebbiolo is not the only vine grown. There are noticeable quantities of Dolcetto and Barbera, a little Moscato (mainly in Neive commune) and some of the 'international' varieties. There is also a little production of Langhe Nebbiolo from vines not used for Barbaresco.

GETTING THERE

The vineyards of Barbaresco comprise the three communes of Neive, Treiso and Barbaresco itself, plus an extra strip

Right The impressive Martinenga estate, flanked by its crus, in one of Barbaresco's prettiest spots.

Above *A view across the rooftops of the tiny but well-cared for village of Barbaresco.*

BARBARESCO

RECOMMENDED PRODUCERS

Practically all estates also produce Dolcetto d'Alba and Barbera d'Alba, sometimes from single vineyards and sometimes, in the case of Barbera, partly or entirely *barrique*-aged. Many produce other wines too.

TREISO
Fiorenza Nada
Tel: 0173 638254; E. F.
Leading estate showing rapid and significant improvements in both vine husbandry and winemaking. Resources concentrated on non-*cru* Barbaresco. Can visit any day, afternoons only.
Orlando Abrigo
Tel: 0173 630232; E. F.
Small estate, making quiet, perfumed wines but not without structure. Keen to experiment with new techniques and grapes. Barbaresco *crus* Pajorè, Rongallo and Sorano. Must book. Agritourism.
Pelissero
Tel: 0173 638136; E. F.
One of Treiso's most encouraging estates, family run. Well made Barbaresco, *cru* Vanotu. Must book (as family not always at estate). Will advise on local restaurants, hotels and agritourism apartments.
Eredi Lodali
Tel: 0173 638109; E. F.
Smallish estate, with ancient cellars, traditional ideas and respect for quality. Barbaresco from *cru* Rocche dei 7 Fratelli. Also chance to taste local cheeses.
Villa Ile
Tel: 0173 362333; E. F.
Well organized (and well signposted) small estate with panoramically sited

just west of Treiso, bounded by the Seno d'Elvio stream. They are all within spitting distance of Alba. You'd never know it, though. Innumerable large signposts give clear directions to the various communes of Barolo, but of Neive, Treiso and Barbaresco eastwards, there is nary a hint. To find the way it is best to start from the large road junction by the town's hub, Piazza Savona. Take the road that keeps the square and the sign for the Hotel Savona, strictly behind you. Shortly after, pass through an elongated square and into a rather scruffy part of town and you quickly reach a roundabout. At the first exit, partially obscured is the first, small sign to the communes of the Barbaresco zone.

You cross a stream, then a railway, then begin to see vineyards, (not, as yet, part of the Barbaresco zone). Follow the road for two or three minutes, its large curves giving some entrancing views, forking right at the sign for Treiso.

Alternatively and more simply, there is a direct approach to Barbaresco from the Asti-Alba road, which *is* clearly signposted. Coming from Asti, it is the second turn-off (left) to Neive, at the traffic lights by the large Langa e Roero foodstuffs outlet. You would then start the tour in Barbaresco village, following the route from there (marked with an asterisk ★ in the text below) through Barbaresco and Neive communes, and branching off from the road back to Alba (at the point marked with a double asterisk ★★) to go through Treiso commune, finishing with a further part of Barbaresco.

NB Within the Barbaresco zone all distances are short and vineyards follow each other very closely. The whole route can be completed in half a day and leads on conveniently to the shortish route through Alba's Moscato country (*see* page 85). Many of the important *crus* are signposted: clearly in Barbaresco commune, less reliably in Neive and Treiso. A word of warning, though: don't try a scenic cut-through on one of the lanes leading off the through roads. Without fail they lead to no more than a cluster of buildings before dying out in a narrow, rutted track.

TREISO

The commune of Treiso contains some of Barbaresco's highest vineyards and the road towards the village quickly starts to rise into the hills. After a couple of minutes it takes a large, gentle, left-hand bend, bordering the *cru* of Rizzi. Shortly afterwards you pass the incredibly steep *cru* of Nervo to the right and, to the left, the impressive Bricco di Treiso: high, steep and topped by a house. Just another minute or two brings you to Treiso village. From here, curve back northwards, following signs to Alba/Neive, and descend through the heart of Treiso commune, where lie the steep, straight slopes of its prime sites, all to the left. First is Giacosa, below the first major leftwards bend; next comes the long Marcarini. Casotto nestles below but is hidden from view until the road makes a large leftward sweep, when you can look back on it. Then comes Pajoré:

steep and well-exposed, the commune's *cru* of highest renown. Pajoré finishes just as the road swings sharply right and meets the one between Alba and Neive.

BARBARESCO

As you reach the road junction you cross from Treiso into Barbaresco commune and pass the *frazione* of Tre Stelle. Follow signs for Barbaresco. Down to the left is the poorly known *cru* of Trifolera (a name possibly derived from the local dialect word for truffle). Within seconds, fork left off the road to Barbaresco village. On the left runs the long Rabajà *cru*, southwest facing and on somewhat gentler slopes, with the less extensive *cru* Martinenga below, at the point where the railway line cuts under a sharp U-turn in the road way beneath. (Those starting the tour in Barbaresco will already have taken this road and seen both vineyards from a better vantage point.)

The ridge on which the two vineyards lie is one of Barbaresco's two hill ranges, with spurs that tumble down northwesterly to the Tanaro Valley. After a tiny gap comes the second, more northern range and the Moccagatta vineyard (again, a second sighting for Barbaresco starters), which straddles both sides of the road. Just past this point the road forks, with signs leading to Barbaresco village in both directions. Take the right-hand fork. This leads into Barbaresco's most northern vineyard area, with harder, redder-coloured soils containing more clay. The steep, but well sheltered, south-facing *cru* Montestefano is on the right, between the fork and the next junction. You could, if impatient to see Barbaresco village, take this very sharp left turn into it. It is probably better, however, first to continue straight ahead for a short way, to see *cru* Montefico (right)

vineyards around the cellars and tightly knit, elegant wines. Also produce jams, vegetable preserves etc. Can arrange foot and mountain-bike routes, and other visits. Pay for tastings.

BARBARESCO
Ca' Romé
Tel: 0173 635175; E. F.
Cellars recently enlarged and re-organised. Produce only Barbaresco and Barolo (from Serralunga), *crus* and non-*crus* strictly traditional and only from good vintages. Visits only during working hours, must book, pay for tastings.
Cascina Luisin di Luigi Minuto
Tel: 0173 635154; E.
Friendly estate, with wines improving steadily. Southwest facing Nebbiolo vineyards (others face east and west). Organic cultivation. Barbaresco non-*cru* and *cru* Rabajà.
Giuseppe Cortese
Tel: 0173 635131; F.
Traditionally based, well-reputed small estate based in Via Rabajà. making Barbaresco *cru* Rabajà.
Gaja
Tel: 0173 635158; E. F.
The drive of Angelo Gaja, who single handedly raised the image, the prestige and the prices of Barbaresco, most notably those of his estate's wines, has been widely admired and fully reported. There is barely a word written about Barbaresco that doesn't concentrate on his endeavours. Not only does he make wines that astound by their power, longevity and enticing

Left *The spectacular beginnings of autumn in the Langhe.*
Above *The softly coloured village church in Treiso, home to some of Barbaresco's highest and steepest vineyards.*

suppleness, but he has carried Barbaresco's reputation world-wide. Neither is Gaja afraid of causing a stir. It was he who first put Barbaresco into *barriques* and when he replaced a Nebbiolo vineyard with Cabernet Sauvignon (and dubbed the vineyard Darmagi, dialect for 'a pity', his father's understated expression of disappointment) shock waves reverberated for miles around. Barbaresco comes in three *cru* versions, Sorì Tildin, Sorì San Lorenzo and Costa Russi, all excellent sites, also non-*cru*. From Barolo vineyards comes Barolo Sperss. Also Barbera Sitorey, Nebbiolo Sito Moresco, Darmagi, Chardonnays Gaia & Rey and Rossj-Bass. Cellars are in the centre of Barbaresco, opposite the castle, now owned by Gaja. Construction work linking the two means that visits not possible until, earliest, late 1997, then Tues to Fri am; booking essential. Arrangements for tasting to be made separately.

Carlo Giacosa
Tel: 0173 635116I
Small estate but with well-sited vineyards and careful production. Barbarescos Montefico (traditional) and Narin (*barrique*-aged).

Produttori del Barbaresco
Tel: 0173 635139; E. F.
An astoundingly good cooperative. Sixty members, with 100ha of land on many of Barbaresco's best sites.

then, after a few seconds, Ovello (both sides), the latter just before and between a right-handed U-turn (signed Neive). This is the northernmost extreme of the commune's *cru* vineyards (and the end of the tour for those starting in Barbaresco). Those starting in Treiso commune can now turn back and go into Barbaresco village, benefiting from a much gentler right-hand fork at the turn-off.

Barbaresco★ is a tiny but well cared for village, dominated by its dumpy, squared-off tower which is a local landmark, clearly visible from the Asti-Alba road. A few strides away is a deconsecrated church which houses an *enoteca regionale*, with a small but neatly displayed collection of wines, a good selection of bottles always open and an elegant area for serious *degustation*. (Closed on Mondays.)

Leave the village on the road that passes just right of the church, keeping on this (higher) road at the first fork. It leads past the Ghiga vineyard, immediately below on the right, with Secondine beyond it. Within Secondine is Sorì San Lorenzo (belonging to Gaja). Just before the next junction (those starting in Treiso will already have passed this), there is a slip road to the right, indicating a whole batch of vineyard sites. Take this and begin to descend into some of the most beautiful countryside that Alba has to offer. The road is narrow and full of tight bends. It twists right down to low land, where the single-track railway runs, and back up again, through the most prized and most densely planted land of Barbaresco. Various lanes branch off it too, mostly signposted Via Rabajà or some other *cru* name. Take none of these in order to keep on the right route.

Left *Neat ranks of lush Barbaresco vineyard, overlooked by the hilltop village of Neive (top right).*
Far left *Note how the vines in the foreground have taken on their autumn splendour, while those across the valley, differently aspected, are still green.*

Archetypally sound, typical, full and well-flavoured wines of excellent personality. Wide range of *crus*, including Moccagatta, Montestefano, Rabajà, Rio Sordo, Ovello. Also non-*cru*. Cellars central. Must book.

Albino Rocca
Tel: 0173 635145; E. F.
Small, quality conscious estate with reliably good wines. Cellars in Via Rabajà. Barbaresco *crus* Brich Ronchi (*barrique*-aged) and Loreto. Pay for tastings unless purchases made.

Tenute Cisa Asinari dei Marchesi di Gresy
Tel: 0173 635222; E. F.
Highly individual wines: light, graceful and greatly acclaimed. Barbaresco from *crus* Gaiun (*barrique*-aged), Camp Gros and Martinenga. Must book; visits weekdays until 16.00.

NEIVE
Cantina del Glicine
Tel: 0173 67215; F.
Wines made with care, attention and consideration of vintage character. Cellars are 17th-century, carved from tufa hillside. Barbaresco *crus* Curà, Marcorino and Rio Sordo. Must book.

Castello di Neive
Tel: 0173 67171
Largish, important estate with carefully crafted, beautifully styled wines of class led by Barbaresco *cru* Santo Stefano. Also one of the best Arneis from the Langhe. Ancient cellars.

F.lli Cigliutti
Tel: 0173 677185; E. F.
Small, family-run estate. Classy and powerful, long-lived wines of very high quality. Barbaresco *cru* Sellaboella.

Gastaldi
Tel: 0173 677400; E.
Excellent wines but, despite location produces no Barbaresco. Instead, Dolcetto d'Alba Moriolo is among the area's best. Must book.

Bruno Giacosa
Tel: 0173 67027; E.
Leading light of Neive. Once a firm believer in purchasing grapes, ferreting out the best growers on the best plots; has now bought 9ha of vineyard in Barolo (Serralunga). His knowledge of sites, though, remains unbeatable. Incredibly energetic for his age and brooking no nonsense from anyone, Bruno Giacosa's wines remain exemplary:

On the first part of the descent you pass the steepish, southwest facing Paglieri (also known as Pajé in dialect) on the right and Moccagatta on the left. (For Treiso starters, this is a second, closer sighting of Moccagatta.) The next major *cru* is Asili (left) then, on the right, just before the road takes a sharp U-turn leftward, are Fasèt, one of Barbaresco's finest sites, with its south-facing hill shaped like a shell, and then Porra, just below. Porra abuts the road all round the U-curve and continues past its next, rightward, bend, when the southern end of the Asili vineyard meets it again (still left). Just past this point the vineyards on the left are punctuated by the long, low estate buildings of Tenute Cisa Asinari dei Marchesi di Gresy. The tiny *cru* Gaiun is the last clutch of vines close to the left side of the road, before it bends again to the right. Above Gaiun is Martinenga, then Rabajà (for some a second view), abutting the hill crest and dropping past the far side of the estate buildings. The small Camp Gros vineyard nestles between the two.

The road bends sharply right, over the railway, and begins to re-ascend, giving a superb panoramic view of this whole curved spread of vineyards. It then takes a U-turn leftwards and rises more steeply, after a while gradually meeting the long ridge of the Rio Sordo *cru* (right), which is seen as you rise. You zig-zag beside Rio Sordo before emerging onto the Alba–Neive road at Tre Stelle. Turn left, then immediately fork right (signed Mango). This takes you along between the southern edge of Barbaresco commune and the north of Treiso for a couple of minutes then into the commune of Neive.

especially Barbaresco *cru* Santo Stefano. Must book.

Paitin di Pasquero Elio
Tel: 0173 67343; E. F.
Smallish long-standing estate and owners of top notch Sorì Paitin vineyard since Italy's unification. Underground cellars are 15th-century, but working cellars are more modern. Currently working with better clones of Nebbiolo and new grape varieties.

Sottimano
Tel: 0173 635186; E. F.
Small estate with vines in Treiso too. Barbaresco *cru* Brichet the flagship.

ENOTECHE

See main text.

EATING OUT

Osteria dell'Unione
Treiso, Via Alba 1
Tel: 0173 638303; closed Sun pm, Mon, Tues.
Easy-going, welcoming and popular place despite (or because of?) rarely changing menu. Good basic ingredients, cooked to maximize flavour, complemented by excellent wine list. All good value. Seats outside. Cash only.

Il Tornavento
Treiso, Piazza Baracco 7
Tel: 0173 638333; closed Tues.
Old building refurbished to give

NEIVE

Soils in Neive are sandier and, typically, the wines are the firmest, most weighty and powerful examples of Barbaresco. Although the largest commune of the three, with the highest number of growers, Neive produces less than a third of all Barbarescos (but plentiful Dolcetto and Barbera).

Neive village acts rather as the centre of a wheel of which the important hill ridges form the spokes. So, to see the commune's leading *crus*, you need to head out on each of the roads leaving the village in turn, each time turning back. In most cases, better views are gleaned on the return stretch.

The road from Tre Stelle firstly snakes through patches of woods and fruit tree cultivation but after two junctions passes, to the left, *crus* Basarin and San Cristoforo. Turn right at the Mango junction. Initially you skirt the Serraboella hill ridge but follow until the second hairpin for an excellent view of Sorì Paitin filling the steep, southeasterly facing curve of the ridge end. On the return, head straight towards Neive village, crossing the Tinella stream. You shortly meet the railway line, running parallel on the left. After a while, the road bends right and crosses back over the Tinella. After another couple of sharp bends it heads steadily southeast, now giving views from above of Serraboella, the cru Sorì Paitin at its southern corner and cru Bricco di Neive just a short way further on. A clock tower marks the end of this spoke.

Back across the Tinella, turn right (direction Alba/Asti), cross the railway, head through the built-up part of Neive and continue for a couple of minutes on this road before

Above *Signs to food, wine and culture in a Neive side street.*
Right *The arduous task of removing tartrates from the inside of an old* botte.

turning round at the province border (signed). Now on the right are a series of roughly southeasterly facing hill ridge ends, chiefly planted with vine varieties other than Nebbiolo: first Montebertotto, then Messoirano and Pelisseri.

The modern, functional and aesthetically uninspiring centre of Neive reappears all too quickly. However, Neive has an old centre too, which has much more to offer. Follow the road right round a large walled curve above which sits *cru* Marcarini. Then divert right, forking up steeply into the old town. Be prepared to park some way outside and walk the rest. The form of this cobbled, hilly, medieval centre, though, truly deserves that tired adjective 'charming'.

After descending from Neive, continue on the Asti/Alba road, glancing up at the steep, long and narrow vineyard of Gallina. Just opposite the next junction, leading left to Barbaresco (the approach road taken by those who started the tour there), is *cru* Santo Stefano, better viewed if you continue the short distance to the commune boundary, then turn back to view it on the left on your return towards Neive.

The last spoke leaves Neive on the road to Treiso. This leads back westwards through the densest Nebbiolo plantings and almost half of its *crus*. The road curves right, left, right again, then a bowl of vineyards appears on the left. Cru Valtorta stretches across it, partially hidden behind the trees, with Pastura saddled behind. Half a minute or so later, the road bends sharply left. From here, it starts to follow the base curve of a large, horseshoe-shaped hill formation on the right. The principal slopes are poorly orientated but the furls of the hills give several southerly facing vineyards. Gaia, Curra and Cottà lie just below, Masseria and Tetti are further back; all are devilishly difficult to pinpoint. On leaving the horseshoe you meet the road to Barbaresco and cross back into its commune.

BARBARESCO (WESTERN EDGE)

Now simply follow the road to Treiso/Alba. After Tre Stelle, it begins to descend towards the Tanaro and cuts through a last cluster of vineyards. Past the first turn-off to Treiso is a second sight of Rio Sordo, this time over to the right. Then, a few bends further on, Roncaglia stretches right down across the hill on the left. The road bends right and Roncagliette takes its place, also straddling the left-side hill. At the same time Gaja's southwest facing Sorì Tildin plunges down towards the road from the right. A sharp hairpin bend is visible a short distance in front, as is Gaja's other *cru*, Costa Russi, also southwest facing, under the road past the hairpin. The twist encloses Roncagliette, which has even greater impact seen after the twist, from below. The same applies to Roncaglia, the next sweep of vineyard, which also covers the full slope between the two branches of the road. Very shortly afterwards the second turn-off to Treiso appears.★★ Alba, marking the end of the tour, is just a few minutes away.

Above *Concentrated eating at La Contea di Neive – Barbaresco's top spot.*

restaurant a light, modern feel. Cooking also light and based, rather loosely, on local dishes. Wide choice of local wines and a few from elsewhere. Seats outside – on terrace overlooking vineyards. Good value.

Rabayà
Barbaresco, Via Rabajà 9
Tel: 0173 635223; closed Thurs.
Well-known and highly regarded restaurant, with well-flavoured dishes, traditional but given an individual touch. Good choice of mainly Piedmontese wines. Seats outside. Good value.

Antica Torre
Barbaresco, Via Torino 8
Tel: 0173 635110; closed Wed.
Family-run *trattoria* to frequent for the food, wine and hospitality, rather than the surroundings. Dishes strictly local, some classics, others more unusual (some may need advance ordering). Wines are even more local, the list strongly slanted to Barbaresco. Cash only.

Contea di Neive
Neive, Piazza Cocito 8
Tel: 0173 67126; closed Sun pm and Mon except in autumn.
Top place of the zone. Just a mention gets mouths watering. The joy is the abundant use of fresh vegetables, from the owners' kitchen garden, used in typical Piedmontese ways. Excellent cheese board too but meat not forgotten. Large wine list, the same as in the Enoteca della Contea, situated opposite and owned by the same couple. Surroundings classy, service to match. Expensive but worth the splurge: if budget will not stretch, a more manageable fixed price menu is available. Seats outside.

Barolo

THE WINES

To the uninitiated Barolo is quite simply a tough, astringent wine, slow to age but infinitely rewarding when mature, made from the Nebbiolo grape, grown near to Alba. Yet there is much more to it and one Barolo can differ greatly from another. Some of the differences are due to varying winemaking philosophies. A topic which caused hot debate in the 1980s, for example, was the tendency of some to use shorter skin maceration during fermentation, to lighten the wine and exphasize its fruit, while others sustained the traditional, long maceration, giving greater structure. Now it is more the use of *barriques* that separates estates. Additionally, some prefer the complexity that results when grapes from a number of sites are blended, while most favour the individuality of single-site wines.

Overlaying all this, however, are intrinsic variabilities from the terrain. The zone is partially bisected by the Talloria dell'Annunziata brook, running along the valley between Alba and Barolo village. From this a series of roughly parallel ridges rise up on either side, creating a sort of horseshoe-shape. To the west the soil is Tortonian, a bluish-grey calcareous marl with good clay content, rich in magnesium and manganese; to the east land formations are Helvetian, giving a creamy-grey marl with greater sand and chalk, richer in iron, phosphorus and potassium. The more westerly soils encourage aromas, finesse and quicker developing wines; those of easterly origin derive body, structure, weight and longevity. To simplify things: western wines are exemplifed by those from the communes of La Morra and Barolo; easterly ones by those from Serralunga and Monforte, while those from Castiglione Falletto (central east) are somewhere in between.

Left *Peach trees being sprayed in La Morra; viticulture may be the most obvious agricultural activity in Barolo, but it is not the only one.*

Barolo

	Roads
25	Contour interval 25 metres
	Boundary of Barolo DOC
	Boundary of Verduno DOC
Briccolina	Noted vineyard
	Wine route
....	Commune boundary
Barolo	Commune centre

BAROLO

RECOMMENDED PRODUCERS

Estates also produce Dolcetto d'Alba and Barbera d'Alba, sometimes from single vineyards and sometimes, in the case of Barbera, partly or entirely *barrique*-aged. Many of these are top class. Nearly all produce Langhe Nebbiolo and various other wines too.

VERDUNO
Bel Colle
Tel: 0172 470196; E. F. G.
Verduno's largest estate. Well-made wines especially Barolo *cru* Monvigliero and Verduno Pelaverga. Visits working hours only, must book.
Fratelli Alessandria
Tel: 0172 470113; E.
Smallish estate in splendid 18th-century building, original cellars, just by castle. Much emphasis on viticulture. Barolo from south-facing *cru* Monvigliero.

LA MORRA
Aurelio Settimo
Tel: 0173 50803; fax: 0173 509318; E. F.
Tiny estate, in Annunziata. Classically styled, well-made wines. Barolo *cru* Rocche and non-*cru*. Must book, if possible by fax. Vineyard walks.
Batasiolo
Tel: 0173 50130
Large, important estate with vineyards throughout the zone and several Barolo *crus*. Wines becoming richer and rounder following the change of consultant.
Ciabot Berton
Tel: 0173 50217; E. F.

THE VINEYARDS

The ridge-like structure of Barolo means that most areas give wonderful panoramic views across the valleys and several villages have a spot marked *belvedere* with particularly wide-ranging views. Most villages are topped by castles too, each of a characteristic shape, which, once recognized, make orientation easy. The better vineyards are often at 300–400 metres. The distances are such that, in good weather, the zone would be ideal for for keen cyclists or a walking tour. With motorized transport, you will need a couple of days or more to do it full justice. Just as in Barbaresco, 'off-roading' leads nowhere while, unlike Barbaresco, hardly any of the top vineyards are signposted.

The tour leads first through the western vineyards, then covers the eastern side, finishing along the central-eastern ridge. From Alba, leave on the road to Gallo and Barolo but divert to Roddi as soon as it is signed. The village, well-to-do and topped by a thick-set, stately castle is worth a glance, after which head to Verduno. There is a road that leads straight to it, clearly marked 'Strada Roddi-Verduno' although it is absent from most maps.

VERDUNO

Verduno is the most northwesterly of Barolo's communes, with only its southern edge within the zone. It is, though, the centre of the wine zone Verduno Pelaverga (also called simply Verduno), producing wine from the Pelaverga grape (red). The Strada Roddi–Verduno almost immediately enters the wine zone and quickly rises into vine country. The first major vineyard to the right is Monvigliero, Verduno's most important. About half way along you pass the tiny *crus* of Massara (left), and Pisapolla (right) opposite.

The road then skirts round a wall to its right (inside which is Verduno village). Below is Riva, another good *cru*. Throughout the ascent look back from time to time – the views are a delight. Verduno village, a decent enough small place, has its *belvedere* with views over Riva and across the valley, although short people will find their view impeded by the safety fencing. From there take the road for La Morra and within a minute you cross into La Morra commune.

LA MORRA

La Morra is Barolo's highest producing commune and contains a large cluster of *crus*, mainly to the south of the commune, on the shell-shaped arc of hills betwen the village and that of Barolo. First, though, follow the road from Verduno right to the top of the hill on which La Morra perches, to see the village and, more specifically, in Piazza Castello, its *belvedere*, the zone's most famous. Next, cut through La Morra's more northerly vineyards, on the road to Santa Maria (direction Alba). After the zig zag of the descent and the Annunziata turn off (don't take this), there's a short straight stretch, then the road, descending, bends sharply right and then left. At this point, *cru* Roggeri is on the right. *Cru* Capallotti (left) hugs the next bend rightwards. Bricco Chiesa (right) follows, enclosing the road on both sides, pre- and post- its sharp curve right. Pass the *frazione* of Santa Maria and shortly after you see the long, south-facing slopes of Rive, just back from the road.

From here, slip briefly out of the commune, taking the road back to Gallo, then turn right, south along the main road towards Barolo. Return to La Morra at the junction for Annunziata, about two kilometres along. Above the

Smallish estate with vineyards of good age around and opposite: on Bricco San Biagio, good, south-facing. Elegant, lightish, well-balanced wines.

Corino
Tel: 0183 50219; F.
Fine wines with complex aromas and class, plus the balance to be enjoyable while young yet with strong ageing potential. Barolo *crus* Rocche, Giachini.

Dosio
Tel: 0173 50677; E. F.
High-perched estate (Loc Serradenari). Lightish but firm wines. Barolo non-*cru* and *cru* Fossati. Stocks of numerous vintages of the '60s, '70s and '80s.

Cascina Nuova di Elio Altare
Tel: 0173 50835; F.
Altare, once the outstanding 'modernist', now producer of stunning wines, refined, complex, well-fruited and supple, without lacking concentration or backbone. Barolo best from Vigneto Alborina but Vigna Alborina refers to non-Barolo oaked Nebbiolo. Book.

Fratelli Oddero
Tel: 0173 50618; E. F.
Old, established family estate. Large, with almost 50ha of vineyard in and around Barolo. Traditional but lightweight wines, needing good vintages to shine. Top *crus* Rionda and Mondoca di Bussia Soprana. Pay for tastings; will offer vineyard visit (weather permitting).

Gianfranco Bovio
Tel: 0173 50190
Small estate with gems of wines especially Barolo Vigna Arborina.

Far left *Picking Dolcetto grapes near La Morra. Dolcetto ripens earlier than Nebbiolo – by as much as a month – and tends to be planted on less favourably orientated sites.*
Left *The vine-lined approaches to La Morra village.*
Above *Tall, stainless steel vats in the cellars of high-ranking producer, Renato Ratti.*

Gianni Voerzio
Tel: 0173 509194; F.
Smallish estate with elegant, fine-tuned wines. Cellars close to centre of La Morra. Barolo *cru* La Serra. Must book.

'Monfalletto' di Cordero di Montezemolo
Tel: 0173 50344; E. F.
Medium-sized estate with cellars in Annunziata. Good, traditionally made wines with emphasis on longevity and elegance. Barolo *crus* Monfalletto and Enrico VI. Visits working hours only.

Poderi Marcarini
Tel: 0173 50222; E. F. S.
Estate of high renown. Balanced, complex wines of distinction. Vineyards all in La Morra. Barolo from *crus* Brunate and La Serra. Must book.

Renato Ratti – Antiche Cantine dell'Abbazia dell'Annunziata
Tel: 0173 50185; E. F.
The late Renato Ratti is still talked about in awed terms. No-one had more detailed knowledge of the terrain or worked as tirelessly to improve quality in the entire zone. Estate now run by his son Pietro. Wines are gradually regaining their former style and individuality. Vineyards around the estate. Barolo Rocche Marcenasco, Conca Marcenasco and Marcenasco. Must book for weekend visits; pay for tastings. Don't miss the wine museum (see main text).

Roberto Voerzio
Tel: 0173 509196; F.
10ha of vineyard, mainly of top *crus* in Barolo commune. Viticultural fanatic; very low yields, incredibly concentrated grapes. Wines of powerful intensity but rich fruitiness that, when at their best, are remarkably fine. Barolo *crus* La Serra, Brunate and Cerequio.

Rocche Costamagna
Tel: 0173 509225; E. F.
Cellars in La Morra village. Well set up for visitors. Wines for lovers of heavy oaking only. Barolos from Rocche di La Morra and Vigna Francesco (top part of Rocche).

BAROLO
Aldo Vajra
Tel: 0173 56257; F.
Quiet, thoughtful producer who makes quiet, thought-provoking wines of refinement and class. Notable Barolo Bricco delle Viole. No visits during harvest period. Some old vintages available for tasting (on payment).

road is the long, slim Gancia Luciani vineyard. The road then curves left around a beautiful shell-shaped vineyard, Conca Marcenasco, also known as Conca dell'Annunziata, and continues twisting through the tiny village of Annunziata. The focal point is a 15th-century abbey which now houses the Ratti museum, a wonderful and thought-provoking collection of tools, materials, documents and maps, dedicated to the wine history of Alba in general and Barolo in particular. The road, here called Via Antica Annunziata, then loops back and forth alongside the large and prestigious Rocche vineyard (on the left), curves up through the hamlet of Pozzo and then rejoins the La Morra-Gallo road. Ascend once more to find the road to Barolo. This gives quite amazing views to the left across the lands of La Morra.

As the road snakes round the hamlet of Croera, it starts to pass La Morra's 'golden triangle', an amphitheatre of south-facing vineyards, all on the left. First is Serra, with fanning out clockwise below it, Brunate, Cerequio and Ca' Nere, and below are Sarmassa and Zonchera (although both these lie in Barolo commune). Next to Serra is Fossati, which also sits above Ca' Nere. The *crus* Brunate and Cerequio are justly famous and the names have an almost magical ring to them.

BAROLO

At this point you pass into Barolo commune, which contains the southern tip of Fossati plus a little of both Brunate and Cerequio (and Zonchera and all Sarmassa). It also has many other top *crus* including Cannubi, the most renowned of all. The road towards the village passes the landmark of Castello della Volta, then, on its final descent, gives tantalizing glimpses of Barolo's mesmeric castle, perched on an

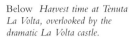

overhanging spur that looks dangerously precarious. The castle dominates the village, looking as if it has been drilled through the rock, speared by some malevolent spirit. Whichever way you go it will eventually block your path. Otherwise, Barolo lives by wine and for wine. The castle accomodates the Barolo *enoteca regionale* and a small museum. Many of the village's buildings house cellars and most of its residents are involved in wine in some way. Bottles sprout from shop windows and restaurants proclaim their selections. So solidly does the village demonstrate its position as the hub of wine country that it is risking getting too twee for its own good.

Next, head back northwest through the heart of the commune, leaving the village on the right-hand road, the Via Alba, opposite the Borgogno cellars. As you go, take the chance to look back at the castle at its most dramatic. The road, the main Alba-Barolo link, cuts through the plain, its verges punctuated by various producers'

Cantina Mascarello di Bartolo Mascarello
Tel: 0173 56125: F. G.
Small, staunchly traditional estate. Mascarello states proudly he has no *barriques*, follows no California model and does not produce *cru* wines and instead blends wines from his vineyards (Cannubi and three others) into punchy, rich, intense, muscular, long-lived wines that can be mind-blowing.

Francesco Rinaldi e Figli
Tel: 0173 440484; G.
Smallish, traditional estate with old barrels and old cellars, hewn out of the hillside. Barolo from *crus* Cannubi and Brunate. Must book.

Fratelli Barale
Tel: 0173 56127; E. F.
Founded 1870. Ancient underground cellars in central Barolo. Barolo *crus* Castellero and Bussia.

Below *Detail from the grounds of the Fontanafredda estate.*
Right *Cellars at Fontanafredda clearly reflect the scale and importance of the estate.*

Giacomo Borgogno
Tel: 0173 56108; E. F. G.
Long-standing, welcoming estate with chunky, long-lived wines – and a few reserves tucked away. Barolo *cru* Liste. Visits weekdays working hours, am weekends (for which booking essential). Not Aug. First wine tasted free, pay for rest.

Giorgio Scarzello e Figli
Tel: 0173 56170; E. F.
Small, unpretentious, family estate, well-typed, mid-weight wines.

Luciano Sandrone
Tel: 0173 56239 E. F.
Elegant and concentrated wines, notably those from wonder-*cru* Cannubi Boschis. Organic leanings. Must book.

Marchesi di Barolo
Tel: 0173 56101; E. F. G.
Large company, wines from numerous vineyards in Barolo and Barbaresco. Rich, balanced, full, well-structured wines. Rare chance to compare Barolo *crus* Cannubi, Cannubi Valletta, Sarmassa, Brunate and Coste di Rose. Must book for weekends and holidays (am only). First wine tasted free, pay for rest.

Guiseppe Rinaldi
Tel: 0173 56156; E. F.
Smallish, traditional, family-run estate.

establishments but giving perfect views (left) of the large, southeast facing Cannubi. The site marks where the Tortonian soils of the west meet the Helvetian of the east and, it is said, from these Cannubi's wines gain both elegance and power, perfume and structure. The entire vineyard follows the road for over a kilometre. The part nearest the village is known as Muscatel, the next section, Valletta, in its lower reaches and San Lorenzo above. Then, half a kilometre along, comes Cannubi itself, followed, after a tiny gap where the hills face due east, by Boschis (also called Monghisolfo). All these fragments are often prefixed with Cannubi (Cannubi-Boschis, for instance) to make their aristocracy clear. After Boschis the hill meets the plain and Barolo commune ends.

GRINZANE CAVOUR

The commune of Grinzane Cavour is marginal as far as wine production is concerned, with few estates of note and just one important vineyard. It would be a great loss not to visit it, though, as it holds a truly magnificent castle, a joy to walk around. The huge, 14th-century, turreted lump gives 360° vistas including, to the south, the one *cru*, the aptly named Castello. On one flank of the castle is a door, subtly marked 'avanti' (enter). This leads to the *enoteca regionale*, one of the region's best and well frequented, with a large selection of wines well displayed. One part of the castle has been turned into a high quality, expensive restaurant; the rest is open to be visited (guide-accompanied only).

From Barolo, follow the road to Alba (keeping on the old road and avoiding the *superstrada*) to Gallo d'Alba, a bustling but rather down-at-heel place, from where Grinzane Cavour is almost immediately signed right. After the castle, you might want to take a brief detour along the road towards Diano d'Alba for a good general impression of the ordered expanses of the zone, best seen as you turn back towards Gallo.

SERRALUNGA

Serralunga is a long, slim commune stretching north to south. It houses Barolo's largest company, Fontanafredda, and a lot of small growers who sell their grapes, but comparatively little in between. From Grinzane Cavour, return to Gallo and turn left at the T-junction into its centre. Barely a minute later, a left turn (signposted Serralunga) marks the beginning of the commune. The first vineyard to appear (left) is San Pietro. Next comes Gallaretto, then, after a dip in the hills the tiny Bianca, followed by Gattinera then La Rosa. All these are owned by Fontanafredda and the estate complex sits just under Gattinera. (The best views, however, are from the road to Castiglione Falletto – *see* pages 72-3.)

Continue to Serralunga. The road rises, giving views of Castiglione Falletto a short distance over to the right. There's a double hairpin bend, immediately after which the Costabella vineyard stretches across, again, to the right. Within a couple of minutes the road passes through the *frazione* of Borgata. Below it (right) but invisible from the road, is the prime, south-facing vineyard Sorì Baudana, with its steepest slopes lying just below the *frazione*'s houses. Past the cluster of habitation and by a righthand curve is the edge of Sorì Baudana (with Castiglione Falletto beyond) and, to the left, Ceretto. Then comes another

Barolo vineyards in Brunate, Le Coste, Cannubi-San Lorenzo, Ravera. Must book; visits working hours only.
Sebaste
Tel: 0173 56266; E. F.
Mid-sized estate now settling after several changes. Elegant, well-fruited wines, characterful and long. Cellars adjacent to a 15th-century chapel of San Pietro delle Viole. Must book.
Tenuta La Volta di Cabutto Bartolomeo
Tel: 0173 56168; E.
Welcoming estate with high altitude and soils giving elegant wines of great finesse. Traditional winemaking; tightly pruned vines. Barolo Vigna La Volta.

SERRALUNGA
Gabutti di Franco Boasso
Tel: 0173 613165; F.
Small, traditionalist estate; balanced, classically structured wines, from Serralunga's Gabutti vineyard. Vineyard visits encouraged. Can help with restaurant and hotel bookings.

Below *The impeccably kept Fontanafredda estate in Serralunga. The buildings have the two-tone stripes so traditional of the area.*

Above *Early signs of spring in Serralunga. The steep aspect of the vineyards can be seen beyond.*

Giuseppe Cappellano
Tel: 0173 613103; E.
Long-established estate, now less rigidly traditional. Robust wines. Also Barolo Chinato.

Tenimenti Fontanafredda
Tel: 0173 613161.
The zone's largest estate, over 70ha of vineyard owned and, with bought-in grapes, producing 6½ million bottles. Estate buildings form practically a village, all sparklingly smart and tidy, and well worth seeing. Equivalently large range of wines; most interesting are Barolo *crus* (La Delizia, La Villa, Lazzarito, Gattinera, La Rosa); Barolo Serralunga d'Alba, from selected vines. Wine shop open daily except Tues. Visits Apr–Nov: book. Weekends: reduced opening hours.

Vigna Rionda
Tel: 0173 613138; E. F.
With 2½ha on the prestigious *cru* of Vigna Rionda, this estate represents the best of Serralunga. Big, powerful, firmly structured wines with good aromas and a supple fruit centre giving complexity and balance. Barolo non-*cru* and *crus* Vigna Rionda, Vigna Parafada, Vigna Margheria.

MONFORTE
Parusso
Tel: 0173 78257; F.
Family estate. Careful vineyard husbandry, minimal treatments and strict grape selection. Aim for rounded wines of finesse, as drinkable young as when fully mature. Barolo *crus* Bussia and Mariondino.

Conterno-Fantino
Tel: 0173 78204; E. F.
Highly rated estate with bang up to date cellar on Bricco Bastia, at 600m one of Monforte's highest points.

house on the right and a 'Stop' sign. At this point, stretching away to the left is the *cru* Prapò.

Just by the lane off to Gabutti, the road starts to cut through the marvellous amphitheatre of the Delizia cru, followed on the right by Lazzarito, mostly hidden from view, both of these owned by Fontanafredda. This leads to the final approaches to Serralunga village. Indeed, the slopes of Cucco (left) are hidden behind its first streets.

Serralunga's castle is visible for miles around and its particular silhouette makes it instantly recognizable. It appears to have risen up through the rock, as in some mystical earthquake. The village, residential more than commercial, is calm and unexploited, yet is well cared for, boasts public toilets and glories in some marvellous views. The steep slopes of the *cru* Rivette are just under the village, seen to the right as you enter. Just below it is Marenca. The two, known as Marenca-Rivette are owned by Barbaresco's Gaja (*see* page 57). Immediately beneath the piazza is Vigna Rionda, Serralunga's best known *cru*. It covers the south-facing slopes of a small spur of land that appears on the right just at the sign indicating the village end. Then follows a cluster of vineyards, all on the right. First is Serra with Collaretto beneath; next, following a gentle left-hand bend in the road, Briccolina, Ornato and Falletto (with views of Serralunga back to the left). There is a shortish stretch without any vineyards of note, followed by another batch of *crus* on the right, Bosco Areto, Francia and Arione. Arione marks the southern border of Serralunga commune from where the road crosses into Roddino and, temporarily, out of the Barolo zone.

MONFORTE EAST
About three minutes after leaving Serralunga commune you pass the turn off to Bossolasco and after a similar time gap you enter Monforte commune. The first stretch of this high terrain is outside Barolo; the southern edges of the zone are rejoined just before reaching a cluster of houses punctuated by an ugly furnace chimney. Many of Monforte's *crus* lie in its east, on a series of short, lateral hill ridges, stretching from the commune's central spine, down to the Talloria di Castiglione brook, giving a succession of southeastern facing slopes. No roads go through them but there are several good vantage points, which also give brilliant views of much of Serralunga, across the brook. One such is reached from a sharp turn back right, roughly opposite the chimney. Within seconds you meet a church with several roads forking off. Take the one immediately right of the church. It passes *frazione* Le Coste, then skirts the Le Coste vineyard, below on the right. After a while the asphalted road curves right and down a steep descent. (This is the border between *crus* Le Coste (right) and (left) Ravera). Just past here, on an unmade road, with your back to the line of the road, *cru* Mosconi is straight in front, on the next hill ridge (topped by a tiny cluster of buildings).

On the following hill ridge is Ginestra and on the one beyond both Gavarini and Grassi. Behind Grassi are, sequentially, La Villa, Pressenda and Ceretta, although these become increasingly difficult to see. There are other vantage points further along the narrow, unmade road, including a good view of Monforte village.

Back by the chimney, continue into Monforte village. This is one of the larger commune centres and has the appearance of being the most extensive. The central square, calm but active, is the pivot of the village, with a superb, solid church and clock tower just behind. It is well worth hiking up to the old church at the top of the town, though, for some truly wonderful panoramas. Leave Monforte on the road north, towards Castiglione Falletto, but branch off shortly after to Perno. (It is clearly signed in advance but the actual fork, just past a curve, hits you very suddenly.) From the next junction (signed Loc Grassi) there are occasional good sightings to the right of the eastern lateral ridges. Throughout this stretch the *cru* Gramolere is visible to the left. The road curves inexorably, then appears a 12th-century chapel atop a conical hill. This is the top *cru* Santo Stefano. Getting closer you see its real, elongated form. Within seconds of passing Santo Stefano, you are in Perno.

Rich, broad wines of ample weight and full flavours. Barolo Sorì Ginestra and Vigna del Gris; much admired Monprà (*barrique*-aged Nebbiolo/Barbera). No large groups.

Domenico Clerico
Tel: 0173 78171; F.
Forward-thinking estate, constantly trying to better already top wines. Monforte austerity tamed with perfume, soft fruit and elegant complexity. Arte (Nebbiolo with 5% Barbera, oaked) of highest renown. Must book.

Elio Grasso
Tel: 0173 78491; E. F.
Hard-working, quality-conscious producer. Full, structured, richly fruited wines of great class. Excellently sited vineyards. Must book.

Fratelli Seghesio
Tel: 0173 78108
Smallish, family-run estate. Long experience of grape-growing, recent converts to thrills of winemaking and bottling. Very approachable yet slow-ageing wines. Must book.

Giacomo Conterno
Tel: 0173 78221
Long-standing, traditional family run estate. Enviably high and consistent quality, terrific wines of huge power, weight, structure and complexity. In good vintages produce Barolo Monfortino, from selected grapes, otherwise all go into straight Barolo. Working hours only, must book, no space for groups.

Poderi Aldo Conterno
Tel: 0173 78150
Mind-blowing wines but this perfectionist producer is sometimes reclusive; visits could be tetchy.

Podere Rocche dei Manzoni di Valentino
Tel: 0173 78421; E. F.
Estate that gained fame with Bricco Manzoni, the first Nebbiolo/Barbera blend to grab attention; now more emphasis on Barolo, firm and mouth-filling, with a broad array of flavours and top class quality. Must book, pay for tastings.

Riccardo Fenocchio di Ferruccio Fenocclo
Tel: 0173 78335; F.
Small estate; traditionally managed. Wines of good weight, style and typicity. Barolo Pianpolvere Soprano.

CASTIGLIONE FALLETTO
Azelia di Luigi Scavino
Tel: 0173 62859; E. F.
High class estate. Barolo *crus* Bricco Fiasco (Bric del Fiasc') and Bricco

Left *Serralunga d'Alba's unmistakable castle shrouded in autumn mists.*

Right *Castiglione Falletto's castle, surrounded by some of its most renowned* crus.

Punta: broad, full and with complex aromas and flavours.

Cavallotto
Tel: 0173 62814; E. F.
Medium-sized, highly traditional family estate. Proudly robust, slow-ageing wines, muscular and rich. Barolo Bricco Boschis, also *crus* from plots Vigna San Giuseppe, Colle Sud-Ovest.

Fratelli Brovia
Tel: 0173 62852; E. F. G.
Welcoming, family-run estate with vineyards dotted about top *crus*. Traditional ideas. Rich, powerful, well made wines following vintage characteristics. Excellent *crus* Rocche, Villero and Garblèt Suè.

Gigi Rosso
Tel: 0173 262369; E. F. G. S.
Largish, long standing estate. Tiny wine museum. Barolo *cru* Sorì dell'Ulivo, from plot including a 50-year old olive tree, attesting to its notable warmth. Must book weekend or group visits.

Giuseppe Mascarello e Figli
Tel: 0173 792126; E. F.
Cellars outside zone, at Monchiero by the Tanaro, originally designed to store ice, and ideal for wine storage. Vineyards are central. Mauro Mascarello owns Monprivato, the super-famous Castiglione Falletto vineyard, and other prized plots (Bricco Villero in Castiglione Falletto, Santo Stefano (di Perno) in Monforte). Barolo Monprivato has legendary ageing capacity, although Mascarello accentuates its finesse and gives it balance, making it accessible early on. Must book and pay for tastings unless bottles already open.

Paolo Scavino di Scavino Enrico
Tel: 0173 6285; E. F. G.
Stunning wines from perfectionist viticulturalist with top sites. Wines complex, dense and elegantly perfumed. Legendary *crus* Bric del Fiasc' (Castiglione Falletto), Cannubi (Barolo), Rocche dell' Annunziata (La Morra). Working hours only.

Terre del Barolo
Tel: 0173 262053; E. F.
Barolo's main cooperative; over 500 members, grapes from 800ha of vineyard all over zone. Wines of good qualitative level, showing truly typical characteristics of the territory. Several *crus*. Open working hours Mon-Sat, Sun am; unless just buying wines, must book.

Vietti
Tel: 0173 62825; E. F.
Lively, family-run estate with vineyards in several communes. Classic wines

Throughout this route, anyone travelling in late autumn will see more red-leaved vines, indicating Barbera or Dolcetto, than elsewhere in Barolo. (Nebbiolo's leaves turn yellow.) Both these grapes do extremely well here, as do some other varieties, and are treated with attendant respect.

CASTIGLIONE FALLETTO

On the descent from Perno it is the village of Castiglione Falletto which catches the eye. As the road drops towards the boundary of Monforte, Castiglione Falletto's castle looms over to the left, with the vineyards Rivera and Scarrone just below it. *Cru* Pira sits just below Rivera, while a little further back along the ridge, to the left, stretches the wonderful, long, southeast facing Rocche vineyard, falling steeply to the valley (*see also* below). The sharply twisting road gives three separate prospects of the *cru*.

The commune is small but lacks neither top sites nor top producers and enjoys its reputation of producing the most balanced Barolos, from soils neither distinctly Tortonian nor strongly Helvetian. To go through it, firstly continue north back towards Gallo (travelling along the valley floor, along the edge of Serralunga, and repeating a small stretch of road covered earlier). On meeting the Alba-Barolo road, turn sharp left (direction Barolo), then left again a minute later, to start rising into the commune's

Left *Small sunny garden in
Castiglione Falletto – sheltered
enough to grow lemons.*

of intensity and structure, lifted by
good fruit and an overlying vein of
elegance. Glorious range of Barolo
crus, each with own characteristics:
Rocche, Brunate, Lazzarito, Castiglione,
Villero. Visits working hours, not Sun.

ENOTECHE

Cantina Comunale di La Morra
Via Carlo; closed Mon, Tues.
Wines from locality; tasting and buying.
Alberto 2VinBar
La Morra, Via Roma 46
Wine bar. Can buy wine too as
well as local food products.
Enoteca Regionale
Barolo. See main text.
Enoteca Regionale
Grinzane Cavour. See main text.
Bottega del Vino Serralunga
Summer weekends only.
All'Infernòt del Castel
Serralunga, Via Roma 2
Shop; some intriguing food products.
Infernòt Monforte, Via Palestro 2
Good wine shop, also food products.

EATING OUT

La Crota
Roddi, Piazza Principe Amedeo 1
Tel: 0173 615187; closed Mon pm, Tues.
Quiet, informal restaurant. Menu
includes traditional, old dishes now
infrequently seen. Good service.
Short local wine list. Seats outside.
Gogabigoga
Roddi, Piazza Caduta in Guerra 1
*Tel: 0173 615454; pm only, closed
Tues.* Inexpensive, fun place. Good,
substantial food. Good wines,
several by glass. Cash only.
Albergo Real Castello
Verduno, Via Umberto 1 9
Tel: 0172 470125; closed winter.
Not cheap but eating in castles never
has been. Dishes local. Excellent
cheese board, good desserts. Mainly
Piedmontese wine list. Seats outside.
Belvedere
La Morra, Piazza Castello 2
Tel: 0173 50190; closed Sun pm, Mon.
One of Barolo's highlights. La Morra's
most panoramic spot (seats outside).
Satisfying, carefully prepared,
flavoursome, typical dishes. Wide
wine choice, mainly local. Mid-price
range but very good value.
Locanda del Borgo Antico
Barolo, Piazza del Municipio 2
Tel: 0173 56355; closed Weds.
Take the tasting menu and try
numerous wines by the glass or just
order one of nearly 100 Barolos listed

ridge of land. This is the Alba–Monforte road. At several
points early on there are impressive views over to the left of
the extensive Fontanafredda estate buildings and the
landforms of its surrounding *crus*.

When the initial series of sharp bends begins to straighten
out, *cru* Parussi folds up away from the road on the right
(unusually, signposted). Very shortly afterwards you start
passing the beautiful Bricco Boschis vineyard (right), facing
south-southwest and stretching above the road for about
two-thirds of a kilometre. As it bends, it gives sight of the
Cavallotto estate and the full extent of the vineyard. At the
same time the lesser-known Pernanno banks steeply on the
left. Next comes the junction to Castiglione Falletto
village. The village is small, with narrow, twisting streets,
but densely inhabited, with dwellings partially hiding the
castle. By the junction, on the right is the westerly point of
the long, slim, southwesterly facing Monprivato vineyard,
best seen from a lay-by a few metres further on. Justifiably
famous, it stretches along the upper slopes of a spur of land
which heads northwest towards the Alba-Barolo road.

A few metres further along are two lanes on the right
leading to the vineyards Fiasc' and Villero respectively.
Shortly after, there is a sharp right-hand U-bend. From
there, Rocche juts downwards beside the road (left),
following it all the way to the border with the commune

– it won't break the bank. Food's good too and as good value as the wines.

Del Castello
Grinzane Cavour
Tel: 0173 262159; closed Mon.
Another castle, but one of the best (see main text). Spacious, elegant, good views. Classic fare, large wine list, mainly local. Quite costly.

La Salinera
Grinzane Cavour, Via IV Novembre 18
Tel: 0173 262138; closed Mon pm, Tues.
Restaurant also *enoteca*, bar, food shop. Grab a table and pluck your wine from the shelves. Dishes recited. Lunch is quick and simple, dinner more relaxed, with more choice and the odd frill. Seats outside (but trafficky). Cash only.

Antica Trattoria del Castello
Serralunga, Fraz Baudana 63/a
Tel: 0173 613375; closed Wed pm.
Lively, bustling, casual spot for empty stomachs, with all the classics, cooked as well as anywhere. Go for better known wines. Mid-priced. Cash only.

Italia
Serralunga, Piazza M Cappellano 3/a
Tel: 0173 613124
Classic old-style *trattoria*, food tasty and abundant. Owner has vines on top *cru* Vigna Rionda so choose house wine. Cheap. Cash only.

Il Giardino da Felicin
Monforte, Via Vallada 18
Tel: 0173 78225; closed Sun eve, Mon.
Barolo's top spot. Nothing outlandish. Just local ingredients, the best available, and traditional dishes. But the quality, the flavours and lightness of touch make them appear as new. Fine wine list; superb value. Seats outside. Also rooms for overnight stays.

Della Posta
Monforte, Piazza XX Settembre 9
Tel: 0173 78120; closed Thurs.
Long-standing, once rough and ready *trattoria*, now smartened up a bit. Good selection of good local wines. Mid-price range. Very popular.

HOTELS

Brezza
Barolo, Via Lomondo 2
Tel & fax: 0173 56354
Officially Hotel Barolo. Refurbished, comfortable, convenient, family-run. Houses the more than decent Brezza restaurant. The tireless Brezza family make wine too.

Le Torri
Castiglione Falletto, Piazza V Veneto 1
Tel & fax: 0173 6296
Central spot. New, just a few rooms, simply furnished, traditionally but with mod-cons, most rooms with cooking facilities. Spacious, cool and relaxing.

of Monforte (about a kilometre). The *cru* is very highly esteemed and ownership is remarkably fragmented, giving chances to taste the heights it can reach via a number of different producers. Above the road is first the vineyard of Serra. This is, however, usually regarded as part of Rocche and at its highest point is normally called Bricco Rocche. To emphasize the point, the modernistic Ceretto estate called Bricco Rocche sits astride it, giving magnificent views across the zone. Beyond Serra/Bricco Rocche is Meriondino (also right), while Rocche continues below. Looking back, you may also see *cru* Villero behind to the right. There is then a small junction and Castiglione Falletto commune gives way to Monforte.

MONFORTE WEST

Back in Monforte, the downwards stretch continues. To the right is the vineyard of Bussia Sottana, just past which a lane forks off right towards Bussia Soprana (upper Bussia), an excellent *cru*. To the left an isolated, easily visible building draws the eye. This is the estate of Aldo Conterno, brought closer as the road curves left. There is then a sharp right-hand bend and the road heads towards the Gabutti vineyard, meeting it after a few seconds and abutting its western-facing slopes (on the right) for another couple, before a dividing track announces its replacement by the large, southwest facing *cru* Pianpolvere. It follows it until the next large right-hand bend. From there, there are few vineyards of special merit and all that remains is to enjoy the overall panorama of western Monforte before returning to Monforte village, the southern extreme of the Barolo zone, where the tour ends.

Above left *The perfectionist Aldo Conterno supervising the grape crush.*
Above *Aldo Conterno's cellars in Monforte.*
Left *Monforte's stately church.*

FOOD SHOPPING

Panetteria Corino
Verduno, Via V Emanuele 16
For true Piedmontese *grissini* and the local *Sfoglia di Verduno*.
Fava Verduno, Via Umberto I 34
Try the *salame al Pelaverga*.
Panetteria Soncin
La Morra, Via Roma 4. Irresistible hazelnut tart and *Lamorresi al Barolo*. And for similar goodies:
Cogno Via Vittorio Emanuele 18.
La Contrada
Serralunga, Via Roma 48. Speciality food products (including wines) and original photographs of the Langhe.
Antica Dispensa Bricco Bastia
Monforte, Via Bava Beccaris 3
Glorious delicatessen with mouth-watering range. Puts new slant on word 'take-away'.
Costantino Rocca
Monforte, Piazza Umberto 20
Honey, cheese and everything in between. Also local wines and *grappe*.

Alba's Dolcetto country and the Alta Langa

DOLCETTO COUNTRY

RECOMMENDED PRODUCERS

Poderi Luigi Einaudi
Dogliani *Tel: 0173 70191; E. F.*
Sited among magnificent views.
Dolcetto di Dogliani non-*cru*, *cru*
Vigna Tecc and selection I Filari. Also
an oddity: white from non-local variety
Tocai Rosso, plus others. Tastings for
purchasers only. Agritourism.

Fratelli Pecchenino
Dogliani *Tel: 0173 70686; F.*
Consistently good wines, thanks to
dedicated vineyard husbandry and
knowledgeable winemaking. Dolcetto
crus Sirì d'Yermu and Pizabò.

Quinto Chionetto
Dogliani *Tel: 0173 71179.*
Smallish estate with vineyards tended
with love and intense dedication.
Resulting wines concenrated, full,
elegant and complex, but clear
difference between the two Dolcetto
crus, Briccolero and San Luigi.

Gillardi G Battista
Farigliano *Tel: 0173 76813; F.*
Tiny, well-rated, family-run estate.
Two Dolcetto crus, Cursalet and
Maestra, with distinctive characteristics.

Ca'Viola
Montelupo Albese
Tel: 0173 617570; E. F.
Fairly new, small estate, already
making high quality, concentrated
wines from well-exposed vineyards.

THE WINES

Dolcetto is grown widely throughout Barbaresco and
Barolo and many think the wines from these zones
(denominated Dolcetto d'Alba) represent the pinnacle of
Dolcetto production. Others regard the livelier, fruitier
Dolcetto that comes from outside as a truer expression of
the grape. The argument is muddied by the abundance of
Dolcetto d'Alba and the relative paucity of other types:
from the zones of Dogliani and the Langhe Monregalesi,
plus the aristocratic Diano d'Alba, all three in Alba, not to
mention Dolcettos from Ovada and Acqui in Alessandria
province, considerably further east, and Asti. There is little
option but to try for yourself.

THE VINEYARDS

From Monforte, head southwards towards Dogliani. Almost
immediately the hill format changes from the neat ranks of
Barolo to rougher, less disciplined hillsides and more
foresting. About five minutes along the road, roughy
halfway between the two villages, Dolcetto d'Alba ends and
Dolcetto di Dogliani begins. There are practically no vineyards to be seen, however, until reaching Dogliani itself.
Dogliani is a great spot for a quick stroll, with its narrow,
cobbled, porticoed medieval centre, tranquil but alive, even
on Sunday morning – shops are open! It also glories in a
huge, majestic church, containing an impressive crucifix and
16th-century frescoes.

From Dogliani, first divert along the *statale* to Monchiero.
The road is flat and dull but shows a few clusters of vineyards
on the dumpy hills to the right. (Any on the left are Dolcetto

Above *Diano d'Alba.*
Right *Well-tended Langhe
vineyards to the south of Alba.*
Top right *Dolcetto country.*

delle Langhe Monregalesi). On returning to Dogliani, head up behind the church (direction Savona), past a cemetery and then past the leading Einaudi estate on the right. Next make for Belvedere Langhe and the height of the road gives superb panoramic views over the vineyards and much else besides. At Belvedere Langhe, the zone of Dolcetto delle Langhe Monregalesi begins, a large rambling area stretching west to the Tanaro and south practically to the Ligurian border. Its centre is towards the river around Mondovì and Vicoforte but production is minuscule so better to continue across its outskirts, up to Murazzano, a wonderful village with a glorious medieval tower and a delightful 8th-century church. Murazzano gives an option to turn off to Ceva, which gives access to the *autostrada* to Savona and the Ligurian coast (*see* pages 94–109). The route, however, goes on to Bossolasco, out of the wine zones. From here it is sheer scenic bliss, even if vine free. It cuts through the heart of the Alta Langa, and high it is indeed, mostly over 700 metres, with some extraordinary mountain views. Bossolasco is the hub and a natural magnet for visitors. Continue along the ridge, before starting a slow descent at Serravalle Langhe.

Very shortly after, just past the junction for Cerreto Langhe, you re-enter the Dolcetto d'Alba zone and, at the turn off for Sinio, a couple of minutes later, Barbera d'Alba vineyards join in. Continue through Montelupo Albese, from where there are good views of the Barolo zone and after which the road takes a couple of large loops. Just past these you enter the commune of Diano where Dolcetto di Diano d'Alba (or simply Diano) replaces Dolcetto d'Alba. Suddenly, vines once more surround you, splayed across angular hills. Many of the south-facing slopes have long been recognized as of very high quality, with *crus* truly worthy of the name.

Diano is but a short hop from Alba with panoramic views over the Barbaresco zone on the way. Two hours will be enough to complete the circuit.

Rossetto di Destafanis Gianpaolo
Montelupo Albese
Tel: 0173 617240; F.
Small, family-run estate. Vineyards over 550m high with splendid views. Traditional Dolcetto d'Alba.

ENOTECHE

Griva Dogliani, Via V Emanuele 43
Good choice of Dolcetto di Dogliani. Also tempting local food products.
Enoteca Regionale di Diano d'Alba Palazzo del Municipio, Via Umberto I 22

FOOD SPECIALITIES

Murazzano The local cheese – a type of Robiola.
Hazelnuts In the Alta Langa quality is supreme.

EATING OUT

Albero Fiorito
Dogliani, Piazza Confraternità
Tel: 0173 70582; closed Weds.
Simple, largish *trattoria*, good choice of the best of Dogliani wines, plus others. Also rooms for overnighters.
Del Peso
Belvedere Langhe, Via Merlati 26
Tel: 0173 797105; closed Weds.
Long standing *trattoria*. Food has the home made touch. Well chosen wines. Cash only. Lunch only, unless book for dinner. Also rooms in small hotel.
La Coccinella
Serravalle Langhe, Via Provinciale 5
Tel: 0173 718220; closed Mon.
Good value, unpretentious, popular trattoria. Well-flavoured local dishes. Fair wine list, good spread. Cash only.
Locanda dell'Arco
Cissone, Piazza dell'Olmo 1
Tel: 0173 48200; closed Tues.
Good value, welcoming restaurant. Excellent wine list: strong on Barolo. Light, flavoursome seasonal dishes.
La Pedaggera
Cerreto Langhe, Loc La Pedaggera
Tel: 0173 520373; closed Tues.
Simple spot; simple light dishes; good wine choice. Cash only.
Antica Trattoria del Centro
Diano d'Alba-Ricca,
Via Alba-Cortemilia 91
Tel: 0173 612018; closed Mon pm, Tues.
Inexpensive, comfortable *trattoria*, traditional in style and dishes. Local cheeses. Well chosen wines. Cash only.

FOOD SHOPPING

Manzone
Dogliani, Via V Emanuele 29
Salumi and good local cheeses.
Co Zo Al Murazzano, Loc Crovera
Main sales point for this local cheese producing cooperative.

Asti and Southern Piedmont

Despite images of fizzy wine Asti is above all a town, a pleasant one, not too large but big enough to service every need, reflecting its wine links in a relaxed manner. The wine patrimony of the surrounding province is hugely important; it is frustrating to the Astigiani that their wines are often treated as mere adjuncts to those from the Langhe.

Asti's main wine districts are south and east of the town. There are five grape varieties strongly linked with the province and adjacent lands, and although nowhere is one grown to the exclusion of the others, each has its fiefdom.

Foremost is Barbera, grown throughout the province and its lifeblood. Its merits are discussed endlessly, its many sustainers are passionate in its defence and are often puzzled by its lack of popularity. (More on Barbera in the next section page 128.) Then there's the wonderfully grapey Moscato. Unlike Barbera it is popular, populist and, in some circles, highly fashionable. The grapes for sparkling Asti and the non-fizzy Moscato d'Asti grow across a large half-moon-shaped area southeast of Asti. However, it is the much smaller area between the Belbo Valley and the Tinella stream where the finest Moscato wines are made. Visually, it is wondrous. Hills roll away on all sides and there are the bright colours and harmonious forms of vines everywhere.

Dolcetto is most at home in the eastern part of the area. Its style changes vastly in the 20 kilometres or so between the first appearances of Dolcetto d'Asti, light and softly fruity, the in-between area of Dolcetto d'Acqui, and its most eastern strip, producing firm, powerful Dolcetto di Ovada. Rounding off the grape handful is Cortese, floral and elegant, to start a meal and the startling Brachetto to finish it.

Edging gradually east and a little south almost imperceptibly the climate starts to change, as does the look of the land and, more obviously, the foods, until the warm, dry breezes of Ovada reveal the proximity of Liguria and the coast.

Left *Small vineyard plots below the calm village of Moncalvo.*

Above *No shortage of choice at this stall in Moncalvo market.*

The town of Asti

Above *Chestnuts, an abundant local crop, in Asti's market.*

ASTI

ENOTECHE

Boero Corso Dante 7
Wine shop with tasting area next door. Also sells wine artefacts.
La Cantina Via Pallio 15
Wine shop with large range.

FOOD SPECIALITIES

As a town, Asti has few of its own special foods, but you can find **Castelmagno** – a wickedly good cheese: soft and elastic, yet at the same time crumbly and *grana*-like.

 ### EATING OUT

L'Angolo del Beato Via Guttuari 12
Tel: 0141 531668; closed Sun.
Restaurant in simple but elegant surroundings; varied menu of well flavoured, local dishes. Good wine choices. Mid-priced, good value.
Barolo & Co Via Cesare Battisti 14
Tel: 0141 592059; closed Sun pm, Mon.
In an old, medieval building in town centre. *Enoteca* attached. Hence large wine list, mainly local. Two tasting menus. Also wines by glass.
Il Convivio – Vini e Cucina
Via G B Giuliani 4/6
Tel: 0141 594188; closed Sun.
Smart, modern-looking spacious restaurant, with ample choice of wines including little known names. Good quality, well presented food with a light touch. Open in late afternoon serving wine by glass.
Da Dirce
Loc Caniglie, Via Valleversa 53
Tel: 0141 272949; closed Tues lunch, Mon.
Just outside town. Well-established *trattoria*, simply furnished; simple, traditional food at its best. Short but excellent wine list. Cash only.

For anyone happy to settle in just one spot as a touring base, there is no better place than Asti. Not only is it within easy striking distance of most of the areas on the route but it is a friendly, open, attractive wine town, the sort of place easily warmed to; large enough to have all you could need but small enough for everything to be close to hand. Parking, while not a doddle, is surprisingly unproblematic. There are reasonable hotels and the dearth of night life means you can sleep untroubled, even in its centre. It is also a good, mixed community, not class-ridden and, if there in autumn, you can witness (and sniff) the real, commercial daily truffle market in Piazza Alfieri.

Piazza Alfieri is the central square of the town although 'square' is the wrong word for this elegant, porticoed but triangular meeting place. From the apex of Piazza Alfieri sprouts Corso Dante, with a mix of useful and more luxurious shopping, while across the apex swings Corso Alfieri, the main shopping street but not without a good smattering of architecturally fascinating old buildings, villas, and churches. Behind Piazza Alfieri is the Campo del Palio, a large, hexagonal area, where Asti's Palio is run (*see below*). Rather like Turin, a vital branch of social life is the elegant coffee bar. Bar Dante, in Piazza Alfieri was once the focus and still looks the part. Youngsters still gather outside to chat about everything and nothing (*angolo dei fessi*, this spot was consequently dubbed: idiots' corner) but the real meeting point has moved to Bar Ligure in Corso Alfieri.

To add to Asti's draw, in September it goes festival mad, with a series of beanfeasts that takes over the town and scoops up everyone in a welter of ceremony and jollification. Foremost of these is the Palio.

THE PALIO
Even though non-Italians tend to think that there is only one *Palio* in Italy, in Siena, there are others. Of these, Asti's is in leading place, held each year on the third Sunday in September, preceded three days earlier by a magnificent and colourful display of flag-tossing. The *Palio* starts with a large parade, again very colourful, with everyone in period costume. Then comes the horse race. The rituals surrounding it are as deeply entrenched as in Siena, the rules and regulations lengthy. But once the bareback race starts anything, it seems, goes. Afterwards there is more spectacle, with the ceremony of the presentation of the *Palio* itself, a special piece of cloth. Preparing for, celebrating and reliving the *Palio* takes many hours of animated chat. But then, the quiet, industrious Astigiani just love to party.

THE FESTIVAL OF THE SAGRE
Many Italian villages have a festival, known as a *sagra* once a year to celebrate the crop most closely associated with

them; it is rather like a harvest festival with more merry-making. Asti's, held on the second weekend of September, is the *sagra* of the *sagre*. It is a huge bash, with folk from each of the surrounding villages bringing a different foodstuff. They each set up stall (and kitchen) and everyone sets to 'sampling'. Suffice it to say that no-one goes hungry, or thirsty and early bedtimes are forgotten. In the morning there's a parade (a *festa* without a parade? Unthinkable!) of traditionally costumed farmers on floats, each designed and built with massive amounts of pride and effort. These illustrate themes relevant to each village and its leading crop. It is all fiercely competitive and participated in with great gusto. Then there's more eating and drinking.

THE DOUJA D'OR

In 'the festival town', it would be very strange if wine, so central to everyone's life, livelihood and culture were left out. It isn't. Between the Festival of the Sagre and the Palio is the Douja D'Or, several days of judging wines from anyone, anywhere in Italy who cares to enter: the somewhat garish certificates awarded to wines that score highly can be seen adorning cellars the length and breadth of the country. While serious judging takes place on one side, on the other there are more stalls and chances to taste, drink and buy dozens of different wines, and for the whole period of the Douja Asti overtly glories in its wine links.

Gener Neuv Lungoranaro 4
Tel: 0141 557270; closed Sun pm, Mon.
By River Tanaro. Expensive, hushed and formal despite vaguely rustic design and emphasis on dialect. If hungry try tasting menu. Can opt for three included wines or choose from vast list.

HOTELS

Lis Via F.lli Rosselli 10
Tel: 0141 595051; fax: 0141 353845.
Asti's friendliest spot. Central, modern, with spacious, comfortable rooms. Affable, helpful, wine-interested staff who have created homely feel.
Salera Via Mons Marello 19
Tel: 0141 410169; fax: 0141 410372.
Run by same family as Lis, just outside the centre. One quality level up, also has restaurant.
Rainero Via Cavour 85
Tel: 0141 353866; fax: 0141 594985.
Central with garage. Good 3*.
Reale Piazza Alfieri 6
Tel: 0141 530240; fax: 0141 34357.
Historical hotel (1793), Asti's most elegant and very central. Frequent meeting spot. Rooms refurbished with all mod cons. Garage.

FOOD SHOPPING

Gastronomia San Secondo
Corso Dante 6; closed Mon.
An enormous choice of top class products; dishes to heat up at home; cheeses, *salumi* and other cold foods. Locally called 'Asti's best restaurant'.
Main fruit and veg market
Bright, clean and in a building in Piazza Libertà. Open also pm except Thurs.
Laboratorio Caseario Artigiano
Corso Matteotti 150/a; Viale Pilone 3
The freshest of cheeses.
Macelleria Piero Rosso
Via Giobert 36
Fine meat from small farmers and good *salumi*.
Pasticceria Giordanino
Corso Alfieri 254
For the best of the local goodies.
Ponchione Corso Alfieri 149
Wide range of food specialities and wines. Good, own-roasted coffee.

SPECIAL EVENTS

Apart from the three major festivals, the first Tuesday of May Asti celebrates San Secondo, its patron saint. The Saturday before comes the ceremony of approval of that year's *palio* cloth. There is also a drama festival in the summer months.

Left *A quiet moment on market day in Asti.*

Asti

Legend:
- Autostrada
- Main road
- Other roads
- Railway
- Regional boundary
- Provincial boundary
- Wine route

- Boundary of Moscato d' Asti DOC
- Boundary of Barbera d' Asti DOC
- Boundary of Barbera del Monferrato DOC
- Boundary of Brachetto d' Acqui DOC
- Boundary of Cortese dell' Alto Monferrato DOC
- Boundary of Dolcetto d' Acqui DOC
- Boundary of Dolcetto d' Asti DOC
- Boundary of Freisa d' Asti DOC
- Boundary of Freisa di Chieri DOC
- Boundary of Gabiano DOC
- Boundary of Grignolino d' Asti DOC
- Boundary of Grignolino del Monferrato Casalese DOC
- Boundary of Malvasia di Cosorzo d' Asti DOC
- Boundary of Malvasia di Castelnuovo Don Bosco DOC
- Boundary of Rubino di Cantavenna DOC
- Boundary of Ruchè di Castagnole Monferrato DOC
- Boundary of Monferrato DOC
- Boundary of Langhe DOC
- Boundary of Loazzolo DOC

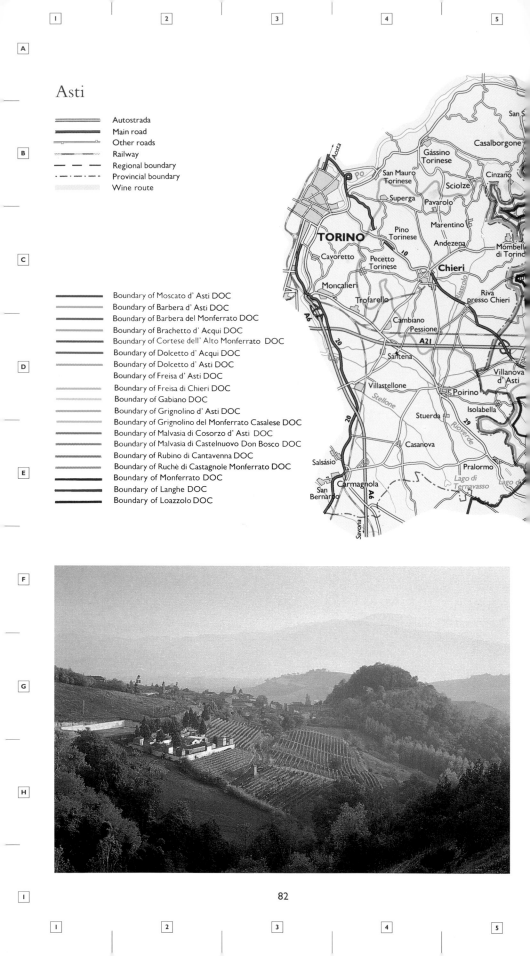

Left View near Canelli, *famed for* spumante *production and the base of several vermouth houses.*

1 : 355,000

Km 0   5   10

Miles 0   5

Moscato Country

MOSCATO COUNTRY

RECOMMENDED PRODUCERS

Fratelli Bera Neviglie
Tel: 0173 630194; F.
Well-respected estate on small hill.
Reputation based on rounded,
refined Moscato d'Asti Su Reimond.

**Cascina Fonda di Barbero
Secondino** Mango
Tel: 0173 677156; E. F. G.
Increasingly noteworthy family-run
estate. Vines scattered around
highish sites in Mango and Neive,
nearly all for Moscato d'Asti. Tiny
production of highly-rated Asti. Best
to book for weekend visits.

Vignaioli di Santo Stefano
Santo Stefano Belbo
Tel: 0173 282582 (Ceretto).
Owned by Ceretto. The *vignaioli* are
four growers with vineyards near
Santo Stefano. Elegant, deeply
aromatic, purely flavoured Moscato.

La Morandina Castiglione Tinella
Tel: 0173 855261; E. F.
Moscato experts. Beautifully fresh
Moscato d'Asti of finesse from fiercely
steep vineyards. Also Barbera. Can
request snack of salami, cheese and
wood-oven baked bread when booking.

Scagliola Calosso
Tel: 0141 853183; E. F. G.
Carefully crafted Moscato d'Asti
'Volo di Farfalle' of length and balance.
Can suggest local restaurant and
agritourism. Vineyard walk offered.

Fratelli Gancia Canelli
Tel: 0141 8301; E. F.
Well known name but, despite size,
reliably high quality standards. Large
range of sparkling wines produced.
Most dry, of varying styles. Visits
working hours Mon–Thur only. Must
book and confirm in writing: Corso
Libertà 66 14053 Canelli (AT).

Luigi Coppo e Figli Canelli
Tel: 0141 823146; E. F.
Although based at Moscato's hub
(cellars in Via Alba) and producing a
refined Moscato d'Asti, (Moncalvina),
the focus of the Coppo brothers'
activities is Barbera d'Asti, with three
types: L'Avvocata (traditional),
Pomorosso (oaked, old vines), Camp
du Rouss (aged in barrels previously
used for Pomorosso). All of fine
quality, and clear personality and
individuality. Visits working hours
only, must book. Groups contribute
to tasting costs.

Forteto della Luja Loazzolo
Tel: 0141 831596; E. F.
This estate *is* Loazzolo. The wine
not overly sweet, with a clear oak

THE WINES

Although Moscato grows throughout Piedmont's south-eastern corner, it is the area rising from just east of the Barbaresco zone and then sloping down to the *torrente* Belbo where the grape proliferates. Much of this is actually within Alba's territory, rather than Asti's, but the wines are still named Asti or Moscato d'Asti, rendering the administrative boundaries, for once, little more than incidental.

It was once fashionable to be rather sniffy about Asti (the wine). Once called Asti Spumante – and this is still an alternative denomination – these joyous, life-enhancing mouthfuls of light, grapey froth were much dismissed with that damning pronouncement, "It's *sweet*!" As a side consequence the word *spumante*, meaning neither more nor less than 'sparkling', became synonymous with the Asti-type of sparkler and the full range of Italy's sparkling wine production was condemned by implication. Asti is sweet, but it is not some cheap, nasty gloop, even though there is still quite a lot made that is depressingly mundane.

Unlike most sparkling wine – where the grape juice is fermented fully to form a dry base wine before a yeast and sugar mixture is added, provoking a second fermentation, this time with the resultant carbon dioxide gas being trapped – Asti is an all-in-one production. The grape must ferments just part way before its container is sealed. The continuing stages of the fermentation are then under pressure and the fizz is retained. The wine is fully sparkling long before all the grape sugars have been used up and so the wine has a delicate sweetness, from the residual grapiness. An additional benefit is that being only part-fermented, the alcohol is low, giving further lightness and verve to the wine. Moscato d'Asti is even better. It is, roughly, like Asti Spumante without the Spumante. Usually the best grapes go into Moscato d'Asti, they ferment about half way and then that's it. The wine is then bottled. It may be still or, more commonly, have a light beading of bubbles but is the epitome of light, fresh, youthful, grapey delight.

There are also producers who want to do something more 'serious' with their Moscato crop, resulting in richer dessert wines, made from *passito* Moscato grapes, although these are not eligible for the Moscato d'Asti denomination. For grapes grown in the small area of Loazzolo, however, the DOC Loazzolo has been created, specifically for this type of wine. This area, on the eastern side of the Belbo, also comes into the Dolcetto d'Asti zone, whose westerly border roughly follows the valley floor.

THE VINEYARDS

The area is quite compact and the route, taking barely two and a half hours could be tacked onto the end of the Barbaresco tour: from the road to Alba from Tre Stelle, shortly before reaching Alba and just before crossing the railway line, turn sharp left towards Benevello. Alternatively, you could start from Alba, taking the route out of town described for Barbaresco (page 56), and turn right at the sign to Benevello after crossing the railway line. From Asti, it is quickest first to zoom down to Alba.

From the Benevello turn-off the road rises into vineyard country and within no time there is nothing but vines as far as the eye can see. In fact, the whole area is remarkably densely planted, and the expanse and concentration of vine cultivation is quite mind boggling. At first there is an intriguing spread of cultivation methods: vines more or less densely planted, trained low and high, pruned longer and shorter depending on the grape variety. Although Moscato dominates, it is by no means planted exclusively, especially in this early stretch where Barbera and Dolcetto are also important. Moscato's domain has, though recently increased, with growers switching to it from Barbera. Large quantities of grapes are greedily hoovered up by the large producing companies that dominate the market, and, despite wine snobs' sneering, there's been plentiful demand for the wines.

Above *A hard choice to make.*
Top *Vineyards at Rocchetta Palatea.*
Bottom left *A glass of Moscato at the end of a meal gives a wonderful lift especially with cakes and biscuits or these carnival fritters.*

overlay to its gentle muskiness. Walking routes are marked through the most picturesque parts of estate's butterfly-rich woodland. Must book. Pay for some wines. Third weekend of each month runs tie-in visits with Nizza's antiques market (see page 92).
Michele Chiarlo Calamandrana
Tel: 0141 75231; E. F.
The main base of this large company. Wines from various sites on 135ha of vineyard. Best known as influential producer of Barbera d'Asti, notably Valle del Sole; Barolo *crus* Cerequio and Cannubi also arousing much interest. Visits working hours only.
Elio Perrone Castiglione Tinella
Tel: 0141 855132; F.
Emphasis on two Moscato d'Asti *crus*, Clarté and Sourgal, displaying the scope for stylistic differences. Visits working hours only.

ENOTECHE

Enoteca Regionale
Mango; see main text
Bottega del Vino
Castagnole Lanze, Via Ener Bettica 15
Tel: 0141 877219.
Small, attractive place, local wines
only, but only open weekends and
public holidays unless pre-advised.
Enoteca Regionale Canelli
Undergoing relocation and
reorganisation in late 1996.
Ask locally for details.

EATING OUT

Ristorante del Castello
Mango, Piazza XX Settembre
Tel: 0141 89141; closed Tues.
Spacious, refined surroundings;
classic dishes with modern touches;
good selection of local and regional
wines; and cheaper than most of
the restaurants in castles.
Della Stazione
Santo Stefano Belbo, Piazzale Mango 6
Tel: 0141 844233; closed Tues.
Long-standing, popular *trattoria*. Local
dishes, based on fresh seasonal
ingredients. Limited but reasonable
wine choice.
Da Palmira Castiglione Tinella,
Piazza XX Settembre 18
Tel: 0141 855176; closed Mon pm, Tues.
Well known, much admired *trattoria*:
spot-on traditional dishes from first
rate ingredients. Good local wines too.
**Trattoria della Posta 'da
Camulin'** Cossano Belbo, Via
Negro 2
Tel: 0141 88126; closed Sun pm, Mon.
Long-standing, well-known and highly
reputed for local food at its best.
Well matching wine list, mainly local,
some regional. Charge cards only.

Above *Moscato grapes in a tangle
of vineyard growth.*
Top right *San Damiano d'Asti.*

Carry on for five to ten minutes to the first junction, there turning left towards Treiso and then following signs to Trezzo Tinella. After curving down to the village of Trezzo continue to Neviglie, passing some vineyards where the hillside has been stepped, like partial terraces. After Neviglie, head to Mango. Of all the villages en route, Mango is the most worthy of exploration. It has a fascinatingly higgledy-piggledy formation, with slopes, twists, cobbles and arches vying for attention with the well-kept, often overhanging houses. The village is topped by its castle, originally medieval but rebuilt in the 17th century. This now houses both a smart restaurant and a smallish *enoteca regionale*. If the *enoteca* is not open, someone in the restaurant may be willing to give you a look round.

From Mango, head towards Santo Stefano Belbo via Camo. The road passes through a somewhat rougher zone, steeper, with more woodland and some great panoramas, before twisting steeply down from Camo to the Belbo Valley. The *torrente* Belbo can indeed be a torrent when in flood (in the disastrous floods of autumn 1994 it became a monster) but usually it is little more than a dribble. At the valley floor turn left onto the *statale* and into the uninspiring Santo Stefano Belbo whose sole claim to fame is as the birthplace of the Italian writer, Cesare Pavese.

This whole stretch from Trezzo Tinella has led in a roughly easterly direction, now the route branches northwest, back towards the Tanaro. Leave the centre of Santo Stefano following signs to Asti/Alba across the river, then turn left towards Valdivilla and almost immediately right to Castiglione Tinella. The road heads back up into scrubby countryside while giving good views down onto Santo Stefano. By-pass Castiglione Tinella, turning left at the T-junction that gives access to the village to continue to Valdivilla. From there, take a sharp V-turn right to Castagnole Lanze. Within a couple of minutes you cross the provincial border into Asti.

From now on the route remains in Asti province. The only noticeable change, however, is that the area is fairly densely inhabited, mainly because Castagnole Lanze is built up due to the accessibility of the Asti-Alba road. At Castagnole Lanze, the route changes direction again, along the Tinella Valley to Boglietto, with views up into the vineyards on the left. At the T-junction just by Boglietto, turn right (signed Santo Stefano), then fork left for a short southeasterly stretch to Calosso and Canelli, optionally diverting through San Marzano Oliveto (all signposted).

CANELLI

Canelli, situated on the Belbo like Santo Stefano Belbo, is also remarkable for its unloveliness. Unfortunately, not every wine town can be full of captivating charm, especially one that has as important a part to play as Canelli – not just for Piedmont but for the whole of Italy. Its Piedmont role is as home to many of the important Asti cellars, those of

Contratto, Bosca, Gancia and Riccadonna among others. Country wide, it supplies the nuts and bolts of wine production; the corks, bottles, bottling lines and other equipment without which no producer can survive. Just a short hop along the *statale* from the town, in either direction, will lead past concrete monstrosities all involved in some way with the industry surrounding wine production.

Aesthetic relief comes in the form of the Castello Gancia, perched on a spur guarding over the town. From Piazza Cavour (with the river behind) follow the road to the right past the petrol station, from where the Castello is signed.

LOAZZOLO

Loazzolo is the other side of the Belbo. Its *passito* Moscato is produced in tiny quantities by no more than a handful of producers. Even so, it is a worthwhile optional diversion. If skipping it, cross the river from central Canelli and follow signs to Nizza Monferrato. However, to see the zone, having crossed the river, curve left (direction Bubbio), after which signs to Loazzolo appear. Once clear of the valley, the road quickly becomes twisty and steep, with scattered vineyards mainly on the less steep slopes. The heart of cultivation is around a large left-hand bend, where Azienda Loazzolo is signed down a slip road. Continue into almost alpine-looking countryside before descending into Loazzolo village, which boasts a *belvedere* worthy of the name.

From here turn back but shortly fork right to Cassinasco. You are soon presented with the weird sight of the road leading round an isolated arabic-styled church. Needless to say, this spot, Caffi, is quite a tourist haunt. Past another crumbling church, follow the sign for Canelli then take first right by a chapel. This isn't signed, although there is a batch of signs on the wall on the left. It leads through a wooded area, on a single track road full of bends. This is a prime spot for hazelnuts, some of Italy's best. Eventually you reach a T-junction. Turn right, pass Calamandrana and shoot along the plain towards Nizza.

Da Elsa
Calosso, Via S Siro 4
Tel: 0141 853142; closed Mon.
Well-flavoured, traditional menu served in homely surroundings, with fair selection of local wines. Seats outside. Cash only.
San Marco Canelli, Via Alba 136
Tel: 0141 823544; closed Weds.
Classy but comfortable, relaxed and good value restaurant. Impressively flavoured food with traditional roots. Wine list a browser's delight.
Del Belbo da Bardon
San Marzano Oliveto, Via Valle Asinari 25 (the Nizza-Canelli road)
Tel: 0141 831340; closed Wed pm, Thurs.
Known simply as 'Bardon', this large, easy-going, welcoming restaurant serves dishes from fine ingredients, prepared with élan. An enthusiast's wine list, enormous; strongest in Piedmont but spans world. Excellent value. Seats outside.
Enoteca Ristorante I Caffi
Cassinasco, Loc Caffi 28
Tel: 0141 826900; closed Sun pm, Weds.
Mixture of more and less traditional dishes. Tasting menu plus, if wished, wines to match from list or well-stocked shelves of *enoteca* by entrance. Fair pricing, cash only.

AGRITOURISM

Antica Borgo del Riondino
Trezzo Tinella, Via dei Fiori 13
Medieval farmhouse. Only six rooms, all different. Meals provided, mainly from home-grown produce; all organic including wines.

FOOD SHOPPING

Ferrero Valdivilla for *salumi*.
Bosca Canelli, Piazza Amedeo d'Aosta 3 and **Giovine** Canelli, Piazza Gancia:
Both for pastries. Selections quite different but equally tempting.
Ezio Canelli, Piazza Gancia
Ice cream (try Moscato flavoured).

PLACES OF INTEREST

South and west of Loazzolo is the Alta Langa Astigiana, an area of great scenic beauty, notably around Monastero Bormida, Olmo Gentile and Roccaverano. Also known for its Robiola cheese, not dissimilar from that from Murazzano.

SPECIAL EVENTS

Hazelnut fair
Castagnole Lanze, August.
Assedio di Canelli June – jousting in 17th-century costumes.

Nizza to Ovada

NIZZA TO OVADA

RECOMMENDED PRODUCERS

Guasti Clemente e Figli
Nizza Monferrato
Tel: 0141 721350; E. F.
With underground cellars in central
Nizza, owns five properties in the
surrounding hills, yielding estate
wines, notably Barbera d'Asti (two
from separate properties and one,
oaked, from grapes from both).
Also buys in grapes to produce large
range of other wines. Strong links
with America as forebear Secondo
Guasti emigrated in 1881, creating a
huge vineyard in California from
propagated Barbera cuttings. Visits
working hours, must book for
weekend visits.

Cascina La Barbatella
Nizza Monferrato
Tel: 0141 701434; F.
Owned by Milanese wine enthusiast
with serious investment undertaken
in modern, efficient cellars. Estate
concentrates on forward, well-fruited
but structured Barbera d'Asti,
particularly top rated *cru* La Vigna
dell'Angelo. Must book. Large
groups pay for tastings.

Scarpa
Nizza Monferrato
Tel: 0141 721331; E. F.
Absolutely traditionalist estate (a
barrique-free zone) run by strongly
opinionated and firmly quality
orientated Mario Pesce. Despite
cellars in Nizza and major vineyard
holding south of Castel Rocchero,
near Acqui, known as much for
Barolo *cru* Tettimorra (from La
Morra), Barbaresco *cru* Tettineive
(Neive) and, especially Rouchet
(Ruché) from near Castagnole
Monferrato, as the locally produced
Barbera d'Asti and unusual, dry
Brachetto. Tastings held in old cellars,
with accompanying local specialities
as nibbles. Must book.

Bersano
Nizza Monferrato
Tel: 0141 721273
This colossus of the Piedmont wine
scene, producing millions of bottles a
year from all the main wine zones of
the region, is also based in Nizza.
Adjacent is the company's museum
(see page 92).

*Right 'La Bollente': monument
in the spa town of Acqui Terme
to the hot water that steams out
continually below.*

NIZZA TO ACQUI

Nizza Monferrato, situated where the *torrente* Belbo meets
the even smaller *torrente* Nizza, is no great shakes as a town;
it's just a functional commercial centre for the surrounding
villages, although it was once a more important market
town with a leading cattle market, whose site still dominates
the place and it remains a good hunting ground for
craftworks. It is also home to a few producers and lies within
the zone of Cortese dell'Alto Monferrato.

Cortese is the grape variety used for Gavi (*see* page 112-
115) but is also grown in a vaguely rectangular zone,
stretching from a north–south line passing just west of Canelli
eastwards to the edges of the Gavi district, part of the area
known as the Alto Monferrato. (More on Monferrato on
page 126.) Cortese produces firm, structured white wines
with a minerally tang. In youth, when the Alto Monferrato
versions are usually best, they have a delicate florality; in Gavi
they can mature to a spicy, roundedly fruited presence.

Left *Quiet, cool, underground cellars harbouring a priceless store of old bottles.*

Araldica Vini
Castel Boglione
Tel: 0141 762115; E.
Large company with innovative approach producing wide range of well-honed wines styles.

Marenco
Strevi
Tel: 0144 363133
Largish estate, built up by Giuseppe Marenco and now run by his daughters, with vineyards in seven plots, mostly around Strevi. Main emphasis on light, refreshing Brachetto d'Acqui Pineto and Moscato d'Asti Scrapona. Will provide English translator if requested when booking.

Banfi
Strevi
This large Tuscan company also has an outpost at Strevi, for production of its Brachetto d'Acqui, Dolcetto d'Acqui, Moscato d'Asti, Gavi, dry sparkling wine and others. For information, contact their Tuscany office (*tel: 0577 840111*).

Cascina Bertolotto di Traversa Giuseppe e Fabio
Spigno Monferrato
Tel: 0144 91223; E.
About 25km south from Acqui along the Bormida Valley, 400m above sea level. Estate organises tasting days, matching its wines with cheeses from local producers. Two differently styled Dolcetto d'Acqui, Ca Muietti e Ca Cresta; Cortese dell'Alto Monferrato Il Barigi; Piemonte Brachetto (estate outside Brachetto d'Acqui zone). Plans to develop agritourism.

La Guardia
Morsasco
Tel: 0144 73076; E. G.
Mid-sized estate with vines on amphitheatre-shaped, sun-drenched vineyard and wines carefully and attentively produced. Three Dolcetto di Ovadas. Bricco Riccardo is the most typical, both of Ovada style and the estate's production: large, chunky, lively, long, packed with lively fruit and long lived. Il Gamondino is from very old vines, Villa Delfini is matured in *barrique*. Also attractive, well made Cortese dell'Alto Monferrato. Comfortable tasting room. Can also see the 18th-century Villa Delfini and its old cellars carved from the rocks.

Nizza also marks the edge of the zone of Dolcetto d'Asti. Asti's Dolcetto is light, lively, refreshing, zestful and gulpable; well, at least the better and more typical examples are. The production area is a slim strip across the southwestern tip of the province, its eastern edge running roughly along the Belbo, thereby cutting through both Canelli and Nizza.

From Nizza head towards Acqui Terme. It's a pretty route, quite open, with gentle slopes, mostly vine covered. You may see the dome of Fontanile gleaming in the distance, over to the left. Roughly at this point, shortly before a junction on the right to Castel Bordone, you enter the zone of Brachetto d'Acqui. It forms a roughly triangular area, bordered to the northwest by the lowish lands abutting the Belbo Valley and to the south and east by the Bormida River valley. The variety Brachetto is also grown outside this area; you may well already have come across examples of its wines. The denominated zone, however, marks the focus of its cultivation and production. Brachetto makes wines that are the antithesis of what one would expect from a red Piedmontese grape. They bear more similarities to Asti and Moscato d'Asti than anything else. (Both are also produced in the zone but are usually a little fatter than the Moscatos from across the Belbo.) Brachetto wines are pale red to lightish pink; mainly *frizzante* or fully sparkling, but can be still; low in alcohol and sweet or sweetish, with perfumes of straw–berries and Muscat grapes plus, sometimes, violets and roses. Good examples have the attraction of well made Moscatos with an additional layer of flavour and interest.

Cascine Olive-Scarsi di Ratto Giuseppe

Rocca Grimalda (Loc San Lorenzo)
Tel: 0143 831888; F.
Giuseppe Ratto proudly demonstrates the notorious longevity of Dolcetto di Ovada, claiming lives of up to 30 years for his powerful, firmly structured wines. Two Dolcettos, Gli Scarsi and Le Olive. Estate badly damaged by the 1994 floods and is slowly being restored. Must book to ensure someone will be there when you call.

Castello di Tagliolo

Tagliolo Monferrato
Tel: 0143 89195; E. F.
Three Dolcetto di Ovadas, Barbera and others. Tasting room with display of old wines. Wine shop. No need to book.

Contero

Strevi
Brachetto, Dolcetto and delightful Moscato owned by the same company as Tenuta La Giustiniana in Gavi, which is the contact point for any visits (see page 115).

ENOTECHE

Enoteca Regionale di Acqui Terme

Tel: 0144 770273
Tastings free for serious wine enthusiasts. *See also* main text. Check for opening hours.

Enoteca Dionisos

Acqui Terme, Vicolo della Pace 7
Anything you could want, from Chilean wine to an unusual whisky, or a speciality food. Oh, and a good range of Italian wines too.

La Schiavia

Acqui Terme
See Eating Out.

FOOD SPECIALITIES

Chocolates

Also other sweetmeats.

Haunch of Veal

Most notably from Nizza.

Cardoons

Known as *Gobbi di Nizza*.

Fruits

Peaches, apples and other fruits, plus fruit preserves.

Hazelnut tart

Stoccafisso

The Ligurian influence appears increasingly from Acqui onwards with the appearance of this speciality: dried cod, along with anchovies and other dried, salted or occasionally fresh fish. More use of vegetables and increased use of olive oil and aromatic herbs is also evident.

Within five minutes you pass Castel Rocchero, a little over to the right, although the view is spoilt somewhat by the encroaching presence of the round cellars of Torre di Castel Rocchero, a *cantina sociale*. Moments past this the road sweeps to the right and enters the province of Alessandria. This marks the introduction of yet another denominated zone, Dolcetto d'Acqui, which replaces that of Dolcetto d'Asti. Acqui's Dolcetto is not desperately dissimilar from that of Asti, but tends in general to be a little fuller and more richly fruited. The hills here are still soft and rounded but tumble into the more easterly Bormida valley, rather than the Belbo.

Acqui Terme will be reached within about ten minutes along this road and the scenery throughout is restfully appealing. There is the option, though, of diverting leftwards, through Alice Bel Colle and continuing for a short way in the direction of Ricaldone (and Maranzana) before curving rightwards, either to loop back onto the Nizza–Acqui Statale, along a narrow, highly picturesque road, or to divert a little further, to Strevi, and thence come into Acqui along the Bormida valley. The entire stretch will take barely half a hour.

ACQUI TERME

Unlike the uninspiring towns which punctuate the Belbo valley, Acqui, on the Bormida, which rises in the western Ligurian Apennines and flows into the Po, is a delight. It is a small spa town, with all the wealth and sense of well-being that the muds and waters always bring, although it is much more low key now than in the 1950s when it was one of the most important of spas. The main street is neatly cobbled, with a fountain-shaped design picked out on the stones showing the way to the water source. This, known as the *bollente*, is a permanently steaming fountain in a small square, approached through an archway under a clocktower off to one side. Acqui also has a spacious, well-stocked and carefully managed Enoteca Regionale. It is situated beside an alley at the far corner of Piazza Levi (by the *municipio* – town hall). And not to be missed is a coffee at the long-standing and unchanged Bar Pasticceria Voglino, in Piazza Italia (off Corso Dante). Walking through its doors into the old, spacious interior, with its small tables and high counters stacked with tempting goodies is like stepping back into history. The elegantly served coffee is top notch too.

EATING OUT

Farinata da Gianni
Acqui Terme, Via Mazzini 32
Tel: 0144 324283; closed Weds.
The oldest eating place in Acqui, still with its original wood oven for baking *farinata*. Also full meals served. Short menu with mix of Piedmontese and Ligurian dishes. Inexpensive. Cash only. Pm only.

Parisio 1933
Acqui Terme, Via C Battisti 7
Tel: 0144 57034; closed Mon.
Reliable menu from local Liguria/Piedmont ingredients; good wine selection. Not expensive and good value.

La Schiavia
Acqui Terme, Vicolo della Schiavia 1
Tel: 0144 55939; closed Sun.
Acqui's smart spot, set in a rather impressive 250-year old building. Food is the Liguria-Piedmont mix traditional in the area, with positive flavours, excellent textures and lively taste matches. Broad wine list, from local through to international but real wine interest is upstairs where there's a full scale enoteca. Restaurant mid-priced and good value.

Cacciatori
Cartosio, Via Moreno 30
Tel: 0144 40123; closed Thurs.
Well out in the countryside, about 14km from Acqui. Long-standing, family-run, comfortable and welcoming place. Classic local cuisine, with good use of vegetables, flavoursome dishes, well presented. Good wine list, not just local. Mid-priced, cash only.

Osteria del Nonno Carlo
Montechiaro d'Acqui, Via delle Scuole 1
Tel: 0144 92366; closed Tues.
About 20km south of Acqui, up a very twisty road but food absolutely typical with speciality of anchovies in an original sauce unique to this spot. Pasta home made, good quality meats simply cooked (or *stoccafisso*), good goats' cheeses and local hazelnut tart. Mainly local wine list with some little-known producers. Cash only.

La Volpina
Ovada, Strada Volpina 1
Tel: 0143 86008; closed Sun eve, Mon.
Restaurant – more Ligurian than Piedmontese, with plenty of vegetables and fish lightening very

Left *Traditional, large botti in a spacious, purpose-built cellar. These casks are usually made of Slavonian oak and store about 25 hectolitres of wine.*

filling dishes. Pasta home made. Menu offers dishes of the day and wines of the day. Seats outside. Not overly expensive.

Bel Sogiorno
Cremolino, Via Umberto I
Tel: 0143 879012; closed Weds.
Old country house setting. Food more Piedmontese than Ligurian. Go with large appetites. Good service. Large regional wine list. Mid-priced, good value.

FOOD SHOPPING

Centrale
Acqui, Corso Italia 15
Acqui's best salumi but go for the small goat's or mixed goat's/sheep cheeses.

Pasticceria Bellati
Acqui, Piazza San Francesco 2
Something different to take home: special cakes and chocolates made in special form in memory of the old spa water carriers.

PLACES OF INTEREST

Bersano museum
Nizza, Piazza Dante 24
Tel: 0144 721273
Contains artefacts relating to farm workers' lives and old wine prints. Open Mar–Oct, by appointment only.

SPECIAL EVENTS

Antiques Market
Especially important for coins, medals, philately, vintage cars and agricultural machinery. Nizza: third Sun of each month.

Vintage festival
Nizza: end Aug–beginning Sept.

Dolcetto di Ovada market
Ovada: end Aug–beginning Sept.

Truffle day Nizza: Nov.

Calf fair Ovada: Oct.

Medieval jousting Nizza: June.

ACQUI TO OVADA

Acqui marks the start of the transition of Piedmont into Liguria and the climate becomes drier, breezier, sunnier and less prone to winter fogs. Just a short distance south are the first rises of the Apennines, which plunge down to the long arc of coast either side of Genoa. A potter among any of the small roads heading towards the coast from Acqui itself or from the Acqui-Ovada road can be enthralling. To join this road leave Acqui in the direction of Genoa. You should catch sight of the part-standing Roman bridge over the Bormida and pass the more important thermal centres before crossing the Bormida and following signs to Ovada.

Within a couple of minutes you go through Visone and re-enter vineyard country. At the next junction (with four yellow signposts) you switch from the Dolcetto d'Acqui zone to that of Dolcetto di Ovada. This stretches in a large circle around Ovada town, brushing the Ligurian border to the south and overlapping the western flank of Gavi in the east. Ovada's Dolcetto is traditionally chunky, rich, structured and ages well, influenced by the dominant dry winds from Liguria and the rather poor soil that helps keep yields down. Comparatively few producers are bothered to invest in this heritage, however, most preferring the easy route of uncomplicated, light wines they can sell within a year. The best vineyards lie just north of the Acqui-Ovada road. Therefore either come into Ovada straight along the *statale* (via Cremolino) or, better, take a longer route, looping north. Even so, Ovada is still reached within half an hour. To take the detour, turn left at the clutch of yellow signs (to Orsara, Rivalta). This is a truffle hunting zone; the woodlands harbour good hazelnuts too. After a minute or two, cut across right on a slim road that snakes up to Morsasco. Here, turn left and sweep through to Trisobbio and its castle on a wonderful road with vineyards forming neat patches on the soft, shouldered hills. Some even think it was such hills that gave Dolcetto its name, a possible derivation of Dossetto, meaning gentle slope.

Next is Santo Stefanodi and a further choice of routes. Either follow signs straight into Ovada or branch right to Cremolino to rejoin the *statale*. Alternatively, a road to the

Above Dormant vines almost submerged in a thick blanket of snow near Ovada.

left will take you up to the scenic spot of Rocca Grimalda, from where a narrow road follows the Orba Valley to Ovada. Ovada itself is a large commercial centre. It is also the best point at which to head down to Genoa for a long-awaited glimpse of the sea and the very different wines and food of Liguria. The *autostrada* is a miracle of construction, tunnelling through mountains and overhanging narrow valleys. Before joining it, though, you could see the remaining important Dolcetto vineyard areas, the other side of Ovada.

Cross the Orba and head towards Lerma. This road would lead to Gavi (*see* page 112) for anyone not including Liguria in their trip at this point. Just after crossing the *autostrada*, there is Tagliolo Monferrato, with its *castello* which is the first of the two leading cultivation areas. The second is Lerma itself, also with a castle and very pretty, another few minutes further on. Then turn back and follow signs to join the *autostrada*.

Below A splash of colour on a sunny balcony above a sun-bleached wooden door.

Liguria

Genoa marks the centre of the long arc of slim coastal land, closely backed by the protective Apennines, which forms the Ligurian Riviera. The mountains protect this coastline from cold northerly and easterly winds and the sea has its usual softening effect on the climate. The Riviera thus has a special and quite glorious microclimate. Even in deepest winter when, under the dominant high pressure systems, most of Piedmont is suffering a damp, cold, foggy isolation, the Ligurian coast will be stunningly bright, sunny and even roll-your-sleeves-up warm.

There is space for few roads, particularly in the east. The only through routes are the Aurelia (the coastal *statale*) and the *autostrada*. There are, though, routes inland, up into the Apennines, particularly in the west, and these cool sites, often with stunning views and pretty, unspoilt small villages, are a real draw.

To see either the western (*ponente*) or eastern (*levante*) side of Liguria, the obvious method is to go out on one of the main roads and back on the other, ducking inland from time to time in the west, as the mood takes you. Since many of the best views are from the extremities of the region, heading towards Genoa, it is best to whizz out on the *autostrada* and then potter back on the *statale*. Each motorway stretch will take roughly an hour and the journey back at least three times as long.

The *autostrada* down from Ovada hits the coast at Voltri, about 15 kilometres west of Genoa, so you may prefer to continue west, first exploring the *riviera ponente* (western riveria) before having a look at this arresting city. If you do wish to see Genoa first, though, keep on the *austostrada* to do so, because however beautiful the rest of the Ligurian coastline may be, the stretch between Genoa and Voltri is built-up, semi-industrial, heavily trafficked and ugly.

Left *The tip of the Portofino promontory, behind the bay; a haven of tranquility.*

Above *The famous bay of Portofino, glistening in the early morning sun.*

Genoa

ENOTECHE

Vinoteca Sola Piazza Colombo 13/r
Well selected wines; can taste.
Sola, Cucina e Vino
Via Barabino 120/r
Similarly good wines but also
serve typical local dishes.

FOOD SPECIALITIES

Genoa is famous for its snack foods,
farinata, *focaccia*, vegetable tarts and
other savouries, and fried foods, fish,
vegetables etc.
Farinata Made from chick pea flour,
with olive oil, water and salt, cooked
in the oven in large, flat baking dishes.
It's best hot and fresh and sometimes
prepared with added flavours,
rosemary or onions, for example.
Focaccia A cross between a lightly
oily flat bread and a pizza base.
Some make it flatter and crispier,
others thicker and more spongy;
either way it's irresistible. Among
the best spots in town for these
mouth-fillers are:
Antica Osteria della Foce: Via
Ruspoli 72/r; Da Guglie: Via S
Vincenzo 64/r; Sa Pesta: Via dei
Giustiniani 16/r; Sciamadda: Via
Ravecca 19/r; Spano: Via Sta Rita 35/r.

EATING OUT

Antica Osteria del Gaia
Vico dell'Argento 13/r
Tel: 010 2461629; closed Sun.
In old town on the edges of the new.
Friendly and young. Hearty portions
of very tasty food; carefully chosen
list of wines from small estates
(including Ligurian). Cash only.
Da Maria Vic Testadoro 14/r
Tel: 010 581080; closed Fri pm, Sat.
In old town. Good, flavoursome
food, typically Genoese, simple and
satisfying. House wine only. Cash only.
Per Bacco
Piazza del Cavalletto 9–11/r
Tel: 010 540889; closed Sun lunch.
In new town. Small, family-run and
friendly. Excellent quality and very
fresh raw materials. Mainly fish based.
Small choice of wines.
Gran Gotto Via Brigata Bisagno 69
Tel: 010 564344; closed Sat lunch, Sun.
Smart restaurant in new town.
Beautifully prepared food, with
sound emphasis on vegetables.
Good use of herbs. Carefully chosen
wines. Expensive but not overly so.

Ligurians, they say, are closed in on themselves, secretive, isolationist and mean. Not at all. They may turn their backs on the rest of Italy but that is the geographic imperative; cut off from the mainland by the severe Apennine chain, they look outwards to the sea instead.

Genoa is the archetype of this. Its lifeblood is the sea. It was a Maritime Republic and once a thriving mercantile port of huge importance. As trade declined, Genoa, still Italy's number one port, started to grow into a major stop on the European cruise circuit. Now Caribbean cruises are more popular and the festive atmosphere of a cruiseship's arrival is an infrequent luxury. The main traffic is in ferries – hardly the stuff of romance and excitement, let alone the affluence brought about by a ship load of folk eager to spend. Yet Genoa, somehow, retains its prosperous air, it just has a rather low key feel.

The city is long and narrow, filling the limited space between the coastline and the surrounding ring of hills, breached by two narrow valleys and stretching up to the highest point of its protective hill ridge, from where it overlooks the high plain behind. As a result of its postition, Genoa is often swept by strong breezes, at times quite chilly.

There are four sides to Genoa and the swiftest but shallowest way to see three of them is to whizz through the city on the *sopraelevata*, the newish dual carriageway road that gives a bird's eye view of the coast and fragments of the new and old towns. New Genoa is spendid. There are wide, elegant avenues, fringed by smart buildings, some new, others once summer residences and built in typical Genoese style. Between the large Piazza della Vittoria and the lively Piazza de Ferrari is the shop-lined Via XX Settembre, the main axis of this modern part.

The old town is a different world and is the largest old centre remaining in Italy. It lies in a tight web of streets and alleyways behind the old port. Until recently this fascinating area was off-limits, with tales of muggings and low life rife. But although the Genoese still huff and puff at the more rundown parts, the old town has been revitalized – and it is far safer. From the arcades just behind the port come tantalizing aromas of frying, exactly as they have for generations. Within the maze of lanes are individual domains: the street of butchers, for instance, the *stoccafisso* merchants' patch and the essential fruit and veg market (Piazza Banchi). This is the place to come for any specialist craftsman or food shop. Even though many sold up when the area was at its most depressed, there has not been a total exodus. There is also a great deal to interest history and architecture buffs, especially the Royal Palace, facing the port.

The coast is where Genoa lets its civic pride flourish and displays itself to the world. From east to west are the airport with its runway built out into the bay; the new and old ports,

Above *Piazza Banchi, the famous market area in Genoa's old town.*
Left *The splendid edifice of Genoa's town hall in Piazza Caricamento.*

HOTELS

As a major commercial centre, Genoa is liberally dotted with hotels, many of a very good standard. Those listed below are a small sample of the nicest.

Bristol Palace Via XX Settembre 35
Tel: 010 592541; fax: 010 561756.
Well renowned. For indulgence in real luxury. Traditional style. Garage.
Cairoli Via Cairoli 14/4
Tel: 010 206531; fax: 010 280041.
In the old town, on edges of the new. Extremely comfortable. Terrace overlooks city. Not expensive. Garage.
Capannina Via Tito Speri 7
Tel: 010 363205; fax: 010 3622692.
East of centre. Relaxing, comfortable rooms. Not expensive. Small garage.

FOOD SHOPPING

Everything of interest is in the old town (see main text) but not to be missed is:
Pasticceria Romanengo
Three shops throughout the town; best is in Via Orefici. Shop itself is ancient and has been left in its original, beautifully ornate style. Service is personal and attentive and the goodies are quite delicious.

between them the 'lantern' (actually a lighthouse), Genoa's symbol; the *darsena*, shipyard; the aquarium, one of international renown and quite stunning to visit; the modernistic Columbus memorial, built to celebrate the 500th anniversary of the voyage to the Americas; the clean lines of the exhibition centre and, finally, the point where town and sea meet. Here the Genoese walk, jog along the promenade, or just sit and watch the sea lapping the rocky beach.

Finally, there is hillside Genoa. The higher locations were and are the residential areas of the well-to-do although, as the city expanded, more ordinary housing spread into the lower rises, and several parts are served by a regular funicular service down to the centre. There are also numerous panoramic spots from which to look down on the city, some giving views over the old town and the port, others overlooking the modern town and the commercial areas.

All in all, Genoa is a splendid place. Yet it is hardly known by most Italians, who rarely go there: it's their loss.

The Ligurian Riviera

Right *Awaiting the day's visitors
in Portofino.*
Far right *Two views of the elegant
resort of Santa Margherita.*

If only high pressure could be guaranteed throughout the winter, Liguria's coastal spots could become all-year resorts. As it is, they throb with tourists in summer and are left to the residents in winter. These residents, donned in the finery that is the reward for many summers' hard labours, take full advantage of the peace to take long walks along the prom or merely sit in some sunny spot, discussing who knows what with their neighbours.

Portofino is a case in point. This highly-fashionable promontory, the zenith of the super-smart boating set, attracts so many visitors to its tiny centre that road signs warn of the queuing time necessary, in half-hour multiples, just to get into the car park. The bay is so packed that it takes a powerful imagination to see this spot as the fishing village it once was. In January, however, the car park is nearly empty, the atmosphere relaxed and fishermen repair their nets at the water's edge unperturbed.

That's not to say that the Riviera is only attractive out of season. Spring and autumn are delightful; and high summer has a real buzz, if you're patient with the busy roads.

The western resorts tend to be more commercial (Alassio, Diano Marina, San Remo, for instance); the more extensive the stretch of sand, the larger and more bustling

the town around it is the simple and obvious rule of thumb. San Remo, despite the thrall of its name, is the most frustrating, with traffic a nightmare even out of season and hellish parking. The others, despite the buzz, have retained the relaxed, easy-going charm of a good holiday resort. Ventimiglia, just a leap from the French border, and nearby Bordighera are particularly well-scrubbed and welcoming. The part nearer Genoa, east of Savona, is less well known and as a consequence less overtly touristy. Among them, Arenzano is particularly pretty but you will usually need to come off the Aurelia to see these resorts at their best. Overall, however, the western coast is patchier than the east. Parts are quite wonderful, sometimes exotically tranquil, sometimes resoundingly dramatic. Then there are intervals where it is no more picturesque than okay. Yet, without fail, just as you begin to think it might be better to get on the *autostrada* and skip the rest, another wonderful sweep of landscape magically appears. Until Voltri, that is, where Genoa's populated hinterland descends like a curtain and picturesque goes to seedy and drear in seconds.

The real gems of the Riviera are in the east. Sestri Levante, Chiavari, Rapallo and Santa Margherita, not to mention Portofino, are all delightful and quite distinct from each other. There are fewer sandy beaches on this side, more yachting harbours and more small, coastal villages clustered round tiny bays in the rocks that otherwise fall sheer to the sea. West of Portofino are increasing signs of the nurseries that punctuate the riviera all the way to the French border: not for nothing is Liguria known as the Riviera dei Fiori (the Flower Coast) and flowers from here are despatched all over Europe. Pride in the surroundings is tangible. Houses are kept pristine and regularly painted, often in convincing *trompe l'oeil* designs. Even the approaches to Genoa on this side exude confidence and care. It makes returning to the city quite joyful.

HOTELS

No shortage of hotels along the coast but many are closed in winter, heavily booked in summer. These are among the more characterful in the lesser-known resorts:

Stella Maris
Levanto, Via Marconi 4
Tel: 0187 808251; fax: 0187 807351.
Large, traditional rooms, antique furniture in an elegant, old building in town; separate modern site on coast.

Clelia
Deiva Marina, Corso Italia 23
Tel: 0187 815827; fax: 0187 816234.
Spacious, bright, thoughtfully furnished rooms and good bathrooms, in a traditional, old building. Gardens, tennis court, private beach.
Also sells good ice-cream!

Bristol
Lavagna, Corso Mazzini 23
Tel & fax: 0185 395600.
Centrally located, family-run, neatly furnished rooms, excellent value.

Cenobio dei Dogi
Camogli, Via N Cuneo 34
Tel: 0185 770041; fax: 0185 772796.
Beautifully kept, elegant hotel in 16th-century villa by the coast. Swimming pool, tennis court. Private beach with restaurant. Costly.

Villa Pagoda
Nervi, Via Capolungo 15
Tel: 010 323200; fax: 010 321218.
Old villa with large gardens, fully refurbished. Welcoming.

SPECIAL EVENTS

Fish Festival
Camogli – 2nd Sun in May. See huge quantities of fish cooked in an enormous frying pan, then join the crowds eating it – for free.

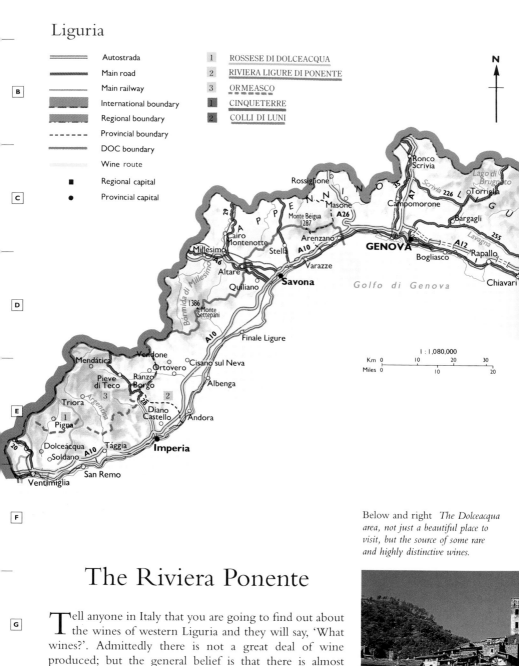

Liguria

Legend:
- Autostrada
- Main road
- Main railway
- International boundary
- Regional boundary
- Provincial boundary
- DOC boundary
- Wine route
- ■ Regional capital
- ● Provincial capital

1 ROSSESE DI DOLCEACQUA
2 RIVIERA LIGURE DI PONENTE
3 ORMEASCO
1 CINQUETERRE
2 COLLI DI LUNI

N

Below and right The Dolceacqua area, not just a beautiful place to visit, but the source of some rare and highly distinctive wines.

The Riviera Ponente

Tell anyone in Italy that you are going to find out about the wines of western Liguria and they will say, 'What wines?'. Admittedly there is not a great deal of wine produced; but the general belief is that there is almost nothing, that what there is is barely worth consideration and that bottles are produced for the tourists, bearing the relevant labels but with the contents possibly coming from goodness knows where. The truth is, as you will discover, that there clearly are vineyards and they are certainly in production. But as their number is limited and their size usually small, producers often need look no further than friends and a few long-standing clients to sell their entire production. It is the market in these wines that is lacking, not the wines themselves.

DOLCEACQUA

Dolceacqua (sometimes called Rossese di Dolceacqua) is a small zone near the French border, cutting across from Ventimiglia and Bordighera on the coast to the heights of the Apennines. Vineyards are, however, generally clustered in the centre of the zone, on the mid-height slopes (below 600 metres) mainly along the Nervia and Crosia valleys. Scenically it is quite stunning. To have a look give yourself a good hour.

Come off the *autostrada* at the Ventimiglia exit and travel back east through the town. A little past the centre take a left turn, inland, signposted to Apricale and Dolceacqua. This leads up the valley of the *torrente* Nervia. The lowest slopes sprout a huge wealth of flowers and plants of all sorts, for nursery cultivation and in some seasons the splashes of colour are remarkable. Lemon trees grow too, clusters of herbs spring out from the rocks and, higher up, olive trees are everywhere. Early spring is mimosa time when the flowers from these glorious trees turn the entire valley bright yellow – a magnificent sight. Among this abundance of cultivation are small plots of vineyards, mainly terraced. The grapes are the Ligurian variety Rossese, a red capable of making ripe, well fruited wines, with good depth and suppleness. The greatest concentration is just across the *torrente* from Dolceacqua village, on steep slopes dropping down the valley side.

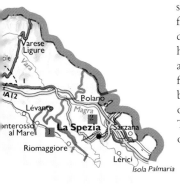

RIVIERA PONENTE

RECOMMENDED PRODUCERS

Terre Bianche
Dolceacqua, Loc Arcagna
Tel: 0184 31426; E. F. G.
Good, rounded, weighty wines
from youngish, forward-looking
estate. Pigato particularly promising.
Attractive agritourism apartments.
Small restaurant attached. Must book.
Large groups may have to pay for
the tastings.

Enzo Guglielmi
Soldano (Dolceacqua)
Tel: 0184 289042
Great attention to its well-sited,
well-exposed vineyard and
progressive refinements in the cellar
have made this one of Dolceacqua's
most noteworthy estates.

Mauro Feola
Diano Marina
Tel: 0183 495049; E.
Founded by current generation's
grandparents who, coming from
southern Italy, were attracted by
the Diano Marina coastline. Very
attentively made wines, in
well-equipped cellar. Afternoon
visits only.

Cascina Feipu dei Massaretti
Albenga, Fraz Bastia
Tel: 0182 20131; F.
Leading, highly-regarded estate
with vineyards on lowish, sandy lands
close to coast. Pigato is the flagship.
Good olive oil.

Anfossi
Bastia di Albenga
Tel: 0182 20024; E.
Based in a grand villa at 500m above
sea level. Also grow other fruits and
vegetables and make high quality
bottled sauces from them (including
pesto). Visits during working hours
only; tastings not offered.

Vio
Vendone
Tel: 0182 76338; E. G.
Family-run estate with south-facing,
terraced vineyards at 300m. Pigato
and Vermentino only. Winemaking
aimed at full intensity of perfume,
good weight and richness in the
mouth. Vio also produce good
olive oil.

A Maccia
Ranzo
Tel: 0183 318003
Up and coming estate. Elegant
Pigato and Rossese wines . Also
olive groves for olive oil, olive pâté
and olives in brine.

Continue up the valley, past Dolceacqua to Isolabona, and
from there head across to Apricale. Just past Apricale, there
is a longish detour for those who prefer mountain heights
to the lap of the sea and who would rather avoid the
lunacy of San Remo. Instead of turning back towards the
coast and Perinaldo, fork off left up to Baiardo and then
down through Ceriana, rejoining the coast at Poggio. The
wine route, however, continues to Perinaldo, diverting up
into this high, spur-hung village for the wonderful views
it gives of the surrounding landscapes, especially from
behind the village – including, if you can find them, a
vineyard or two. Then resume the descent, now following
the Crosia Valley, passing Soldano and one or two other
small clusters of houses before rejoining the coast road.
Vineyard land is quite scarce but 'hunt the vineyard' is not
a totally worthless game.

RIVIERA LIGURE DI PONENTE

Most wines of western Liguria come under the
denomination Riviera Ligure di Ponente. This is hardly
surprising as the zone covers the best part of the entire
western arc west of Voltri, even including the Dolceacqua
zone, giving producers there a choice of denominations for
their wines. Riviera Ligure di Ponente wines come from
one of four grape varieties: Rossese, Ormeasco (the local
name for Dolcetto), fragrant, white Vermentino and the
local, sturdy, white Pigato. Ormeasco is also made into a
rosato, called Sciac-trà. You may spot the odd vineyard from
time to time wherever you wander in the zone but most
production is concentrated in two or three areas. The more
western part, within the province of Imperia, forms the
sub-zone Riviera dei Fiori and is reputedly the area where
whites excel. What vineyards there are mainly cluster in the
hills behind the towns of Imperia, the provincial capital,

Far left *A soothing sight –
full moon over the Appenines.*
Left *Quiet corner reflecting
Liguria's warm climate.*
Below *Fisherman quietly
repairing nets by the sea.*

Tommaso e Angelo Lupi
Pieve di Teco
Tel: 0183 36161; E. F.
Lupi is the grand name of western
Liguria. Starting with an *enoteca*, the
family sought out the best wines of
the area, and were provoked into
making better themselves. Grapes
now bought from reliable growers/
sites. Wines classy and characterful.
Traditionally produced olive oil.
Newly built agritourism.

ENOTECHE

Bacchus
San Remo, Via Roma 65
Good range of tasty snacks or, at
lunchtime, full meals at very good
trattoria level, to accompany
whatever wine takes your fancy.

Enoteca Marone
San Remo, Via San Francisco 61
Wine shop: huge range from Liguria,
Italy and around the world. Oils too.

Pane e Vino
Imperia, Via Des Geneys 52
Drink your way around Italy and the
world or choose a bottle from one
of the five daily specials on offer.
Delicious range of accompanying
nibbles. Cash only.

Enoteca Lupi
Oneglia, Via Monti 3
Wine shop with wide range from
throughout Italy plus Sauternes.
See recommended producers.

San Giorgio
Cervo Alta, Via Alessandro Volta 19
Wine shop with mainly Ligurian
wines and olive oils.

Del Vascello
Albenga, Via G.M. Oddo 16
Wine shop. Huge number of wines
from all over the world. Also spirits,
olive oil, vinegars etc. Tasting
accoutrements too.

FOOD SPECIALITIES

Stoccafisso dried cod.
Olives, olive pâté and other olive
products.

EATING OUT

Gastone
Dolceacqua, Piazza Garibaldi 2
Tel: 0184 206577; closed Mon eve, Tues.
Classic inland Ligurian fare, simple
and without pretensions. Small
selection of local wines. Inexpensive.

important for olive oil and pasta production, and Diano
Marina, one of the larger resorts.

Diano Marina is the best starting point for a quick run
inland to get a feel of this sub-zone. Head up to Diano
Castello, itself worth a short pause, with its well-restored,
striking medieval castle. Then go on upwards to meet the
main cultivation area, a fairly large tract of neat, low-
trained vineyard. Shortly after, the road forks. Take the
right arm towards Diano Borello. You are now deep into
olive country, with a sea of olive trees reaching as far as the
horizon. At the next fork, go right once more (not towards
Evigno), this time downwards, across the steep valley. Cross
the stream and turn right once more, starting the return to
the coast. Viticulture here is quite different, with vines
cultivated on the small, flat patches between the hillsides,
rather than the more usual slopes. There's also some
intensive market gardening in these protected, raised areas.
Olives continue to dominate, however, until lower altitudes
and warmer coastal air prevail when it is but a short hop
back to Diano Marina.

La Casa del Priore
Andora, Via Castello 34
Tel: 0182 87330; closed Mon.
In a restored, 200-year old priory.
Food is strongly based on Ligurian
traditions. Very large wine list. Also
a brasserie and piano bar. Expensive.
Moisello Ranzo, Via Umberto 1
Tel: 0183 318073; closed Mon pm, Weds.
Simple, local dishes, prepared skillfully.
Drink Pigato. Soft background music.
Cash only, good value.
Lilliput
Noli, Loc Zuglieno 49, Fraz Voze
Tel: 019 748009; closed Mon.
Dishes based on fresh, good, local
ingredients, classically prepared.
Good wine list. Slightly costly. Cash
only. Eves only (except weekends).
Vino e Farinata
Savona, Via Pia 15r; closed Sun, Mon.
Long standing *locale* in old Savona.
Typical food including *farinata* and the
other local snack foods. Drink house
rosato. Inexpensive. Book in person.
Bacco
Savona, Via Quarda Superiore 17–19r
Tel: 019 8335350; closed Sun.
Eccentric, jovial place, facing port.
Mainly fish and seafood. Local wines;
sound house wine. Not expensive.

Below *Apricale, above
Dolceacqua, one of the Riviera
Ponente's cool, inland villages.*
Right *Time to watch the world
go by in Dolceacqua.*

A further sub-zone is that of Albenga, or Albenganese, primarily known for Pigato and secondarily Rossese, covering the hills behind Andora and close to the town of Albenga, just a short way along the coast past Alassio. Ormeasco is excluded from this sub-zone but, oddly, its end marks the beginning of the main Ormeasco zone, which stretches west and inland from Albenga along the Arroscia Valley and covers much of the centre and west of the zone, all inland. There are two ways to explore this part. If starting from Albenga, first follow signs to Turin, then to Pieve di Teco. The road follows the Arroscia Valley which is at first broad, flat and quite intensively cultivated, vines included.

Gradually the valley narrows and you begin a slow but continual rise, peppered with occasional vineyard plots. There are, it must be admitted, one or two dull bits along this road but shortly you pass Ranzo and will reach Pieve di Teco about 35 minutes after leaving Albenga. From there it is an exhilarating climb to Pornassio, the nucleus of Ormeasco cultivation. Pornassio is just a few kilometres from the Piedmont border so, unless you only wanted to dip a toe into Liguria, you should turn round now and return to Albenga.

To avoid having to return the full distance on the road on which you came, try starting from Imperia, returning there after touring the lands behind Diano Marina. Then take the road north from Imperia to Pieve di Teco. That way you are only duplicating the section between Pieve di Teco and Pornassio, seeing a little more Ormeasco country

and the Arroscia Valley vineyards on the return to Albenga. The disadvantage is, of course, that you would miss out on a rather lovely stretch of the coastline.

Not too far further along the coast from Albenga, you pass through the village of Pietra Ligure, followed shortly after by Finale Ligure and, a little later by Noli, with its amazingly perched castle. The hills behind these three small centres form yet another sub-zone, called Finale or Finalese, once more only for Pigato, Vermentino and Rossese. There are, however, few producers of any substance in this area.

SAVONA

Noli is but ten minutes or so from Savona. The approaches to the city are rather dulled by the pall from the port but Savona itself is quietly elegant, in an old-fashioned sort of way. In some ways it is like a miniature Genoa, with the contrast between the graceful newer part and the old town, behind the port, with its maze of narrow alleyways. In other ways it more resembles a miniature Turin, with colonnaded streets and grid-like road system. But it lacks the spaciousness and verve of both Genoa and Turin, feeling more closed-in and less airily bright, and seems firmly set in older, more stately times. There are some very ornately decorated buildings, one or two over-exaggeratedly so and some quietly refind piazzas but there's a strong sense that the true Savona does not reveal itself easily and that more than a casual glance is needed to get under the skin of this oddly intriguing, small city.

HOTELS

Kaly Ventimiglia, Lungomare Trento e Trieste 67
Tel: 0184 295218; fax: 0184 295118.
One up from a typical seaside 3* right on the coast. Not expensive.
Enrica Bordighera, Via Novaro 1
Tel: 0184 263436; fax: 0184 261344.
Near the sea. Small and welcoming, familial feel. Bright rooms. Inexpensive.
Corallo Imperia, Corso Garibaldi 29, Loc Porto Maurizio
Tel: 0183 666264; fax: 0183 666265.
Fronting sea. Sizeable rooms. Large terrace, gardens. Friendly.
Holiday Finale Ligure, Via Ulivi 45bis, Loc Varigotti
Tel: 019 698124.
Clean, simple, friendly and cheap. Officially a 2* but spacious, tranquil and near sea. Good breakfast. Homely dinner also provided.
Miramare Noli, Corso Italia 2
Tel: 019 748926.
Converted fort, parts of old walls still integrated into hotel. Cool, spacious rooms with original ceilings and sea view. Garden.
Garden Savona, Via Fareggiana 6, Loc Albissola Marina
Tel: 019 485253; fax: 019 485255.
On coast. Modern, bright. Large, attractive, air-conditioned rooms with terrace. Swimming pool. Gardens.
Grand Hotel
Arenzano, Lungomare Stati Uniti 3
Tel: 010 91091; fax: 010 910944.
Grand indeed. Large, air conditioned rooms. Private beach. Fitness centre. Elegant reception and bar areas. Not overly expensive, considering.

FOOD SHOPPING

Olive oil Good, local pressing plants selling direct are: Frantoi Roi Badalucco, Via Argentina 1 (traditional, granite mill); Bensa, Dolcedo; Marco Romagnoli, Castello di Perinaldo.
Anchovies Pescheria U Balinciu, Calata Cuneo 77; Persico, Via Cuneo 39; both in Imperia
Honey from local hives is available from Apicoltura Antonio Ferrari, Via Gramsci 33, Cisano sul Neva and Apicoltura Fernandez, Via Calice 186, Finale Ligure (Loc Perti).
Savona has a large market near the port. Abundant fish, but famous for its tripe.

SPECIAL EVENTS

Stoccafisso (dried cod) festival
Badalucco, 3rd Sunday of September. The cod comes from Norway and a Norwegian contingent joins in with the festivities.

Riviera Levante

COLLI DI LUNI

RECOMMENDED PRODUCERS

Il Monticello
Sarzana, Loc Bratia
Tel: 0187 621432; F.
Small estate above Sarzana. Mainly Vermentino: clean wines with strong varietal typing. Also *grappa*, olive oil. Must book. Agritourism.

Cascina dei Peri
Castelnuovo Magra
Tel: 0187 674085
Hilltop site above Castelnouvo Magra. Wine mainly Vermentino, slightly chunky but perfumed. Also grow many agricultural food products. Agritourism (meals included); can offer lunch or dinner (must book).

CINQUETERRE

RECOMMENDED PRODUCERS

Cooperativa Agricola di Riomaggiore, Manarola, Corniglia, Vernazza e Monterosso
Manarolo
Tel: 0187 920435
The company primarily responsible for upholding and enhancing standards in the Cinqueterre; successive directors have dedicated supreme efforts to improving wine quality. If the wine's fortunes are revived it will be thanks to this coop.

Walter de Battè
Riomaggiore
Tel: 0187 920127
New estate, built up by great wine enthusiast de Battè with frightening dedication. Tiny, fragmented plots on steep gradients, terraces reformed by hand. Unusually, prefers Bosco variety to Vermentino and with good

COLLI DI LUNI

The Colli di Luni zone covers practically the entire south-eastern tip of Liguria and extends into adjacent Tuscany a short way too. Vineyards are quite sparse, with abandoned terraces at least as common as planted areas. Nevertheless, people from La Spezia regard it as their wine and tend to be more proud of it than the just as local and far more chi-chi Cinqueterre. The proximity of Tuscany has a clear influence on the grapes grown. The red majors on Tuscany's super-grape Sangiovese while the white, far more sought-after for the diet of these coastal towns, is based on Vermentino but supported by the Tuscan Trebbiano. (A single varietal Vermentino is made too.)

The best way to get a feel of this well-drained zone of limestone-clay soils is to come off the *autostrada* from Genoa at Brugnato and take the Aurelia the rest of the way to La Spezia, the focal point of the Colli di Luni and the launch point for exploring the Cinqueterre. Do check the state of the road first. The area is subject to landslips in winter making the Aurelia impassable and repairs can take longer than expected. The road, following the River Vara, loops towards the *autostrada* a couple of times, before winding roughly southeast through the Luni heartland.

The eastern side of the area is reached by heading from La Spezia to Lerici and then across the River Magra to Sarzana and up to Fosdinovo (just into Tuscany). Back down to Sarzana, briefly take the main coast road (the Aurelia once

more) and turn off left to Castelnuovo Magra, where most of the top producers in the Ligurian part of the Colli di Luni are clustered (and some good eating spots too). A further quick detour along the coast leads to the easternmost point of Liguria and the archeological site of Luni, which gives its name to the wine and to the surrounding area, called the Lunigiana. In Roman times Luni was the marble town of the area, now usurped by Tuscany's Carrara.

CINQUETERRE

Cinqueterre, the 'five lands', is the most remarkable area of the entire northwest corner of Italy; mountains plunge practically sheer into the sea. The road is well signposted from the western side of La Spezia: just follow signs for Riomaggiore or Cinqueterre. Quickly after the roads to Riomaggiore and Portovenere divide, the road rises and within minutes there are marvellous views back over the city and the sea. A bit of twisting through the hills, a short tunnel, and suddenly the awe-inspiring sight of the Cinqueterre explodes in front of you. The view is literally incredible: tiny terraces, hewn out of the steepest of slopes, buttressed by lengths of dry stone wall and the railway line cutting through the hills below you – it must be impossible to remain unmoved by the heroism required to create and cultivate such sites. The vineyards are interlaced by thick wires, for hauling equipment and grapes up and down the precipitous slopes, and dotted with small huts to store small equipment and shelter vinyard workers. Gradually you begin to pick out the carefully constructed steps that get the workers from terrace to terrace. It is all quite amazing.

proportion of Alborola. Winemaking aimed at enhancing structure and perfumes. Must book, pay for tastings; no space for large groups (and precious little time for small).

Forlini e Cappellini
Manarola
Tel: 0187 920496
Perfumed but well-structured Cinqueterre, hand cultivated by the owners on the steep rocks above Manarola and Riomaggiore.

RIVIERA LEVANTE

ENOTECHE

Franco Baroni
Lerici, Via Cavour 18
About a hundred wines available by the glass; sandwiches and snacks.

Bar-Enoteca Franco Lanata
Lerici, Fraz Solaro, Via Militare 72
Excellent wines, fine snacks and tempting sweets; well run.

Er Botteghin
Sarzana, Fraz San Lazzaro,
Via Aurelia 312
Another good spot to try a glass or three in the evening, with excellent snacks and light dishes.

Mulino del Cibus
Castelnuovo Magra, Loc Canale,
Via Canale 46; pm only, closed Mon.
Huge wine list, mostly local, hearty snacks, good bread and very good cheeses. Open late. Cash only.

Enoteca Internazionale
Monterosso Mare, Via Roma 62
Wine shop. If you can get there, the best place to find Cinqueterre wines, notably from small producers.

FOOD SPECIALITIES

Mes-ciüa
Substantial soup of short pasta (home made), greenbeans, olive oil and seasonings. Filling and refreshing.

EATING OUT

La Pettegola
La Spezia, Via del Poplo 39
Tel: 0187 514041; closed Sun.
Fish-based restaurant. Home-made desserts. Well-balanced, fairly-priced wine list. Seats outside, air conditioned.

Antica Osteria da Caran
La Spezia, Via Genova 1
Tel: 0187 703777; closed Tues.
Spacious, easy-going *trattoria*; owners make customers feel at home even if they don't speak Italian. Short menu. Small wine selection and house Colli di Luni. Good value. Cash only.

Left *Vernazza, one of the Cinqueterre (the Five Lands).*
Far left *Sunset over Vernazza.*

Il Moccia
La Spezia, Pegazzano, Via Chiesa 30
Tel: 0187 707029; closed Weds.
In an old part of town, with
old-fashioned ambience and large,
loyal clientele. Home-style cooking,
traditional dishes, with several
vegetarian. Sit outside, under a
pergola. Excellent value.

La Pia
La Spezia, Via Magenta 12
Long-standing place for great *farinata*.

Locanda dell'Angelo
Ameglia, Viale XXV Aprile 60
*Tel: 0187 64391; closed Mon
(not in summer).*
One of the great names of Italian
cuisine and therefore furiously
expensive. Try a tasting menu.
Delicate food with full, well-matched
flavour. Air conditioned inside or
sit outside. Decent hotel attached.

Dai Pironcelli
Ameglia, Loc Montemarcello,
Via delle Mura 45
Tel: 0187 601252; closed Weds.
If funds won't stretch to the Locanda
dell'Angelo, try this welcoming
trattoria with its Ligure-Tuscan food.
Good selection of Colli di Luni. Dinner
only, except weekends. Cash only.

Vallecchia Bianchi Livia
Castelnuovo Magra, Loc Vallecchia
Tel: 0187 674104; closed Tues.
Traditional, family-run *trattoria* with
terrific views over the coastline.
Wholesome fare for hearty appetites.
Small choice of Colli di Luni. Cash only.

Osteria a Cantina De Manan
Corniglia, Via Fieschi 117
*Tel: 0187 821166; closed Tues
(not summer), pm only in summer.*
Ancient hostelry, now a welcoming
trattoria with fresh fish and more
traditional dishes. Home-produced
carafe wine, Cinqueterre from the
coop or red from Piedmont or
nearby Tuscany. Cash only.

Il Maestrale
Lerici, Loc Zanego 8
Tel: 0187 966952; closed Tues.
Fish restaurant – and excellent value,
with impressive wine list makes this
a popular spot. Cash only.

La Palmira
Lerici, Loc San Terenzo, Via A Trogu 13
*Tel: 0187 9710940; closed Weds
(not summer).*
Another very good value fish place,
informal and with hearty portions.
Unusual desserts. AmEx, Visa
cards only.

Miranda
Lerici, Loc Tellaro, Via Fiascherino 92
Tel: 0187 968130; closed Mon.
Lerici's smart spot, fairly costly,
but high quality. Good tasting
fish-based menu. Excellent service.
Seats outside. No charge cards.

From here, the fun begins. It is natural to want to see the
'five lands': the coastal villages of Riomaggiore, Manarola,
Corniglia, Vernazza and Monterosso al Mare, which
punctuate the hills. Riomaggiore is not too bad. A fairly
short series of hairpin bends down a well-made road and
you reach a carpark. Stroll round this small village,
fashioned around an inlet and carved into the hills. Return
up to the road that runs through the vineyards and go on for
a few minutes before turning off down again to Manarola,
another delightful, tiny place clustered round a minute bay.
By this point the road is higher and the bends tighter but
once more a car park heralds your arrival, for another visit
on foot. Back up on the 'high' road, it soon degenerates to
little more than a narrow, twisting track. From now on the
roads become increasingly poor, narrow and full of bends,
the 'high' road gets increasingly high, the distances between
successive descents get longer and the descents themselves
(maybe 15 or 20 minutes) best reserved for those with strong
nerves, good tyres and keen brakes. Believe your map when
it shows no more than mule-track-standard roads. To see
the Cinqueterre properly you need to use a boat or a
mountain bike, find a mule or get out the hiking boots!

If you do decide to plough on by car, put aside best part
of a day and you'll still be left with long stretches of difficult
roads for the return to the Aurelia or the *autostrada*. It seems
impossible that a corner of western Europe could be left
with such poor road communications but maybe that just
enhances its charm.

THE WINES
The results of all this travail? Well, there's not a great deal of
wine anyway, despite the visual impression, and growing
numbers of abandoned terraces point to an increasing
decline. Sadly, much Cinqueterre is not very good. It is
mainly sold locally, to tourists more interested in the name
and image than the flavours. Only white is produced; of the
three grapes used, the local Bosco (in theory at least 60
percent of the blend) and Albarola appear to have little
quality potential. The best wines have as much of the third
variety, Vermentino, as possible. There is also a scarce variant
called Sciacchetrà, a *passito* version, sometimes fortified too.

OTHER WINES OF EASTERN LIGURIA

The coastline from La Spezia to Genoa is dotted with vineyards and each wine bears a local name and is drunk in the immediate vicinity. Grape varieties, styles and qualities vary so widely it is impossible to generalize except to say that if you come across one, try it.

LA SPEZIA

La Spezia is a surprisingly good city. Situated at the top of a vast natural inlet, it makes a perfect natural port. The surprise is that even around the docks it lacks the seediness that most ports seem unable to avoid. La Spezia is small, squashed, like most Ligurian towns, between the coast and the hills, but basks in its long coastline, a promenade to die for. The city exudes quiet prosperity and earnest (but profitable) endeavour; there are shops to fulfill practically any consumerist need but it is anything but flashy. The grid-like road system is nearly all one-way but, generally, the flow of traffic alternates between roads, which makes navigating the city comparatively trauma-free. Parking, though, can be difficult.

Left   Cinqueterre vineyards in front of the tiny village of Manarola.
Below   Classic Genoese tromp l'oeil, here on Columbus's house.
Below left   La Spezia from the road up to the Cinqueterre.

Osteria del Monsignore
Sarzana, Via Cisa 98
Tel: 0187 624195; closed Weds.
Simple, local dishes produced with care. Own olive oil. Home made desserts. Short wine list, mainly Tuscan reds (this is a meat place). Seats outside. Popular. Eves only. Cash only.

HOTELS

Firenze e Continentale
La Spezia, Via Paleocapa 7
Tel: 0187 713200; fax: 0187 714930.
Near the station (but no train noise), recently refurbished, but comfortable, 'lived-in' feel. Continental breakfast but plentiful. Mid-price range.
Genova
La Spezia, Via Fratelli Rossetti 84
Tel: 0187 731766; fax: 0187 732923.
Lowish priced, simple, fairly small hotel, centrally located.
Marina Piccola
Manarola, Via Discovolo 38
Tel: 0187 920103; fax: 0187 920966.
Small, attractive, with sea view. Not expensive.
Doria Park
Lerici, Via Doria 2
Tel: 0187 967124; fax: 0187 966459.
Set high, with superb views. Five room levels (different prices, none exaggerated, special offers in low season). Excellent service.

FOOD SHOPPING

Gelateria Riccardo
La Spezia, Via Manzoni 26
Rich, creamy ice-creams.
Gelateria La Fiorentina
La Spezia, Via Manzoni 27
Best for sorbets and ice-cream sponges.
Panificio-Pasticceria Meg
Castelnuovo Magra, Loc Colombiera
For plumcake and, in winter, goodies from nuts.
Pasticceria Oriani
San Terenzo
Glorious sweet *focaccia* with various flavourings. On the promenade.
Paneficio Brondi e Cargioli
Lerici, Via Petriccioli 58
Excellent breads and biscuits, including Lerici specialities.
Gelateria-Bar Paolo Biagi
Sarzana, Via Genova
Ice-cream too good to miss.

The East: wines of Alessandria and Pavia

The east of Piedmont has a feel all of its own. It has a warmer, more benign aspect, although winters can be every bit as icy as further west. It also seems quieter and more rural. The scenery mixes gentle, rolling hills with steeper and more rugged terrain and numerous river valleys flowing north into the Po, the most important being the Scrivia.

The terrain divides naturally into three main areas. Gavi, the most western and southern of the three, lies west of the Scrivia and tucks into the Apennine foothills just before they grow into the mountain barrier separating Piedmont from Liguria. Gavi's white wines made from the Cortese variety are well renowned and have long led the field among Piedmont's whites, although competition from elsewhere is hotting up. Nevertheless, despite Cortese's strong domination, not even Gavi is a simple, one grape area.

East of the Scrivia and further north is the lesser-known zone of the Colli Tortonesi. It is linked with Gavi by the cultivation of Cortese but more important is the production of Barbera, although the potential from these well-aspected, eye-catching hills still tends to exceed its realisation.

The Cortese theme continues into Lombardy and the Oltrepò Pavese zone, again further east and north. Here too, however, Barbera plays a more focal role, even though no one grape dominates the multi-varietal scene that characterizes the Oltrepò. More than any tributary it is the Po itself that defines Oltrepò Pavese with vines clustering on the first slopes rising out of the river's broad, flat valley.

The Oltrepò marks where the northwest of Italy gradually dissolves into the central north countryside and some of its varieties are more central than western. Nevertheless, there is little doubt that it belongs in the northwest, historically and culturally, as well as viticulturally.

Left The remote hamlet of Parodi
Ligure just southwest of the
sweeping hills of Gavi.

Above Detail from the Certosa
of Pavia – outside the area but
well worth visiting.

Gavi

Above *Neat rows of well-tended vines near Tenuta la Meirana in the zone of Gavi.*

THE WINES

If you let Gavi's reputation colour your judgement, you'll probably never get beneath the surface of this curious wine zone, nor even get much pleasure out of the wines. The stumbling block is that some years back Gavi was hailed as one of Italy's best white wines and was suddenly the one everybody who was anybody had to be seen drinking. Prices rose accordingly. Then somebody screamed, 'The emperor has no clothes,' and it was as fashionable, from then on, to decry Gavi as an overpriced con as it had previously been to laud it. The truth, of course, encompasses both extremes as well as a broad spectrum between them.

Gavi is made from the Cortese grape which here, in its most classic area of production, gives attractive, floral wines with a firm backbone. Drunk young, as is normally the case, these wines can be enjoyable and may even yield finesse but they are hardly heart-stoppers. In the hands of the most assiduous producers, however, Cortese grown in Gavi can give firm, spicy, tangy wines of great presence. Some are rich and powerful, others are more elegant and complex; either way they have great class. These wines, though, need time to develop, a luxury the Italian market (obsessed with drinking whites as young as possible) rarely allows.

Some estates enjoy an extra cachet from labelling their wines 'Gavi di Gavi' although it has no official qualitative significance whatsoever. For some its use is a convenient way of distinguishing their top wine from their secondary product. Only those with vineyards actually in the Gavi commune can use the double-barrelled term though others have developed variations on the theme.

There are also small quantities of sparkling Gavi made, with notable success.

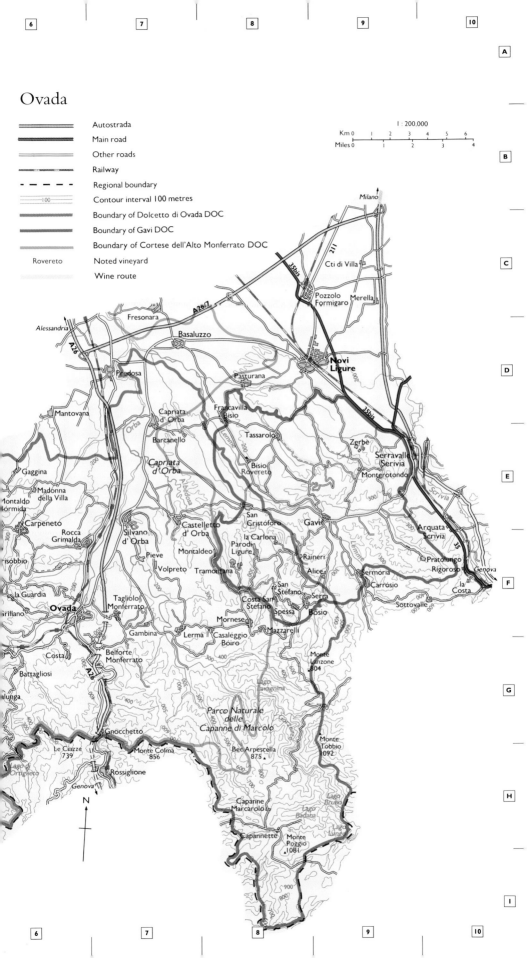

Ovada

Autostrada	
Main road	
Other roads	
Railway	
Regional boundary	
—100—	Contour interval 100 metres
	Boundary of Dolcetto di Ovada DOC
	Boundary of Gavi DOC
	Boundary of Cortese dell'Alto Monferrato DOC
Rovereto	Noted vineyard
	Wine route

1 : 200,000

Km 0   1   2   3   4   5   6
Miles 0   1   2   3   4

Milano

Cti di Villa

Pozzolo
Formigaro   Merella

211

35bis

A26/7

Fresonara

Alessandria

Basaluzzo

A26

Prodosa

Novi
Ligure

Pasturana

35bis

Mantovana

Orba

Capriata
d'Orba   Francavilla
Bisio

Barcanello

Tassarolo

Capriata
d'Orba

Bisio
Rovereto   Zerbe

Serravalle
Scrivia

Gaggina

Madonna
della Villa

Montaldo
Bormida

Carpeneto

Rocca
Grimalda

Silvano
d'Orba

Castelletto
d'Orba

San
Cristoforo

Gavi

la Carlona
Parodi
Ligure

Monterotondo

Scrivia

Arquata
Scrivia

35

Pieve

Montaldeo

Tramontana

Raineri

Pratolungo
Rigoroso   Genova

Volpreto

Alice

Sermoria

la
Costa

risòbbio

la Guardia

Tagliolo
Monferrato

Costa San
Stefano

San
Stefano

Serra

Carrosio

Sottovalle

rillano

Ovada

Spessa   Bosio

Gambina   Lerma   Casaleggio
Boiro

Mornese

Mazzarelli

Costa

Belforte
Monferrato

A26

Monte
Lanzone
804

Battagliosi

Lago
Lavagnina

alunga

Parco Naturale
delle
Capanne di Marcolo

Gnocchetto

Le Ciazze
739

Monte Colma
856

Bec Arpescella
875

Monte
Tobbio
1092

Lago di
Ortiglieto

Rossiglione

Genova

N

Capanne
Marcarolo

Lago
Bruno

Lago
Badana

Lago
Lunga

Capannette

Monte
Poggio
1081

| A |
| B |
| C |
| D |
| E |
| F |
| G |
| H |
| I |

6   7   8   9   10

GAVI

RECOMMENDED PRODUCERS

Villa Sparina
Gavi, Fraz Monterotondo
Tel: 0143 634880; E. F. S.
Well equipped, well run, impressive estate with carefully tended vineyards and cellars that blend excellent functionality with aesthetic appeal. Gavi *normale* and *reserve* La Villa: the latter good, rich, buttery, balanced with lively acidity and with fine ageing capacity. Also long-matured Gavi Brut, also with good longevity, firm, elegant and rounded. Plus Cortese dell'Alto Monferrato and others.

Tenuta San Pietro
Tassarolo, Loc San Pietro
Tel: 0143 342125; E. F.
Small estate run with determination and hard grind by Maria Rosa Gazzaniga, who has a long-standing attachment to the area's traditions. Vineyards on well-exposed, steep slopes, with good views. Fine, quirky wines that will never please everyone: the essence of personality. Gavi *normale* plus *crus* Bricco del Mandorlo, from 30-year old vineyard underneath a century-old almond tree (*mandorlo*), and Vigneto La Gorrina, from, remarkbly, a 2ha vineyard over 80-years old and therefore planted before the arrival of the phylloxera bug, which forced grafting of vines onto American rootstock. Visits working hours only, must book.

Gian Piero Broglia
Gavi, Loc Lomellina
Tel: 0143 743267; E. F.
Large estate producing full, well-structured wines of rounded fruit character needing time to come round. Five different styles of Gavi, including one oaked (Vigna Fasciola) and one *frizzante* (Roverello). Also sparkling Gavi and *grappa* from Gavi. Must book.

La Scolca
Gavi
Tel: 0143 682176. E. F.
All the fuss surrounding Gavi has its focus on this estate, the one that spearheaded the wine's fortunes, the one whose price tags can still cause apoplexy, the one that represents for many the apex of its potential and the one whose name is often

THE VINEYARDS

On a map the zone of Gavi looks fairly extensive, stretching over eleven communes scattered around Gavi village. On the ground, though, the zone seems small and compact, since practically all the vineyards are in the sector north of Gavi village, mainly in the communes of Gavi itself and Tassarolo, but also in adjacent segments of Novi Ligure and Francavilla. As communes go, Gavi is fairly large and so directions often involve mention of its most important *frazione*, Rovereto. Unfortunately, being a *frazione*, it remains absent from maps making orientation particularly frustrating. In compensation, most estates are well signposted. Allow an hour and a half or or so for the route.

Anyone having skipped Liguria and arriving directly from Ovada will make for Gavi village then continue, on the road to Serravalle Scrivia, turning left a minute or so outside the village to Monterotondo. Otherwise leave Liguria on the Genoa-Milan *autostrada*. This is another marvel of Italian engineering with the two carriageways of this major artery often separated and even crossing each other to make efficient use of the almost non–existent space through the gorge of the Scrivia Valley. Take the Serravalle Scrivia exit and go through this bustling town (direction Genoa), itself just inside the eastern edge of the Gavi zone. Just beyond the town fork right at the first sign to Gavi.

The road starts to rise and ducks under a small tunnel. Continue for a little under five minutes until a sharp right turn to Monterotondo. You may wish, firstly, at this point to go into Gavi village for a look round. However, the approach to it is far more impressive from the other direction – as you will discover at the end of this route.

The road crosses a stream and heads relentlessly upwards on a narrow, twisty road almost hemmed in by lush woodland. Eventually the view opens out and vineyard at last appears. (The estate is Villa Sparina.) Continue to the clock tower and turn left (direction Novi Ligure). The single track road winds through partially vined countryside showing clearly the relief forms of the land, with its fairly steep clay-rich hills. Five minutes along you pass the back entrance to the large La Raja estate, after which is an area of almost fake-looking, dark, egg-yolk coloured, sandstone soil. Next there appears on the left a huge area of regimentally neat vineyard, following the entire slope of a long, low hillside. This belongs to the enormous Tuscan company Banfi, for their Gavi, Principessa Gavia. After another five minutes there's a stop sign, where you take a sharp turn left, almost doubling back on yourself. The direction signed is Lomellina (a non-mapped *località*) but as the signpost is for the benefit of those coming in the opposite direction it is practically invisible until the turn has been effected.

synonymous with the wine itself. Run by the Soldati family, now in their fifth generation. The estate's style is typified by the Gavi *normale*, from younger, more vigorous vines, but concentrated in the Gavi dei Gavi, informally called Etichetta Nera (Black Label), from the oldest vineyards – a wine of great power and character, needing several years to round out and lasting for several more. Plus Gavis Valentino, lighter and for easier drinking; Zunot, bottled early for enhanced freshness; Villa Scolca, from mid-aged vineyards; Rugré, *frizzante*. The Soldatis are also strongly involved in sparkling wine making, with four of these, all based primarily but not exclusively on Cortese. Pay if tasting more than a pair of wines.

Castello di Tassarolo
Tassarolo
Tel: 0143 342248; E. F.
Well-styled wines. Three Gavis: Tassarolo S, soft and forward; Castello di Tassarolo, partially oaked; Vigneto Alborina, strongly oaked. Also red and white from non-local varieties. Visits welcome from purchasers only.

Nicola Bergaglio
Gavi, Fraz. Rovereto
Tel: 0143 682195.
Well respected estate producing rounded, well-fruited wines with good perfume. Gavi *normale* and more intense *cru* Minaia.

Castellari Bergaglio
Gavi, Fraz. Rovereto
Tel: 0143 645910; E. F.
Fourth generation, family-run, smallish estate at 350m, on iron and clay-rich soils. Low yields from long established vineyards and slow, controlled fermentations give enhanced perfume and concentration. Gavi *normale*; Brise, *frizzante*, fresh and lively; Di Rovereto, from the best grapes from over 75-year old vineyard; Barric, oak fermented. Also Grappa di Gavi.

Tenuta la Giustiniana
Gavi, Fraz. Rovereto
Tel: 0143 682132; E. F.
Behind the imposing pomp of the villa, the image of this estate is of the cheerful, friendly but concernedly diligent Enrico Tomalino who runs it. The three Gavi *crus* Lugarara, Centurionetta and Montessora, whose differences become more marked as they mature, are refined, elegant, complex wines, needing a good year to show their class. Also *barrique*-fermented Gavi Vignaclara, Giustiniana Nature (sparkling) and an oddity, Campoghero, late harvest Sauvignon. Visits working hours only.

Right *The fortress of Gavi
with its commanding view across
the countryside.*
Far right *Scattered vine plantations
over Gavi's rolling hills.*

La Chiara
Gavi
Tel: 0143 642293; E. F.
Apart from the vineyards around
the cellars there are some in
Rovereto. Light elegant Gavi
normale plus *barrique*-aged *cru*
Groppella and sparkling versions.

FOOD SPECIALITIES

The Lemme Valley produces
high quality honey.

 EATING OUT

Cantine del Gavi
Gavi, Via Mameli 67
Tel: 0143 642458; closed Mon.
Rather ornate surroundings but
carefully prepared and elegantly
presented dishes, of powerful, clear
flavours. Strong Ligurian influence
in the food. Given the restaurant's
name it is not surprising the cellars,
which can be visited, hold a strong
range of regional and national wines
(plus some from abroad).
Tramontanino
Tel: 0143 681109; closed Mon, Tues pm.
Parodi Ligure, Fraz Tramontanino
Small *trattoria*, despite the address,
actually at Tramontana, about 10km
west of Gavi on a narrow, twisting
road. Ligurian influence noticeable
mainly in the intelligent use of herbs;
in general, classic local dishes
are served, simple and satisfying.
House wine only, but not to be
sneezed at. Inexpensive, cash only.
Locanda San Martino
Pasturana, Via Roma 26
Tel: 0143 58444; closed Mon pm, Tues.
Small, neat, welcoming restaurant
with typically Piedmontese dishes
(rather than Ligurian influenced) plus
some determinedly untraditional.
Very good wine list with ample
choice of Gavis. Seats outside.

 HOTELS

Sereno di Gavi
Gavi, Loc. Cheirasca
Tel: 0143 643232; fax: 0143 642428.
Once a monastery, now anything but
(but still peaceful). Large rooms,
cleanly furnished. Tennis courts,
small gym, sauna. Good breakfast
and general 4* comforts.

In this segment of the area numerous estates are sited, as the
large clutch of estate signposts confirms. Fork left at the
next junction, which you reach very shortly, still going
towards Lomellina. Another pair of estate signs, and then
the road begins a big curve downwards into the vine-free
valley, past more egg yolk soil, before climbing another
large lump of hillside. The eye is next drawn to the
beautifully kept vineyards of La Battistina, in a large sweep
across a hillside to the left, with the estate buildings beyond.
Two more estates are indicated, Il Vignale with its small
vineyard plot and yellow villa over to the left and Castel di
Serra, up to the right and best seen from behind after
passing it, before La Raja reappears. This time its far more
impressive front entrance is seen. Next on the right is a lane
leading up to Tenuta San Pietro. You could use this to get
up to Tassarolo (*see* below) but it is better to continue past
Broglia and the side of the estate La Scolca, and turn
sharply right at the next junction, towards Rovereto.

This is a pleasant, open road with no shortage of
vineyard, which soon passes the main entrance to the estate
La Scolca (right). Once you reach a stop sign with a
crucifix on the left, continue straight ahead, towards
Tassarolo. This is a tiny, tranquil hilltop hamlet, completely
dominated by the heavily set Castello di Tassarolo, one of
Gavi's major landmarks. Now return back down to the
junction with the crucifix (direction Gavi), and turn right
(towards Loc Pesenti). This is an area dotted with small
estates, most of them practically unknown outside the
immediate locality. Past the first group of estates there is a
stretch of plain land, then vineyards recommence. The first
batch of those are in Rovereto Superiore, the next, at lower

altitude, are in Rovereto Inferiore. The road takes a large curve to the left and crosses a brook, then passes the estate Bergaglio Nicola on the left, the first of a closely packed clutch of estates. As the road dips the hilltop town of San Cristoforo starts to appear up ahead in the distance and shortly after you see the soft yellow, 17th-century villa of La Giustiniana on a hillside to the left. Finally, the road hits the Lemme Valley at a road junction known as Bisio.

If the idea of seeing another castle appeals, first turn right and shoot along the valley for two or three minutes to Francavilla, which sports a none too threatening, small, neat, squat one, before turning back. Otherwise turn left and follow the valley towards Gavi village. Within seconds you pass (left) the front entrance of La Giustiniana. Not to be hurried past – this is a truly magnificent villa. There is a short stretch of vine-free road then vineyards reappear as the road sweeps drastically right and then left. Both San Bartolomeo, the estate on the right, and La Chiara, an important estate on the left are clearly signed. A few seconds later the road begins to rise and the fortress of Gavi appears high above, atop an impossibly steep rise of land.

GAVI VILLAGE

The mound on which the fortress of Gavi perches is a classic scarp and dip hill. The village spreads along the dip side, with mainly narrow, cobbled roads spreadeagled across it. The central piazza is large but mostly a transport and commercial hub. Historical Gavi requires a determined plod upwards. Strangely, for a wine centre, there's a serious dearth of good eating places in the village; locals possibly take 'eating out' to mean eating out of town.

PLACES OF INTEREST

Castello di Tassarolo
Built originally around an 11th-century tower, although has on occasions been extended and restructured, including removal of its rooftop towers. Adjacent is the mint where the Spinola family, its owners since the 14th century, used to mint money. The Spinolas, still owners of the eponymous estate, gained their wealth by levying taxes on anyone using the road past their property, at the time the only route between the Genoese Republic and northern Europe.

SPECIAL EVENTS

Cortese Festival Gavi: September.
Festival of honey (From the Lemme Valley) – Gavi: first week September.

Colli Tortonesi

COLLI TORTONESI

RECOMMENDED PRODUCERS

Vigneti Massa
Monleale
Tel: 0131 80302; E. F.
The only one of the Colli Tortonesi's estates so far to have really hit the mark. Three Barberas: Campolungo, fresh and slightly *frizzante; cru* Bigolla; Monleale, perfumed, rich and well balanced by acidity. Also produces the mysterious Timorasso and others. Must book; may pay for some wines.

FOOD SPECIALITIES

'Baci di dama' (ladies' kisses)
The sweetmeat of Tortona.

 ## EATING OUT

Antica Locanda del Groppo
Pozzol Groppo, Fraz Biagasco-Groppo
Tel: 0131 800164; closed Mon.
For snacks or full meals from locally produced raw materials. Good choice

Below *Vineyard-clad valley sides rising steeply above the River Po.*
Right *Throughout the year the Colli Tortonesi boast stunning views.*

The Colli Tortonesi is probably the least well known wine area of Piedmont. This is, in one sense, only a little surprising; in other ways it is extremely odd. The main grape varieties are Barbera and Cortese. Barbera is grown so widely in Piedmont that an additional band of countryside in the very east of the region might perhaps be considered of minimal importance. Cortese, on the other hand, is grown in quite a limited area. Its heartland is Gavi and lands further west, so a strip out to the northeast of Gavi could just be an insignificant outpost. Yet such hypotheses scarcely ring true. Italians, generally, are so proud of every centimetre of their viticultural heritage and so keen to demonstrate the multiplicity of *terroirs* and resultant wine styles that one would expect them to glory in any additional production zone. To add to this, the Colli Tortonesi nurse a unique variety, the unbelievably obscure Timorasso. It's a white gem, its wines weighty, rich, nutty yet with ripe, floral overtones but practically unknown outside the zone. To complete the indignity, the natural beauty of Tortona's hills is quite sensational.

THE VINEYARDS

The full extent of the Colli Tortonesi zone spreads from the Sesia River valley, between Tortona and Novi Ligure, east to the border of Piedmont with Lombardy. In effect,

though, the vineyard area is mostly concentrated in a much narrower strip fairly close to the regional border. To some extent the lands could be considered a western extension of the Oltrepò Pavese (*see* following pages) although there are clear differences, so it is better not to take the comparison too far.

The starting point is Tortona. This is easily reached from Gavi by returning towards Serravalle Scrivia and whizzing up on either the *statale* or the *autostrada*. In order to appreciate the extent of the main vineyard area you could take the road to Viguzzolo (clearly signed) then continue south on the same road, following the valley down through the eastern side of the vineyard strip, almost to San Sebastiano Curone. This little town roughly marks the southern end of this core area. Here you would cut across through the hills on some very narrow roads towards Garbagna and head back northwards towards Tortona through the more western valley. However, it is every bit as good, maybe better, to take a shorter route, cutting across from the eastern to the western valley through the middle of the area – the point where the growing area is concentrated and the views at their most breathtaking. The round trip (from and to Tortona) will take barely an hour.

From Tortona, take the road through Viguzzolo. At first, peach trees predominate; later vines and peach trees alternate in a wonderful patchwork of toning colours. Within a minute or two you pass Castellar Guidobono. As the name suggests, a castle is situated there but it has succumbed to modern demands and been turned into a disco. A fork in the road follows. Keep right, signposted Caldirola. Vineyards now begin to emerge to the right on low, soft hills. As you progress, the hills gradually get steeper, higher and more rugged and there are vineyards to the left as well. At any point, Monleale, for example, you could take a short diversion off to the right, up into the hills where, within seconds of starting to rise, a wide and superb panorama presents itself. (There is also a hilltop route from Monleale as an alternative for good navigators.) Otherwise keep on the Caldirola road until, within 30 minutes of leaving Tortona, Casasco is signed on the right. This is the point at which to cut across the hills.

The narrow road curves up to Casasco, giving quite fabulous views of the countryside. It goes through the village then, descending, makes a large curve to the left after which you should turn right towards Garbagna. This road passes a magnificent old mulberry tree, used for silk worms. The road down gives no less stunning scenery than the ascent, but finally the valley is reached where you should turn right, back towards Tortona. This road passes near to Montemarzino, the most densely planted bit of the Colli Tortonesi and later Sarezzana, also a heavily planted area, after which vineyard land declines along with the altitude of the hills, until they vanish completely. The road rejoins the Tortona–Viguzzolo one and the tour ends.

of vegetable dishes. Wines mainly from Oltrepò Pavese. Seats outside. Cash only.

Locanda del Diavolo
Cecima
Tel: 0383 59123; closed Weds.
Good home-produced salami, pasta and desserts. Main courses of meat, game. Good choice of local wines. Fairly inexpensive and good value.

Forlino
Montacuto, Fraz Giarolo
Tel: 0131 785151; closed Mon.
Welcoming restaurant using mainly home-grown ingredients. Broad range of Piedmontese wines. Mid-priced but good value.

Stevano
Cantalupo Ligure, Fraz Pallavicino
Tel: 0143 93136; closed Mon.
Some way off route but useful as overnight stays possible. Richly flavoured dishes, with Ligurian aromas and vegetables lightening robust Piedmont classics. Pasta is home made. Good local and regional wines. Reasonably priced.

HOTELS

Villa Giulia
Tortona, Corso Alessandra 3/A
Tel: 0131 862396; fax: 0131 868561.
Very small but smart, comfortable and well appointed.

PLACES OF INTEREST

Caldirola At over 1000m altitude and a skiing centre.
Garbagna 'The cherry village'.
Tortona A prettily attractive old centre, good to stroll round and a modern part that is not bad at all. Focal point is the tall golden madonna atop the Sanctuary of Madonna della Guardia.

Oltrepò Pavese

OLTREPO PAVESE

RECOMMENDED PRODUCERS

Castello di Luzzano
Rovescala
Tel: 0523 863277; E. F.
Run by two sisters. Very clean wines of consistently high quality and dangerously good drinkability, with Barbera and Bonarda particularly strong. Concentration on still wines. Estate straddles zone's eastern border, so vineyards also in adjacent Colli Piacentini zone (in Emilia) from where another five wines come, including *frizzante*. Groups must book. Also arrange guided tastings with a light snack for a small fee. Good agritourism apartments.

CS La Versa
Santa Maria della Versa
Tel: 0385 79731
Produces one of the best known labels of the area, the sparkling wine La Versa Brut.

Vercesi del Castellazo
Montù Beccaria
Tel: 0385 60067; E. F.
On the south facing slopes of Oltrepò closest to the Po Valley. Medium-sized estate with long and often troubled history. Well-made wines, notably the reds. Pay for tastings; Can also provide meals from agrituristic restaurant. Booking essential.

Anteo
Rocca de'Giorgi, Loc Chiesa (off route)
Tel: 0385 48583; E. F.
Up in the hills, the Alta Valle Scuropasso, remote from traffic. Famed for its Pinot Nero and sparkling wines. Organic tendencies. Must book.

Monsupello
Torricella Verzate
Tel: 0383 896043; E. G.
Mid-sized estate close to Po. Innovative techniques in vineyard and cellar. Heart of production are three elegant sparkling wines, mainly from Pinot Nero; emphasis also on barriqued wines.

Le Fracce di Mairano
Casteggio *Tel: 0383 82526*
Hospitable estate with good wines in pleasant surroundings.

Tenuta Pegazzera
Casteggio *Tel: 0383 899256*
Impressively sited estate, with *castello* and good views. Well set up for visits and happy to receive groups.

Right *Picking grapes for Oltrepò Pavese Rosso, Barbera blended with Croatina and other grape varieties.*

The name Oltrepò Pavese may seem complicated for non-Italian speakers but it simply means the part of the province of Pavia lying across (ie south of) the River Po. Once part of Piedmont and still occasionally called Antico Piemonte, the Oltrepò Pavese now sits firmly in Lombardy but retains strong viticultural links with its former home. The area forms a large, fairly slim triangle, with its apex pointing south and its base following the meandering Po. The wine zone, however, covers only a small part of the district, with vineyards lying in a broad band across the centre of the area. Vines are limited to the north by the plains of the Po Valley, in effect, meaning the Alessandria-Piacenza *statale*, and to the south by the increased height of the hills, a part of the Oltrepò known as Alto–Appennino.

The height of the vineyards is a significant factor in wine production. Apart from winter fogs, the Po Valley can be quite humid in summer. The height of the Oltrepò's vineyards, averaging 150–300 metres, keeps the vines clear of this weather, except when fogs are particularly dense. It can be remarkable to stand in clear, bright sunlight among the vines looking down on what appears as a sea of white cloud. Even more amazing is to watch the fog swirl round the lower parts of hills, isolating the higher parts, which then seem to float magically. No wonder, then, that almost every suitable slope has been given over to vines.

THE WINES

The name Oltrepò Pavese encompasses no fewer than 13 different wines, the majority of them single varietals. The diversity of grapes reflects the zone's location: a spur of Lombardy, sandwiched between eastern Piedmont and western Emilia. The varieties Riesling Italico, Riesling Renano, Pinot Grigio (all white) and Pinot Nero (red) have links with the Emilia side; Barbera, Cortese and

Moscato show the Piemontese influence, and Bonarda is the nearest thing to an Oltrepò indigene. The other wines are red (and occasionally *rosato*) and mix Barbera with some Croatina (Bonarda), Uva Rara and Pinot Nero. The Oltrepò Pavese Rosso also comes in a reserve version, with two years ageing. To add to the party are the gloriously named Buttafuoco (derived from 'sparks like fire') and Sangue di Giuda ('Judas's blood'), from the same red blend, produced at the zone's northern limits. Buttafuoco is always dry, Sangue di Giuda may also be lightly or fully sweet. Many other wines are also made according to the producer's fancy.

There is also both white and rosé sparkling wine made from a blend of Pinot Nero, Pinot Grigio, Pinot Bianco and Riesling. This gets closer to the heart of Oltrepò Pavese because the essence of the area is fizz. Although still versions of all the wines exist, you are far more likely to come across *frizzante* bottles. This is how they are best liked, both locally and in Milan, a major market for the wines. Oltrepò is also the prime source of grapes, grape must and base wine for Piedmont's large sparkling wine houses. The remaining wine that becomes legitimate Oltrepò Pavese Spumante is a source of great pride. To ensure reliable quality, growers developed the marque 'Classese' for wines made according to certain criteria by the *metodo classico* (ie, the method used for making champagne) and from at least 85 percent Pinot Nero, although it is being supplanted by the newer marque 'Talento'. This latter is set to apply to most northern Italian sparkling wines from hill-grown grapes, provided certain quality contraints are met.

Above *The tranquil driveway to the Oltrepò estate Castello di Luzzano* (see *listings*).

San Giorgio
Santa Giuletta
Tel: 0383 899168; E. F. G.
Very old estate bought by wine-loving Milanese and completely restructured. Best wines vary with vintage. Must book. Agritourism.

Doria
Montalto Pavese
Tel: 0383 870143; E. F. P.
Owned by the Doria family for well over a century. Wide range of wines with frequent use of *barriques*.

Montelio
Codevilla
Tel: 0383 373090; E.
Well-signed from the centre of Codevilla and vineyards visible from *statale*. Montelio means 'sun hill' (from the Greek), signifying good exposure. Mid-sized estate with over 150 years' history: 100 year-old press and 200 year-old cellar plus other well-preserved structures from the 1800s. Good tasting room, no visits Suns. Overnight accommodation available from 1998.

Fattoria Cabanon
Codevilla
Tel: 0383 940912; E. F.
Well-ventilated spot at 300m. Strictly organic, run by the Mercandelli family. Individual wines. Book.

Above *Reflective Oltrepò countryside. Note how vineyard is restricted to the best aspected slopes.*

FOOD SPECIALITIES

Salami and prosciutto
From goose.
Zuppa Pavese
Light broth, 'fortified' with a poached egg on toast and parmesan.
Polenta

 ## EATING OUT

Da Ottavio
San Damiano al Colle, Fraz Mondonico
Tel: 0385 750015.
Well recommended place with careful attention to food and excellent selection of local wines.
Prato Gaio
Montecalvo Versiggia, Loc Versa
Tel: 0385 99726; closed Mon pm, Tues.
Simple, comfortable restaurant. Well chosen local wines. Not expensive.
Al Ruinello
Santa Maria della Versa,
Fraz Ruinello Sotto 1/a
Tel: 0385 798164; closed Mon pm, Tues.
Seasonal, traditional dishes prepared with intelligence and insight. Short wine list, mainly local.
Al Pino
Montescano, Via Pianazza 11
Tel: 0385 60479; closed Tues pm, Weds.
The sole really high quality restaurant of the Oltrepò. Classic, local dishes but with an individual and uplifting touch. Good value tasting menu. Correspondingly good range of Oltrepò wines. Smart, quite costly.

GETTING THERE

From Tortona it is best to go across to the eastern side of the Oltrepò and gradually travel back west through the vineyard area. The quickest way to reach the start point is on the *autostrada* for Piacenza, leaving at the Castel San Giovanni exit. Head into Castel San Giovanni (keeping left at a fork at the village entrance) and turn right at the traffic lights into the main street. About half way along are signs to Creta and Castelli di Luzzano to the left. Just seven kilometres along this road is the Castello di Luzzano, one of the zone's most important estates and the starting point of the tour. Alternatively, take the *statale*, once more heading for Castel San Giovanni. The road goes right into the main street (only this time approaching from the other direction). The turn for Creta, now to the right, is impossible to miss: it is a compulsory turn-off. Journey time is about an hour on the *statale*, less by motorway.

If there's time, though, it is far more pleasant to amble through the higher, more southern band of the Oltrepò, the Alto-Appennino. It may be a vine free route but the natural beauty is outstanding. A good two hours, maybe more, are needed. However, it may be best to forego the delights of the tight curves and steep ascents and descents if the weather is inclement. To take this hill route, leave Tortona for Viguzzolo and follow the signs for Salice Terme. Follow the one way system round the spa town of Salice until you are in Via Marconi. Go straight ahead at the crossroads, across the Staffora stream, then turn right to Godiasco.

Once through Godiasco you start to rise. The route goes sequentially through the following hamlets and villages, all of which should be signposted: Rocca Susella,

Left *Old vertical press.*
Below *Good cellar hygiene is vital to wine quality; here steam cleaning the grape collection boxes.*

Becco Giallo
Canneto Pavese, Fraz Monteveneroso
Tel: 0385 600037.
Inexpensive, good value spot with good choice of local wines.

San Contardo al Gallo
Broni, Piazza V Veneto 52
Tel: 0385 250075; closed Mon.
Simple, traditional *trattoria* but with large selection of Oltrepò wines.

Antica Osteria Calvignano
Calvignano, Via Roma 6
Tel: 0383 871121;
closed Tues (not summer).
Sympathetically designed, largish, rural place with superb vineyard views when sitting outside. Top quality ingredients, mainly local dishes. Desserts home made. Huge range of Oltrepò wines. Good value.

Antica Osteria San Desiderio
Godiasco, Fraz San Desiderio
Tel: 0383 940574;
closed Mon, Tues lunch.
In a prettily rebuilt old house, next door to a small, 13th-century church. Filling and tasty traditional dishes, notably the pastas and risotto. Good choice of local wines. Seats outside, air conditioned inside.

Il Caminetto
Salice Terme, Via C Battisti 11
Tel: 0383 91391.
On the pricey side but excellent service, well-furnished dining room and carefully prepared food. Good for a break from strictly local fare. Wines are mainly from all over the Lombardy region, plus some from further afield.

Arpesina, Biancanigi, Stefanago, Zebedo, Borgoratto Mormorolo, Villa dei Cavalieri, Villa Galeazzi, Torre d' Alberi, Carmine, Pomero, Canevino, Volpara, Golferenzo, Pizzofreddo (brilliant views!), Vicobarone and Creta. Before reaching Creta you will pass Castello di Luzzano on the left. Turn round at this point to start the main tour.

THE VINEYARDS

Allow a full half day for this route and be prepared to be stared at. The small villages it takes you through do not see vast numbers of tourists, who therefore remain intriguing oddities. The first stage takes you through Barbera/ Bonarda country, then through the Buttafuoco and Sangue di Giuda sub-zone. The central area is where sparkling wine production dominates and the western edge, closest to Piedmont, has a strong showing of Cortese.

From Castello di Luzzano head down the road towards Mula. Two or three minutes later turn right to Rovescala and descend on a narrow, twisty, bumpy road, framed by vineyard. Another minute or two brings you to Mulino di Rovescala where there are a surprisingly large number of training systems cheek by jowl. On reaching Rovescala go sharp left towards Santa Maria della Versa, although you may want first to detour up through the village to see the *castello*. A series of ups and downs leads rapidly through Ca' Nova, Scazzolino and Torrone, straight after which you need to look out for a poorly signposted fork to the right, to Santa Maria della Versa.

Above You may see scenes like this if travelling around the region in late autumn or early winter, when the task of tidying and pruning the vineyards begins.

Selvatico
Rivanazzano, Via S Pellico 11
Tel: 0383 91352; closed Sun pm, Mon.
Family-run restaurant. Short and frequently-changing menu of mainly local dishes. Moreish desserts. All good quality. Well balanced and varied wine list.

HOTELS

President Hotel Terme
Salice Terme, Via Enrico Fermi
Tel: 0383 91941; fax: 0383 92342.
Of the three hotels offering treatments, the President is the only one with spa water on tap, as it were. Only okay rooms (including some family rooms), but a fully fledged fitness and beauty centre where you can pump iron, work up the heart rate or just be pampered to death. Hydromassage, mud treatments, therapeutic pool, normal swimming pool.

After Valdamonte the road plunges down into the valley of the Versa and through Santa Maria, passing the cooperative. Continue to follow the River Versa (on the right) for about five minutes before turning right on a small bridge across the river to Donelasco. Follow the road towards Montù Beccaria. Just before the town centre, in the *frazione* called Poggiolo there is a 'stop' sign. Fork left here and head for Montescano. The road brings you back down, across the Versa then up again. At the top of the incline fork left (avoiding the road to Monteveneroso). Shortly afterwards is a T-junction and another 'stop' sign. Here turn right, north, to Broni. This is the Oltrepò Pavese heartland, where Buttafuoco and Sangue di Giuda are produced. Broni is about five minutes, an attractive small town at the edges of the Po Valley. At the T-junction go left to Pietra de' Giorgi (also signposted Voghera). Turn left at the next traffic lights, then immediately right and continue to follow signs for Pietra de' Giorgi. You are now heading back south.

After Valle Scuropasso and Cigognola comes Pietra de'Giorgi, which boasts an important *castello*, the Castello de Vistarino. Unless viewing the castle, go straight through the village. You now start following signs for Mornico Losana. Before reaching it, though, take a right turn towards Torricella Verzate (the sign is easy to miss). This pretty road goes through more prime vineyard country, following the Torricella stream on the left. Torricella Verzate itself is little more than a five-way road junction, but is an important religious/pilgrim centre. Take the branch to Casteggio, then a few seconds later turn left at the T-junction (direction Mornico Losana). Next comes a fork in the road. Veer right to Oliva Gessi and on to another delightful little road, with some very old vines on the left given counterpoint by some new plantings on the right. The village of Oliva Gessi is pretty appealing too.

Next stop is Montalto Pavese, just a few minutes away, on a tiny but quite lovely, tranquil road. You also pass the renaissance Castello di Conte Balduino which has magnificent gardens but which, sadly, remain closed to the public. From Montalto Pavese, with its excellent views over the Po Valley, proceed to Calvignano. Just beyond it, curve left and you pass the large Travaglino estate. Curve sharply left again and head down into lower country and Borgo Priolo. At the next major road junction go left, towards Pragate. Then take first right to Sant'Andrea. The road makes a sharp incline and as it rises the views improve equally rapidly. Keep straight (ignoring the second sign to Sant'Andrea) following a ridge for about five minutes, until reaching a T-junction. Turn right into a short, rather boring stretch leading to a crossroads which is punctuated by a castle on the right. Here, turn left towards Torrazza Coste. Go through the village centre and look for signs to Codevilla. This leads to the western edge of the zone and a good, straight road. Fork left off it, into Codevilla. Follow the road through the town until reaching a crossroads (where Garlazzolo is signposted to the left). Go straight ahead at this junction onto a long, winding road, up through vineyard and woodland to Murisasco (which, unusually, isn't signposted). The road then starts to descend and at the bottom is a T-junction. Turn left. This road goes through a bit of the Alto-Appennino, past Chiusani and towards Rocca Susella, where you want to fork right to Susella and San Paolo. This small road merges into a larger one which leads to Godiasco which marks the end of the vineyard area.

For the next stage of the tour you need to return to Asti. The best way is by *autostrada*, reached from Godiasco by following the Staffora River to Rivanazzano and Voghera, from where there's a link road. However, unless you passed through on arrival, it's worth crossing the river before Rivanazzano to have a look at the small spa town of Salice Terme before proceeding. You might also wish to have a glance at Alessandria, the provincial capital, skirted by the *autostrada*. Be warned, though, Alessandria is a rather mundane market town whose main claim to fame (apart from being home to a well-known felt hat manufacturer) is to have been the worst affected town in the devastating floods of Autumn 1994.

Cavour
Casteggio, Piazza Cavour
Tel: 0383 890620.
Small, inexpensive; spacious, modern rooms in old building.

Ali due Buoi Rossi
Alessandria, Via Cavour 32
Tel: 0131 445252; fax: 0131 445255.
Luxurious, old hotel for those who prefer traditional to modern fittings, space and comfort.

Londra
Alessandria, Corso F Cavallotti 51
Tel: 0131 251721; fax: 0131 253457.
Small, simply furnished, not expensive, unpretentious but just nice.

PLACES OF INTEREST

Salice Terme
Small spa town, nevertheless with all the glitz and hubbub such resorts inevitably attract; a surprising hub of activity in an otherwise quiet, rural area. Open for business Apr–Oct.

Castello di Rovescala
With notable frescoes. Final approach by foot only.

Castello de Vistarino
Pietra de' Giorgi.
Owned by the Conte Carlo di Vistarini and surrounded by a large game reserve. Also large vineyard holding: a major supplier of the Gancia sparkling wine house.

Bobbio
Well off the route and even out of the region (it's in Emilia) but it's such a glorious place it's well worth the detour, as they say.

Above *Given a sunny spot, as on this balcony, Italians will frequently cultivate flowering plants.*

Monferrato

Despite having cropped up several times already, you may be excused for remaining confused about what Monferrato really is. In fact, it is the name of the large hilly area stretching between the Po and the Apennines within the provinces of Asti and Alessandria. The lower land, the more northern area between the Po and Tanaro rivers, is known as the Basso Monferrato; the higher terrain south and east of the Tanaro is the Alto Monferrato. Hence, many of the zones described on previous pages lie within the Monferrato: for example, Asti's Moscato country; the areas of Nizza, Acqui and Ovada; Gavi and the Colli Tortonesi. Nevertheless, the classic Monferrato is the Basso Monferrato, the soft countryside north of Asti, punctuated by the villages of Castagnole and Vignale, and the town of Casale.

Southeast of Asti is not quite so classic but still rolling Monferrato countryside. It is the best place to take a good look at Barbera, Piedmont's most important variety. The Barbera d'Asti zone covers the whole of Asti province plus much of the grape growing part of Alessandria too. Barbera del Monferrato covers the same territory plus the lands of Ovada and a slightly extended area north of Alessandria town. The main difference between the two DOCs is that Barbera d'Asti is made exclusively from Barbera, while Barbera del Monferrato contains small quantities of any of Freisa, Grignolino and Dolcetto to tweak its style.

Despite the abundance of Barbera, there is the usual choice of varieties to keep palates stimulated. Grignolino is the main 'other', grown quite widely both north and south of the Tanaro. Labelling is clearer than with Barbera as Grignolino d'Asti comes strictly from Asti province, while that coming from north of the Tanaro in Alessandria province is labelled Grignolino del Monferrato Casalese. There is some Cortese grown south of Asti and a few other varieties to its north. To find out which, read on.

Left *Typically mixed countryside of the Monferrato in spring, with dense vineyard interspersed with poppies.*

Above *Barbera, the most widely planted grape variety in Piedmont, is said to originate from Monferrato.*

Barbera Country

BARBERA COUNTRY

RECOMMENDED PRODUCERS

Viarengo e Figlio
Castello d'Annone
Tel: 0141 401131; E. F. G.
Cellars, just metres from the Tanaro, suffered serious damage in the 1994 floods. Best known for oaked Barbera II Falé. Also clean, fresh Barbera Vigneto Morra and others. Visits weekday working hours only.

Braida di Bologna Giacomo
Rocchetta Tanaro
Tel: 0141 644113; E. F.
Giacomo Bologna's famed wines drew crowds wherever he appeared, as did his memorable sociability and hospitality. Since his untimely death, the estate has been run by his wife, daughter and son and, after a few wobbles, the wines have returned to form, as has the atmosphere of warmth and enthusiasm: family motto, 'whoever honours wine by drinking it absorbs its spirit.' Bricco dell'Uccellone, oaked and slow developing, is the wine that made the estate's name. There's also Bricco della Bigotta, aged longer in oak and firmer structured; La Monella, non-oaked and lightly *frizzante*. Must book; visits on non-working days not often possible.

Boffa Alfiero
San Marzano Oliveto
Tel: 0141 856115; E. F.
Up and coming estate with agritourism and linked with sporting and cultural centres. Must book.

Renato Trinchero
Agliano d'Asti
Tel: 0141 954016; E. F.
Mid-sized estate with wines clearly reflecting vintage characteristics. Pay if tasting more than two wines.

Above *The distinctive hills of Asti province with neat, well-aspected vineyards.*

To talk about a small part of the province of Asti and to describe it as Barbera country is in one sense insane. Barbera is the most abundantly grown variety in the Italian northwest and few areas of Piedmont's viticultural heartland are without plentiful amounts of it. Nevertheless, if there is an area where Barbera takes precedence over all other grapes and where there is not another, narrowly diffused variety to draw interest away from it, this smallish territory, immediately south and east of Asti town is it.

THE WINES

Barbera's main characteristic is high, vivid acidity combined with low tannin. In theory, this could be considered a fault, giving unbalanced, sharp wines and certainly, when Barbera is allowed to overcrop and is shoddily vinified it can be pretty unpalatable. But, and it is a big but, when proper care is taken with its cultivation and vinification, it develops such a wonderful vibrant fruitiness that the low tannin isn't a lack at all and the high acidity is an essential element in creating its eminently satisfying, refreshing zip. With *salumi*, especially the local products, there is nothing finer.

Another, equally successful way of handling Barbera is by maturing the wine in *barrique*. The wood softens the acidity and boosts the tannin, giving it more balance. The wine develops a distinct, different style, rather than tasting merely of Barbera plus oak, and this has given the grape a new array of admirers. A number of producers take the middle line of maturing Barbera in oak, but in large *botti*, giving a more subtle softening and bolstering effect. The Barberas of Asti, while not the biggest and richest wines, are, most reckon, the most typical incarnation of the grape.

THE VINEYARDS

If coming directly across from the Oltrepò or Alessandria on the *autostrada*, leave it at the Felizzano exit and take the *statale* towards Asti, turning off left within about five minutes to Rochetta Tanaro (and Nizza Monferrato) to commence a circular route through Barbera country. Starting from Asti, take the *statale* towards Alessandria, pass through Castello d'Annone and then turn right to Rochetta Tanaro.

The road to Rochetta Tanaro is flat, interspersed with classic Po Valley poplars and the village itself, just over the River Tanaro, is no great shakes, despite its 15th-century bell tower and 18th-century church. Its viticultural influence is profound, though. Not only is it home to the Braida estate of the late Giacomo Bologna whose barriqued wine, Bricco dell'Uccellone, was the first wine to convince folk outside of Asti of Barbera's breadth of potential. The village also houses a museum of ampelography (the botanical study of vine varieties) and an *enoteca*. After Rochetta, head for Mombercelli which can

Agostino Pavia
Agliano d'Asti
Tel: 0141 954125.
Small estate with just five hectares of excellently exposed vineyard around the cellars, much of it planted with old vines. Family traditionally agriculturalists, now into second generation of wine producers. Fairly gentle but quite well structured wines. Must book visits. Can advise on local agritourism.

F.lli Castino
Agliano d'Asti
Tel: 0141 954502; F. F.
Small, family-run company with two vineyard plots. Oaked Barbera Vigna Antica from very old vines in Agliano and Grignolino Vigna Scarrone from Moncucco di Mombercelli. Can advise on local agritourism.

Cascina Castlèt
Costigliole d'Asti
Tel: 0141 966651; E. F.
Individual wines, produced with great care by Mariuccia Borio on fairly steep, well exposed terrain. Five types of Barbera: from young and lively to Passum from partially *passito* grapes. Also delicate Moscato d'Asti and Moscato Passito. For groups of 8–10 morning seminars on various aspects of wine can be organized (cost c70,000 lire). Can arrange balloon or helicopter trips over vineyards, if prior-booked. Must book; may have to pay for tasting.

Tenuta La Meridiana
Montegrosso d'Asti
Tel: 0141 956250.
Friendly, smallish estate. Chunky Barberas. Tour includes vineyards. Must book. English or German interpretor can be arranged.

Marchesi Alfieri
San Martino Alfieri
Tel: 0141 976288; E. F. G. S.
Across the Tanaro from Costigliole d'Asti, with cellars beneath and vineyards around the splendid castle owned by the family – a landmark from the Asti–Alba road. Wine producers for generations but renewal of interest in recent years with resultant qualitative leaps. Barberas La Tota (*normale*) and Alfiera (oaked) lead range. Must book.

Alessandra e Ermanno Brema
Incisa Scapaccino
Tel: 0141 74019; E. F.
Forward looking estate, with continuous development and surprises. Willing to show visitors around historic parts of the village.

either be reached directly (go through Via Roma and at the end, with Braida on the corner, turn right, signed Cornalea) or, more pleasurably, go through Rochetta's nature reserve. For this route return to the entrance to the village and on a wall on the left scour for a tiny sign to the 'Parco naturale'. There are patches of vineyard on the road up, as there are in the reserve itself.

From the reserve the road descends to the plain to cross a *torrente*, then rises again. Pass Mombercelli village, fork left towards Vinchio and on to Vaglio, initially along a pretty road with attracive views of open countryside. These two communes have a shared *cantina sociale*, called Vinchio-Vaglio, one of the most qualitatively successful of the entire area. The route then passes into a rougher looking area with poorly-kempt vineyard patches. As the route continues, it is quite fascinating to see how from here, the furthest point of the route from Asti town, the density, quality and husbandry of the vineyards steadily improve. A couple of minutes later, just before Vaglio village, there is a cut across on the right to Noche (not on all maps). At the entrance to Noche, take a left turn along Via S Giorgio (just prior to a Carabinieri sign) to cut through towards Castelnuovo Calcea; this narrow road also is not always mapped. The hills here are lowish, soft and gently rounded, by now about three-quarters cultivated. Looking across the valley to the top of the hill ridge, it is easy to understand how fragmented much of the production is. Houses stand on the ridge and small vineyard strips sweep down from them, like no more than extended back gardens.

Right *The memorable castle of Costigliole d'Asti, near the River Tanaro, southwest of Asti town.*

ENOTECHE

Cantina Comunale
Costigliole d'Asti.
Vineria Da Taschet
Rocchetta Tanaro, Piazza Piacentino 11.

FOOD SPECIALITIES

Lingue di Suocera Crispy, flavoursome, from very fine shavings of bread crust.
Tira Local speciality tart, ring-shaped.
Beef From Piedmontese breed cattle.
Peppers, celery, cardoons, aubergines All produced locally.

EATING OUT

Losanna
Masio, Via San Rocco 36
Tel: 0131 799525; closed Mon.
No doubt of wine's importance in this *trattoria*. Also good, satisfying traditional food.
La Fioraia
Castello d'Annone, Via Mondo 26
Tel: 0141 401106; closed Mon.
Good quality restaurant with good wine selection. Tasting menu available. Mid-priced, good value.
Trattoria I Bologna
Rocchetta Tanaro, Via Nicola Sardi 4
Tel: 0141 644600; closed Tues.
Run by relations of the Braida wine estate, so no problems with wine selection (still plenty of choice, though). Fixed priced menu, changing weekly. Pasta home made. Cash only.
Da Guido
Costigliole d'Asti, Piazza Umberto 1 27
Tel: 0141 966012; closed Sun.
Expensive, but as one of Italy's top restaurants hardly surprising. Meals so good they're impossible to describe. World class wine list. Forget the budget, put on the fine togs and glory in the experience. Eves only.
Collavini
Costigliole d'Asti, Via Asti-Nizza 84
Tel: 0141 966440; closed Tues pm, Weds.
If funds won't stretch to Da Guido (above) console yourselves in this friendly restaurant, with well-flavoured classic dishes and broad wine list. No charge cards.
Da Elvira
Montegrosso d'Asti, Via Santo Stefano 75
Tel: 0141 956138, closed Sun pm, Mon.
Popular agritouristic estate, with Piedmont 'standards' much in demand. Wines home produced. Cash only, not expensive.

When you meet a T-junction turn left (ie, not towards Valeggia). Turn left at the next T-junction too, and head downwards, crossing the railway line. Take yet another left turn at the following T-junction (direction Nizza) and proceed along the valley floor for a short distance, passing the *cantina sociale* of Castelnuovo Calcea on the right, before turning right at the traffic lights to Agliano (and Costigliole). A right turn at the next junction brings you on the approach road to Agliano, a beautiful stretch with vines tumbling down on all sides of a shallow bowl of land. Only the flat base is vine free.

Agliano itself has a clean, sparkly feel to it. There's a circular road around the town, the Viale d'Albea, which gives good views over the vineyards, even though the village is not at great altitude. Agliano, arguably the best of all spots for Barbera d'Asti production, is the place where numerous leading estates have recently bought land, having grabbed parcels from the sale of an unprecedently large estate there. From Agliano take the road signed to the spa of Fons Salutis. At the spa, keep the hotel complex on your right and continue straight ahead, following the signpost to San Zeno/Lovetta/Vianoce. Turn left at each of the next two T-junctions, following signs for Costigliole.

Costigliole d'Asti is a large village, well worth wandering around. It has developed in two sections, separated by a valley spanned by a short bridge. Its focus is a large castle, built tall but not on particularly high ground and which, extensively restructured, falls only some way short of Disneyesque. In front are carefully tended gardens and adjacent, a villa, its facade adorned with one of Asti province's characteristic sundials. After Costigliole, turn back on yourself for a short way through this highly renowned Barbera territory to make for Montegrosso d'Asti, passing the Madonnina sanctuary on the way (all signposted). Early on along this tract you pass the large Cora vermouth establishment down in the valley. As Montegrosso approaches, past another wide, shallow amphitheatre of vines, the density of inhabitation increases quite noticeably. Montegrosso and its various *frazioni* are within easy striking distance of Asti town and, like most around here, act as dormitory villages, and the small vineyard patches do nothing to dispel the impression of being cultivated by these Asti commuters in evenings and at weekends. As Montegrosso looms up in front and slightly to the right, also in front but higher and further left is Vigliano d'Asti, a well-known marine fossil area, and both have plentiful vineyard land.

Cross the Asti-Canelli/Nizza *statale* and the railway line and rise up to Montegrosso. After passing its centre make for Rocca d'Arazzo. You continue to rise and are suddenly in a zone of steeper hills, with vines gradually handing over to woodland as the altitude and slope become more rigid. From the refreshing cool of the woods, descend to Rocca d'Arazzo and from there to the pleasant little village of Azzano. A last chunk of woodland, a sprinkling of vineyards, a cluster of houses and then comes the last sweep of road through the cultivated plain before returning to Asti.

Il Campagnin
Montaldo Scarampi, Via G B Binello 77
Tel: 0141 953676; closed Tues.
Easy going *trattoria*, lunches only, serving mainly classic fare but strong on vegetables. Short list of local wines. Not expensive. Cash only.

Il Cascinale Nuovo
Isola d'Asti
Tel: 0141 958166; closed Sun pm, Mon.
Just off the Asti-Alba road, about half way along. Fine cuisine, filling but not heavy, with beautifully distinct flavours. Inventive dishes from a traditional base. Spacious, modern-looking but relaxed. Excellent wine list, giving rise to separate enoteca. Fairly costly but good value. Also hotel (see below).

HOTELS

Fons Salutis
Agliano, Via alle Fonti 125
Tel: 0141 954018 Fax: 0141 954554
For a spa treatment or two to aid the relaxation.

Il Cascinale Nuovo
Isola d'Asti, Via Asti–Alba 15
Tel: 0141 958166 Fax: 0141 958828
Conveniently located, with simply furnished, spacious, rooms above the top class restaurant (see above). Swimming pool, tennis court and large gardens. Good value.

Locanda del Bosco Grande
Montegrosso d'Asti, Loc Messadia
Tel: 0141 956390.
Peaceful, tranquil spot with seven, bright, unfussy rooms. Spacious gardens. Meals served.

FOOD SHOPPING

Il Panatè Rochetta Tanaro,
Via Giochino Sardi 56
For Lingue di Suocera, Tira and other breads and pastries.

Macelleria Borio Lorenzo
Rochetta Tanaro, Piazza Piacentino
Top quality locally produced beef.

Salumeria Rita Stocco
Rocca d'Arazzo, Fraz Forni.

PLACES OF INTEREST

La Bottega del Fabbro
Rochetta Tanaro
A smith, still using a traditional forge.

Scuola Alberghiera
Agliano
Tel: 0141 950479.
Short courses (3–7 days) on local cooking skills and techniques. Further information c/o Lucia Barbarino.

Left *Costigliole d'Asti: one of several famous sundials in the province of Asti* .

MONFERRATO CASALESE

RECOMMENDED PRODUCERS

Cantine Sant'Agata
Scurzolengo
Tel: 0141 203186; E. F.
Eighty-year old company with cellars dug out of the rock below the family home on a panoramic site. Large range of wines. Also *grappa* and food products. Stables nearby. Agritourism.

Fattoria Augustus, Castello di Razzano
Alfiano Natta
Tel: 0141 922124; E. F.
Largish, forward-looking, quality-conscious estate. Choice between *botte*-aged, *barrique*-aged or non-oaked Barbera. Also Grignolino and others. Must book. Lunch or dinner can be provided for groups if arranged in advance.

Colle Manora
Quargnento
Tel: 0131 219252; E. F.
Important estate working primarily with non-local varieties. Must book.

Liedholm
Cuccaro Monferrato
Tel: 0131 771916; E. F. Sw.
Tranquil estate with well-tended vineyards and thoughtfully made, very drinkable wines.

Bricco Mondalino
Vignale Monferrato
Tel: 0142 933204; E. F. G.
Mauro Gaudio believes strongly in Grignolino and makes a much sturdier version than most; deeper in colour, and richer, firmer and more concentrated – with great success. Also one of the few sustainers of Malvasia di Casorzo. Vineyards, panoramically sited, can be visited; tastings in well-arranged tasting room. Book for visits conducted by Mauro himself or for foreign languages.

Nuova Cappelletta
Vigale Monferrato
Tel: 0142 933135; E. F.
Large estate, run following biodynamic principles. Also grow cereal crops and raise Piedmontese breed cattle, who provide natural manure. Four separate vineyard plots. Working hours only, must book.

Colonna
Vignale Monferrato
Tel: 0142 933241; E. F. G.
Estate that is beginning to make waves, run with drive and energy by Alessandra Colonna on biodynamic principles. Aim to make Grignolino del Monferrato aromatic, soft and appealing, without astringency. Also others. Can suggest restaurants and agritourisms. No evening visits.

Monferrato Casalese

North of Asti and therefore north of the River Tanaro the terrain changes once more into more open countryside, with low hills and vineyard patches interspersed with other crops, much of it wonderfully calming and delightfully pretty. Barbera continues to dominate the wine scene but other varieties, notably Grignolino, Freisa and Malvasia (*see* pages 44-5), and the unusual Ruché, have a significant presence in some parts of the area. You'll need the best part of a day to get the most from the route.

Leave Asti in the Alessandria direction, taking the *statale* for a short distance. Just past the factory of the large bottle manufacturer AVIR, turn left at the signpost to Casale Monferrato. The road ducks under the *autostrada* and passes through Valenzani before starting to rise into vineyard terrain, towards Castagnole Monferrato. This is the centre of the tiny production of Ruché di Castagnole Monferrato, the zone radiating a mere five kilometres or so around the village. Ruché is rather odd. Despite the classic Piedmontese leanness, it also has a soft, perfumed sweetness and despite often being destined for ageing, there is much to be said for drinking it in the full liveliness of its youth. More than anything, though, it is rare, making carefully considered judgements well nigh impossible.

Continue, past Castagnole towards Casale, next passing Montemagno, a small place with a spectacular castle, seen at its most imposing on leaving the village. Next, cut across to Grana and from there continue on a small road to Casorzo, the centre of the even smaller area of Malvasia di Casorzo d'Asti. Production, however, is about twice that of Ruché, mainly in a soft, sparkling, Asti-like style. From there make for Altavilla Monferrato. At the junction that separates the Altavilla road (right) from the Vignale Monferrato road you leave Asti province for that of Alessandria, entering the part of the Monferrato known as Monferrato Casalese. Past Altavilla, start heading down

Far left *Vineyards at Casorzo d'Asti, between Asti and Casale Monferrato.*
Left *San Giorgio Monferrato, classic Monferrato countryside.*
Below *Detail of the vine-clad Monferrato hills.*

towards Vignale, clearly visible atop a nearby hillside but branch off very quickly to Fubine to start a loop through some magical countryside via Fubine and Cuccaro before coming into Vignale's centre.

Vignale itself is quiet and unhurried, with an eye-catching sundial overlooking the main square. Just off the main square is an *enoteca regionale*, in the cellars of a wonderful villa, with elegant gardens giving good views over the countryside below. And although it is grown over a wide area, in Asti as well as the Monferrato Casalese, Vignale is also the home of Grignolino. Grignolino's wines, even though once among Piedmont's most famed, are, frankly, a long way from what modern tastes dictate. They are pale red, sometimes orangish, with fragrant perfumes of cherries and violets. The palate may at first seem innocuously light with distinct acidity but often reveals hidden power and a firm, tannic edge. Because of its chameleon-like structure, however, a good Grignolino, from sandy, calcareous-clay soils, often happily accompanies a wide range of food and, once prejudices are removed, can be wonderfully satisfying to drink.

Cantine Valpane
Ozzano Monferrato
Tel: 0142 486713; E.
Small, long-standing estate, housed in 18th-century farmhouse, with small museum of old agricultural equipment. Organic leanings. Barbera only: d'Asti del Monferrato and Valpane (oaked). New agritourism apartments. Must book, no evening visits; pay for tastings unless purchases made.

Tenuta La Tenaglia
Serralunga di Crea
Tel: 0142 940252; E. F.
Super-smart estate, perched high at over 450m, near the Sanctuary of Crea, with vineyards stretching down from the estate buildings. Cellars partly ancient (estate originally 17th-century) partly bang up to date. Carefully honed, modern wines. No need to book. Elegant agritourism available.

Ermenegildo Leporati
Casale Monferrato
Tel: 0142 55616. E. F.
Non-traditionalist estate housed in a very old villa with vineyards around. Wide range of wines includes whites made from each of Barbera and Grignolino. Working hours only. Can recommend hotels and agritourisms.

ENOTECHE

Enoteca Regionale del Monferrato
Vignale
See main text.

Bottega del Grignolino
Portacomaro
Good range of Grignolino and Ruché but open only for a few hours weekends and holidays.

EATING OUT

Da Rita
Scurzolengo, Via Marconi 19
Tel: 0141 203284; closed Weds.
Friendly, cheerful, popular place. Simple, tasty, sustaining food. Rough and ready but eminently drinkable local wines. Cash only, not expensive, good value.

La Braja
Montemagno, Via San Giovanni Bosco
Tel: 0141 63107; closed Mon, Tues.
Smart restaurant with good service.
Dishes mix tradition and new ideas,
all prepared with great care. Serious
wine list, mainly Piedmontese. Air
conditioning, seats outside.
Mid-priced, good value.

Ametista
Moncalvo, Piazza Antico Castello 14
Tel: 0141 917423; closed Weds.
Small, neat, comfortable restaurant.
Range includes fish dishes. Large,
broad-based wine list, regional, Italian
and foreign. Seats outside. Inexpensive.

Il Giardinetto
Grazzano Badoglio, Via Dante 16
Tel: 0141 925114; closed Sun.
Restaurant with appetizing, unusual
dishes and good wine list. A little
pricey. Evenings only.

Gabriella Trisoglio La Pomera
Vignale Monferrato, Ca' Ravino 4,
San Lorenzo
Tel: 0142 933378
Agritouristic estate serving substantial,
tasty meals, with home grown
vegetables, home made bread and
mouthwatering desserts. Well
chosen local wines. Cash only.

Serenella
Vignale Monferrato, Piazza del
Popolo 1
Tel: 0142 923100; closed Mon.
Homely *trattoria* (and bar) in central
piazza, serving strictly local food
in hunger-abating portions. Strictly
local wines too, fair selection.

Castello di San Giorgio
San Giorgio Monferrato, Via Cavalli
d'Olivola 3
Tel: 0142 806203; closed Mon.
Castle with elegant dining area, and
superb views. Unhurried atmosphere
and attentive service. Refined food
based on classic dishes. Mainly
regional wine list. Rather costly.

Hostaria dal Paluc
Mombello Monferrato,
Fraz Zenevreto, Via San Grato 3
Tel: 0142 94412; closed Mon, Tues.
Interesting, tasty dishes, plentiful use
of vegetables. Tasting menu. Broadly
based wine list including half bottles.
Not costly.

After Vignale, take the road to Camagna, with its neat, rectangular vineyard plots. At the next junction with a cluster of signposts on a wall on the right, turn left to Bonina. Turn left at the Stop sign (direction Alessandria) and then right at the next crossroads to Frassinello. On clear days you should begin to see the mountains of the north from here and the soft, gentle landscapes of these parts are regarded by many as the true Monferrato countryside. The next point on the tour is Rosignano Monferrato, involving a right turn at the T-junction, followed quickly by another right, then a straight stretch before forking right at the Casale/Rosignano junction. Pass the Cantina Sociale del Monferrato and shortly after plunge down into a valley before climbing back up towards Rosignano, a good area for Grignolino, as is nearby Sala and much of the surrounding territory. Then head towards Treville. At the fork offering a choice between Sala and San Giorgio take the former. The road passes along a high ridge and skirts Ozzano. There is no need to divert off this road to go into Treville – but the views are so good it is too irresistible not to. On returning to Ozzano, continue down to the plain and the Casale-Asti *statale*, there turning left towards Asti.

Follow the *statale* west for a while, passing the turn-offs for Serralunga di Crea and Mombello. The flat road, along the valley of the *torrente* Stura, is not itself that exciting but gives an excellent idea of the form of the terrain, with views up onto the variously cultivated, serene, muted landforms. Turn off (right) towards Gabiano, cutting across roughly northwest to meet the Po Valley and coming into the small, overlapping wine zones of Gabiano and Rubino di Cantavenna, both making predominantly Barbera-based wines and neither of any real importance. Gabiano is far better known for its massive castle, situated on a high spur, overlooking the Po. The vast distances that can be seen from its carefully positioned bulk over the broad plain north of the Po make its strategic importance obvious. The castle is also in remarkably fine condition and able to accommodate the most important of dignitaries.

Right *Monferrato vineyard
in spring, well in need of some
serious tidying up.*

Left *Just some of the bottles in the Enoetca Regionale di Vignale Monferrato.*

Tre Merli

Morano sul Po, Loc Due Sture, Via Alighieri 18
Tel: 0142 85275; closed Weds.
Long-standing *trattoria*, just north of the Po with dishes based mainly on freshwater fish from the Stura River and local rice dishes. Short list of well-chosen wines. Cash only.
Plus at **Grana** there is a very simple, inexpensive place with, as speciality, the local *agnolotti d'asino*. To find it, just follow your nose.

HOTELS

Ariotto

Terruggia, Via Prato 39
Tel: 0142 801200; fax: 0142 801307.
In art nouveau-style villa. Few rooms, large, traditionally furnished. Large gardens. Not too costly.

AGRITOURISM

Cascina Alberta

Vignale Monferrato, Ca' Prano 14
Tel: 0142 933313.
Simply furnished rooms, home produced wine and, in evening, good, fresh food, strong on organic vegetables. Produce for sale.

Il Mongetto Dré Casté

Vignale Monferrato, Via Piave 2
Tel: 0142 933442.
18th-century villa with attractive, traditionally furnished rooms. Good meals served; weekends only. Wine produced, with cellars under villa. Also bottled foodstuffs.

PLACES OF INTEREST

Antica Distilleria di Altavilla

Loc Cittadella 1; F.
Well-known, 150-year old distillery making *grappe* for many producers in the area. Visits generally possible without booking.

EVENTS

Grignolino Festival Vignale: May.
Dance Festival Vignale: summer months.
Grape Festival Casale: Sep.

The final stage of the tour leads back east towards Pontestura. It provides more eye-catching sights as the road straddles the top of the scarp slope over the River Po, giving wide vistas over the Po Valley and good prospects of the town of Vercelli. Vercelli is, in fact, the next port of call, marking the beginning of the route through northern Piedmont. You could take the most direct road to the town, descending rapidly from the ridge at Cornale and crossing the Po to Trino, from where Vercelli is a scant 15 minutes away. An alternative route would be to take a more gentle descent to valley level and cross the river just past Pontestura, meeting the direct road to Vercelli just north of the town of Trino.

However, unless in a hurry it is better to contine past Pontestura to Casale Monferrato, the town that gave its name to the Monferrato Casalese (and from where there's a fast road north to Vercelli). The outskirts and modern parts of Casale are none too captivating but the old town is quite different. There are Gothic, Romanesque, Renaissance and Baroque buildings aplenty, numerous churches and grand houses, a maze of colonnaded streets and an important museum of Judaeism – making a stop-off there well worth while.

Northern Piedmont

The wines of Northern Piedmont are almost entirely Nebbiolo based and, with the exception of Gattinara, are renowned more for the paucity of production than anything else. Usually, they are grouped together under the umbrella heading of 'wines of the Novara-Vercelli hills', the hills being the lowest of the Alpine foothills as they start to rise out of the flat Po Valley.

Unlike those from the Langhe and Roero, these northern wines are rarely made exclusively from Nebbiolo (usually called Spanna here): the mix usually includes the local varieties Vespolina and Bonarda. The latter, officially Bonarda Novarese, is also known as Uva Rara. Confusingly, it is a different variety from Oltrepò Pavese's Bonarda.

The wines of Novara province, the obscure Sizzano and Boca, and the marginally less obscure Fara and Ghemme follow these first slopes alongside the east bank of the River Sesia, which rises in the Alps on Monte Rosa and flows down, past the town of Vercelli to the Po, dividing the two provinces as it goes. There is also a denomination, Colline Novaresi, which covers all the wine produced between this stretch of the river and the more easterly River Ticino. There may be single varietal Spanna (Nebbiolo), Vespolina, Uva Rara (Bonarda Novarese), Croatina (the other Bonarda) or Barbera produced. (You need a very clear head when thinking about these varieties!) Otherwise producers may opt to blend Nebbiolo with one or more of these other grapes, Barbera excepted, or make a white from Erbaluce.

Across the Sesia, in Vercelli province, the hills rise north of a line west from the river towards Biella. The leading wine is Gattinara DOCG, which, after a long time in the doldrums, is trying to regain its quality status. Bramaterra and Lessona are Vercelli's famous ghosts. Here too, however, there is an attempt to rationalize the scattered production of the district in a new DOC, Coste della Sesia.

Left *Viticulture in Northern Piedmont has a rich heritage and dates right back to Roman times.*

Above *An ancient wine press – quite a contrast to those used by producers nowadays.*

Novara-Vercelli hills

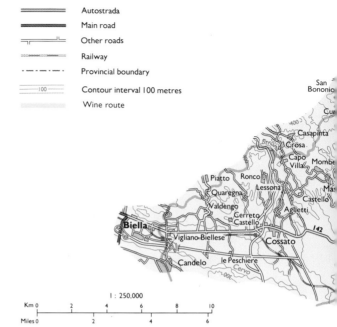

═══════	Autostrada
▬▬▬▬	Main road
╤╤╤	Other roads
▓▓▓	Railway
·—·—·—·	Provincial boundary
═══100═══	Contour interval 100 metres
▓▓▓▓▓	Wine route

San Bononio

Cur

400

Casapinta

Crosa

Capo Villa   Mombe

Piatto Ronco   Mas

Quaregna Lessona Castello

Valdengo   Aglietti

Cerreto Castello

Biella   142

Vigliano-Biellese   **Cossato**

Candelo   le Peschiere   Cervo

1 : 250,000

Km 0   2   4   6   8   10

Miles 0   2   4   6

The towns of Vercelli and Novara

VERCELLI

Vercelli, in the middle of the Po Valley flatlands, is the centre of Italian rice production and all approach roads will take you through the well organized system of ditches and canals that split up the vast expanses of paddy field. As a town whose economy is based on this major, multinational, agricultural industry and which controls Europe's most important rice market, Vercelli appears surprisingly run down. Only the small, old centre offers any relief from the drab, care-worn streets. The main draw is the wondrous, vividly coloured, 13th-century Basilica of San Andrea, one of Italy's foremost Gothic buildings. There is also an adjacent abbey, plus numerous churches and medieval towers and a tight net of narrow streets.

NOVARA

Novara is barely 20 minutes from Vercelli (east across the Po Valley) and is larger, livelier and more affluent in appearance. The old centre is enclosed in an uplifted ring of roads, following the old ramparts of its castle. From the large, central, pedestrianized square, the gathering spot for Novaresi at leisure, it is but a sneeze to the elegant, colonnaded main

Above *Nebbiolo vines (locally referred to as Spanna) in Ghemme. In Northern Piedmont it is usual to blend in small quantities of other grape varieties, principally Vespolina and Bonarda.*

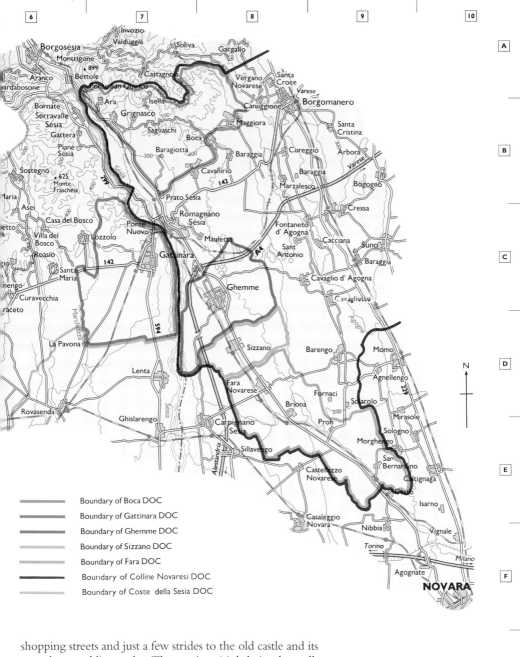

Boundary of Boca DOC
Boundary of Gattinara DOC
Boundary of Ghemme DOC
Boundary of Sizzano DOC
Boundary of Fara DOC
Boundary of Colline Novaresi DOC
Boundary of Coste della Sesia DOC

shopping streets and just a few strides to the old castle and its attendant public park. The major 'sight' is the tall, spectacular Basilica of San Gaudenzio, the emblem of the town, and visible in snatches from a few of the surrounding roads. Sadly, the density of building in the old centre has rather boxed it in, preventing any really good close-up views. The same fate has befallen the large, arresting Duomo. But there are numerous other nooks and crannies sheltering medieval buildings and one or two really pretty, tiny little piazzas, so a good stroll will pay off.

Novara is also an excellent spot to break from wine touring for a short while and spend a few hours or days along the peaceful shores of Lake Maggiore, a scant half hour northwards, while anyone flying to or from Milan's second airport, Malpensa, will find it an ideal pre- or post-flight base.

NORTHERN PIEDMONT

RECOMMENDED PRODUCERS

Bianchi
Sizzano
Tel: 0321 320155; E. F.
Organic production. Cellars and
centre of operations in Sizzano.
Visits working hours only.
Antichi Vigneti di Cantalupo
Ghemme
Tel: 0163 840041; E. F.

Below *Ripe bunch of Nebbiolo
grapes soon to be harvested.*
Bottom *Chickens enjoying the
space to roam under a high-trained
vineyard in Gattinara.*

THE NOVARA HILLS

The road from Novara towards Varallo is barely five
kilometres from the town when, just past Cesto, you officially
enter the zone of Fara. This seems surprising as Cesto is still
right in the middle of rice fields. It is, in fact, one of those
bureaucratic niceties that allows Fara to be produced
anywhere in the communes of Briona and Fara, although
what little there is doesn't appear for a further five kilometres
or so, on the very first, low rises on the right, just before
Briona castle. In the short distance between Briona and Fara
villages there are a number of small, vine-covered hillocks,
plus the occasional patch of old, poorly kempt vineyard. All
in all it doesn't amount to much and within seconds you are
through Fara and have passed into the zone of Sizzano, the
next village along. The pattern is the same: small clumps of
vineyard of various qualities; all on the right facing the road.
In the blinking of an eye you have passed Sizzano and moved
into the zone of Ghemme, once more taking its name from
the next village along the road. It is easy to imagine that the
vines, which go right to the crest of these baby slopes, also go
over and down the other side. But they don't. They cling
purely to the better exposed, southwest facing rises. By
Ghemme, though, the hills are beginning to get higher.

Soils, like most in the Novara and Vercelli wine zones,
are formed from the moraine of what was once the glacier
of Monte Rosa and the climate, similarly typical of the
area, is influenced by cool Alpine air, the warm humidity
of the Po Valley and tempering currents from the nearby
lakes, giving the zone rapid temperature changes.

Left *Washing day in Northern Piedmont.*

The sole serious flag-wavers for Ghemme, with about 20ha of all Ghemme vineyard. Large range of wines led, not surprisingly, by Ghemme; *normale, crus* Collis Carellae and the leading Collis Breclemae, and selection Signore di Bayard. Visits working hours only.
Antoniolo
Gattinara
Tel: 0163 833612; E. F.
Forward looking estate keen, unlike most, to demonstrate the appeal of Nebbiolo when comparatively youthful. Work exclusively with Nebbiolo.
Travaglini
Gattinara
Tel: 0163 833588; E. F.
Quality-conscious estate, traditionally orientated; elegance and longevity the main aims. Two Gattinaras plus a younger Nebbiolo. Must book but tastings not offered.
Luigi Perazzi
Roasio (Bramaterra)
Tel: 0163 860034
Careful traditionalist aiming for slow-maturing wines. Apart from Bramaterra makes *barrique*-aged equivalent, La Sassaia.
Sella
Lessona
Tel: 015 99455
Leading producer of Lessona and Bramaterra who, after many years stuck in a progress-free rut, has now renovated both cellars and ideas with encouraging results.

ENOTECHE

Tutto Doc
Vercelli, Via Crispi 3
Surprising range of new world wines as well as Italian tasting area. Also distillates and a few foody bits.
Enoteca Regionale della Serra
Roppolo, Castello di Roppolo
Tel: 0161 98501
For a last look at the full panorama of Piedmontese wine production before leaving the region for Aosta. Best to check it is open first, though.
Angolo di Vino
Borgomanero, Via Rosmini 9
And for a last glass of one of Piedmont's gems, if leaving in the other direction, towards the lakes.

FOOD SPECIALITIES

Rice From the paddy fields of the Po Valley, especially around Vercelli.

Follow the main road around the village (direction Varallo) for the best views (without off-roading) of what few vineyards there are. As the road joins up again with the one that went straight through the town, you cross out of the zone of Ghemme, although you can still see some Ghemme vineyards across to the right. This is the most northern part of the zone. Continue for five minutes or so through Romagnano Sesia, where the road meets the River Sesia, to Prato Sesia, which marks the beginning of the Boca zone. This wine zone is a little more extensive; it stretches back further from the road and is by far the most scenically exciting of the Novara denominations.

At Prato Sesia, right turn towards Boca to take a large loop through the wine area. At first the road follows the zonal border and although you catch glimpses of scraps of vineyard, most of the area initially is thickly wooded, green and cool. Go through Cavallirio and Boca itself, from there following signs to Grignasco. Shortly past Boca curve round a bend and suddenly, out of nowhere, there is a sanctuary, large and tranquil, facing you. That is the first surprise. Almost immediately after, another bend brings the second. Vines suddenly sprout on all sides. Many are old, often poorly cared for or simply left uncultivated. Others are tended scrupulously. Some are on terraces, others on slopes; some widely spaced, others narrowly. There is also practically every training system known in Piedmont, from current to moribund. In barely a kilometre you can see almost the entire lexicon of Piedmontese viticulture. The road then starts descending towards Torchio and the vines become much more sparse. It continues to descend past Grignasco and rejoins the Novara–Varallo road.

Turn right onto this road and, shortly after, left across the river, signed to Serravalle Sesia. Once across, follow the road to the right and up a slight incline until reaching a set of traffic lights where you turn left (direction Vercelli) heading for Gattinara. You will probably reach this point within an hour of leaving Novara.

Panissa A dish based on rice, *fagioli* and salami.

Cheese Both Gorgonzola and Grana Padana (not dissimilar from Parmigiano) are produced locally, but Novara, the 'cheese town', is the heart of Gorgonzola production. The Sesia Valley is also noted for its cheeses, especially from goat's milk.

Bicciolani Biscuits from Vercelli; Novara also has its own biscuits, called simply *biscottini di Novara*.

EATING OUT

Il Paiolo
Vercelli, Viale Garibaldi 74
Tel: 0161 250577; closed Thurs.
Simple, local dishes, well prepared. Fair wine list.

Moroni
Novara, Via Solaroli 6
Tel: 0321 629278; closed Mon pm, Tues.
Well-known, well-run spot, with carefully chosen ingredients and sound cooking. Large wine list, Italian as well as regional. Not expensive.

Tantris
Novara, Fraz Lumellogno, Via P Lombardo 35
Tel: 0321 469153; closed Sun pm, Mon.
Outside town (towards Vercelli) but seriously good food served in refined surroundings. Huge wine list.

Belvedere
Briona, Fraz Proh, Via Marelli 3
Tel: 0321 826391; closed Fri.
Simple, good, traditional *trattoria*; drink house wine. Cash only.

Roma
Ghizlarengo, Via V Emanuele II 13
Tel: 0161 860143; closed Weds.
Mainly original dishes, mouth-wateringly tempting. Good wine list; mostly Piedmontese; northeastern Italian whites.

Impero
Sizzano, Via Roma 9
Tel: 0321 820290; closed Mon.
Relaxing place. Classic set of dishes, all tasty and satisfying. Can drink the elusive Sizzano or other Piedmontese wines. Walk through bar to reach it.

Ori Pari
Boca, Viale Partigiani 9 ·
Tel: 0322 87961; pm only, closed Tues.
Newish *trattoria* with an excellent wine list. Go just for a snack or a full meal. Daily changing menu, based on local ingredients. Cash only. .

Alla Torre
Romagnano Sesia, Via 1 Maggio 75
Tel: 0163 826411; closed Mon.
Can try several local wines by the glass – even at the bar without eating. Food fresh and flavoursome, with good local ingredients and plentiful use of vegetables and herbs. Home made pasta and desserts.

THE VERCELLI HILLS – GATTINARA

Having crossed the Sesia you are back in Vercelli province. Keep on the Vercelli road and you first pass a landmark castle, then follow the river quite closely until, within a few minutes, you start to approach Gattinara. Keep a look out through the trees up on to the slopes on the right and you will snatch a few glimpses of vineyard – but very little. Indeed, the vineyards are well hidden behind the village you can easily miss them. The easiest (although not the most direct) way to find them is first to have a glance at the village, a rather thick-set place, slightly tatty with a comfortable, well-lived in feel. Then take the road towards Biella. Turn right off the road at the second junction, where there is a sign pointing to the Travaglini estate. This side road is, encouragingly, called Via delle Vigne. At the next junction fork right, upwards, along Via Susa. Very shortly you hit a T-junction. Turn left here and you will come into the vineyard area as well as gaining some more than decent views over Gattinara village. The mesh of vineyards sweeps down from the tower you see up in front, the spot to which the locals gravitate on a Sunday afternoon or when in need of a bit of tranquility.

Follow along the one way system, along Via Monte Rosa, until the Stop sign where you turn left and follow the road upwards. It is steep and narrow, just single track (with passing places) but gives good views of the vineyards and leads right up to the tower. From this vantage point you can see a large part of the Gattinara cultivation zone. There is no option from here but to return on the same road, until reaching the 'Stop' sign, where you turn right

Left *Some of Ghemme's sparse vineyard and an old-fashioned training system. Better vineyard is just visible to the far left.* Below *Freshly harvested Nebbiolo grapes.*

and head back down to the main road. Turn right onto this and, within a few metres, there is the junction marking the beginning of the Biella road. Turn right towards Biella and follow the road past the Travaglini sign (where you turned off to start the vineyard circuit). After a couple of minutes, turn right at the sign to Orbello and Casa del Bosco. Half an hour is ample for this small stretch.

THE VERCELLI HILLS – BRAMATERRA AND LESSONA
Allow another hour for this worthwhile span of countryside. The zone of Bramaterra stretches over seven of the communes west of Gattinara. Most of the terrain is, however, quite densely wooded and the vineyards only sparsely scattered in occasional patches. Bramaterra itself, although a local geographical entity, is not a commune name and has not therefore been plotted on maps. This also means that the production zone does not have a focal point, a role rather loosely taken on by the commune centres of Roasio and Villa del Bosco.

The Orbello road rises into woodland, at first gently, then more steeply. Past Orbello, you pass the Luigi Perazzi estate on the left, one of the two keeping Bramaterra's name alive (the other is Sella). Follow the road left towards Villa del Bosco (and Sostegno), passing some rather better vineyard than most you have seen so far here. Continue towards Villa del Bosco, turning left at the next junction (not towards Sostegno). There is a fair amount of vineyard here, of varying standards and training methods before woodland takes over once more. At the next T-junction, marking the end of Villa del Bosco, turn left towards

Piane di Monolo
Roasio, Strada Statale 65/a
Tel: 0163 87232; closed Mon, Tues.
Gracefully designed restaurant; dishes lean to southern Italy. Broad ranging wine list. A little costly, fair value.

Prinz Grill
Biella, Via Torino 41
Tel: 015 30302; closed Sun.
Small, refined but not overpriced restaurant with great wine list, mainly Italian. Can visit the well kept cellars that house them. Quick turnover at lunchtime, more leisurely in the evening; traditional and fish dishes.

Bersagliere
Borgomanero, Corso Mazzini 11
Tel: 0322 82277; closed Mon.
Smart, popular restaurant with varied dishes, only some local. Well chosen wine list. Seats outside.

Trattoria del Ciclista
Borgomanero, Via Rosmini 34
Tel: 0322 81649; closed Weds.
Long-standing, popular place, bright and spacious. Strictly traditional fare; specialities of donkey- and horse-meat. Good local wine choice, includes scarce Novara DOC's. Cash only.

Pinocchio
Borgomanero, Via Matteotti 147
Tel: 0322 82273; closed Mon.
Refined, expensive and very, very good. Two differently priced tasting menus or choose from the huge menu of widely influenced dishes. Thankfully less vast wine list.

Campagna

Arona, Loc Campagna, Via Vergante 12
Tel: 0322 57294; closed Mon.
Relaxed, neatly laid out *trattoria* with
seasonally changing dishes,
flavoursome and inviting. Good
cheeses, home made desserts. Small
wine list or drink house red. Good
value.

HOTELS

Il Giardinetto

Vercelli, Via Luigi Sereno
Tel: 0161 257230; fax: 0141 259311.
Central but tranquil, with internal
garden. Converted period building,
eight rooms, traditionally furnished.
Decent restaurant.

Modo

Vercelli, Piazza Medaglie d'Oro 21
Tel: 0161 217300; fax: 0161 58325.
On southern outskirts. Modern,
with bright, spacious rooms. The
newer ones have more mod cons.

Viotti

Vercelli, Via Marsala 7
Tel: 0161 257540; fax: 0161 251834.
For those who like the ways of the
past rather than modern comforts.

Italia

Novara, Via Solaroli 10
Tel: 0321 399316; fax: 0321 399310.
Central with high standards. Good
restaurant attached (La Famiglia)
and another next door.

Croce di Malta

Novara, Via Biglieri 2/A
Tel: 0321 32032; fax: 0321 32033.
Small, bright and modern, just
outside old centre. Air conditioning.

Europa

Novara, Corso Cavallotti 38/A
Tel: 0321 35801; fax: 0321 629933.
Neat, well-furnished rooms,
sited just beyong old centre.

Michelangelo

Biella, Piazza Adua 5
Tel: 015 8492362; fax: 015 8492649.
Extremely comfortable 4*.
Plentiful breakfast.

Coggiola

Biella, Via Cottolengo 5
Tel: 015 8491912; fax: 015 8493427.
Nothing grand but neat, clean
and relaxing. Convenient parking.

Principe

Biella, Via Gramsci 4
Tel: 015 2522003; fax: 015 351669.
Close to old centre, long-standing.
Warmly comfortable rooms without
flourishes. Top floor bar (and
breakfast room) with good views.

FOOD SHOPPING

Pasticceria Costantino

Romagnano Sesia, Via dei Martiri 9
Long-standing reference point for all
the local, sweet goodies.

Roasio, then right, away from the village, at the first set of
traffic lights. Follow this road (involving a dog-leg: right at
the T-junction, left immediately after) through some quite
idyllic woodland to the next T-junction, where you turn left,
back down towards the *statale*. Just metres before reaching it,
however, turn right, back through woodland towards
Brusnengo. From here follow signs to Masserano, where
there is another large clutch of vineyard, densely planted and
well tended. Rise into the village, which offers glorious
views, then follow signs to Lessona. Within minutes you are
in the long, slim commune of Lessona itself.

Lessona has such great potential for top class wine
production that it is heartbreaking to see it so little
exploited. Sella, whose name is practically synonymous
with the zone, is in effect the sole producer. Like its neighbours, it is lighter and leaner than southern Piedmontese
Nebbiolo wines and, while still austere, rather more
elegant.

Turn right towards Lessona village. The local road
through the village goes right through the middle of the
commune to Creso, the adjacent commune to the north,
and across the *statale* to the south. To glean an overall idea
of the lie of the commune all you need do is travel along
the full length of this road. It is also worthwhile though
– having first driven through the *frazione* of Capovilla to
the northern border, turned round and returned to the
village – diverting across to the left, where the *chiesa*
(church) is signposted and then following down, passing
the *cimitero* (cemetery). You could then turn right at the
junction where *frazione* Monti is signed and fork right
again where there is a mound of vineyard on the right on
old terracing plus a commemorative stone on the road.
This takes you down into the central valley and back up
again, ready to slip back onto the main road through the
commune. You then pass the Sella estate before emerging

at the junction with the *statale*. Once you have explored the small part of Lessona south of the *statale* your tour of Lessona, of Piedmont and of northwest Italy will sadly have come to an end.

GETTING HOME

The ways of leaving northwestern Italy are as varied and enthralling as the terrrain itself. There is the choice of the *statale* to Biella (via Cossato), an important textiles and wool centre, fairly modern (apart from a small, traffic-free, old centre), prosperous and with no shortage of hotels. From Biella there is a direct but not terribly quick route west to Settimo Vittone and the Aosta Valley or a considerably longer but fast route to the same area, first south to Roppolo and Cavaglià (direction Chivasso/ Santhià) from where there is a further choice between the *statale* (right) or the *autostrada* (left) to Ivrea. Once at this southern end of the Aosta Valley, you could follow it the entire way to Courmayeur and the Mont Blanc tunnel, or branch off at Aosta to the Saint-Bernard pass.

Alternatively, there is the option from Lessona of taking the *statale* back past Gattinara and onwards to Borgomanera and Arona, to finish with some time on the calming shores of Lake Maggiore, possibly stopping off at Stresa, for example, and taking the 'must do' boat trip to the tiny Isole Borromee. Or, from Borgomanero, there's the much smaller and even more tranquil Lake Orta just a few minutes' drive away. Or maybe...

Whichever way you choose it can't fail to be a magnificent end to a marvellous trip.

Gelateria Corradini
Romagnano Sesia, Via Grassi 8
Irresistible seasonal fruit ice-creams.
Pasticceria Ferrura Biella
Traditional *pasticceria* decorated in art nouveau style. Range of local specialities. Try chocolate straws.
Il Tagliere
Borgomanero, Via Rosmini 26
The last chance to stock up on *salumi* to take home.
Salumeria Barcellini
Borgomanero, Via Arona 43
Offers some good, unusual flavours. For cheeses, wait until Arona and search out **Luigi Guffanti's** excellent shop.

SPECIAL EVENTS

Saint's day Novara
22 January. Every Italian town has its Saint's day. Novara's is distinguished by the tradition of selling strings of chestnuts from Cuneo in southwest Piedmont, Italy's best.
Rice festival Vercelli: Sept.
Wine Festival Fara: Sept.
Wine & food fair Sizzano: June.
Grape festival Gattinara: Sept.

Above left *The villa at Meina on Lake Maggiore.*
Below *Angle of the splendid gardens of the Palazzo Borromeo on Isola Bella on Lake Maggiore.*

GLOSSARY

Abbazia abbey

Acquavite spirit, distilled from grapes or other fruit

Alberello traditional training method, vines grown as individual, small, low bushes

Alimentari small, general food store

Aurelia (Via) the first main state road, the SS1, built by Mussolini, following the old Roman road along the coast from Rome to French border.

Autostrada motorway

Azienda estate

Azienda Agricola, Azienda Agraria estate making wine from own grapes

Azienda Vinicola estate making wine from bought-in grapes

Azienda Vitivinicola estate making wine from own and bought-in grapes

Bagna Cauda (or Caoda) raw vegetables dipped into a powerfully flavoured 'bath' of olive oil, garlic and anchovy, kept warm by a small spirit lamp. Typical Piedmontese winter dish

Barolo Chinato strong, aromatized drink based on Barolo

Barrique small, oak cask, mostly of 225 litres, sometimes 350 or 500, made from French oak and used either new or up to the third year of age. Not traditional, but increasingly common

Belvedere panoramic viewpoint

Bollito Misto large array of boiled meats, served with various relishes; classic dish of Piedmont and Valle d'Aosta

Bonet (or Bunet) chocolate-rich custard pudding, Piedmontese speciality

Botte (pl botti) traditional wine cask, usually of Slavonian oak, large (25hl plus) and kept for many years

Borgata hamlet

Bosco a wood

Bric or Bricco a hilltop site, from dialect word for saddle

Caffè coffee; coffee bar

Campanile bell tower

Cantina Sociale (pl cantine sociali) cooperative winemaking and/or bottling cellar

Caprino goat's milk cheese

Casale farmhouse

Castagna (pl castagne) chestnut

Castello large, imposing building; used in sense of both *château* and castle

Chiesa church

Chinato see Barolo Chinato

Classese semi-generic term for high quality sparkling wine, now being replaced by *Talento* (qv)

Colli (sing colle) hills

Colline (sing collina) small hills

Cordon spur training system: vine's trunk trained to an inverted L-shape and new growth starts from a series of spurs left on horizontal, long side of the L

Cru unofficial but frequently used term used throughout Italy for wine from a single vineyard. In the northwest, more often used for wine from a single slope

Dolciaria confectionery

Duomo dome or a domed cathedral

Enoteca/Enoteca Regionale see page 11

Fagioli white kidney beans

Farinata snack food from around Genoa; from chick pea flour, with olive, water and salt, cooked in the oven in large, flat baking dishes; sometimes flavoured (rosemary, onions etc)

Fattoria farm or estate (factory is *fabbrica*)

Festa party

Focaccia snack food, mainly from Genoa area but found widely; cross between lightly oily flat bread and pizza base; may be flat and crisper, thicker and spongier

Fortified wine strengthened by extra alcohol added during or (usually) after fermentation

Frantoio olive oil crushing and pressing plant

Fraz. abb. of Frazione 'fraction'; part of commune or parish with own name and identity

Fritto Misto not to be confused with the more common fishy version, Fritto Misto Piemontese consists of various deep fried, largish morsels, mainly meaty, some vegetable, one or two sweet. Sausage, lamb, chicken, sweetbreads, zucchini, mushrooms, peaches, almond biscuits, can be included. Traditional Piedmontese main dish

Frizzante lightly sparkling (for wine); sparkling (for water)

Fiume river

Gastronomia delicatessen also selling prepared dishes

Gassata sparkling (for water)

Gelateria ice-cream parlour

Grappa (pl grappe) spirit made from grape lees

Guyot training system, particular type of spalliera (qv)

Hectare (Ha) measurement of an area; about 2.47 acres

Hectolitre (Hl) 100 litres

Latteria shop selling milk and dairy products

Levante eastern; mainly Ligurian terminology; more normal expression is *orientale*

Liquoroso fortified (qv)

Loc. abb of Località small locality, similar to *Frazione* (qv)

Macelleria butcher's shop

Marrone (pl marroni) chestnut

Mercantino market with open stands or flea market (also known as *mercato delle pulce*)

Mercato market

Municipio town hall

Must grape juice

Nocciola (pl nocciole) hazelnut

Noce (pl noci) walnut

Normale non-Riserva wine (qv)

Panificio bread shop

Panetteria bread and bakery shop

Panna cotta crème caramel made with pure cream; classic Piedmontese dessert

Passeggiata early evening stroll, an Italian institution; more than a leg-stretch it's an important people-watching, mating and gossip-gathering occasion; each town has its own, never-changing times and routes

Passito wine made from dried or semi-dried grapes

Pasticceria pastry shop

Pecorino ewe's milk cheese

Pergola high training system, more common in steep, narrow valleys

Podere (pl poderi) small farm or plot

Ponente western; mainly Ligurian terminology; more normal expression is *occidentale*

Quintale unit of weight, equal to 100 kilos

Regione region, in the northwest sometimes meaning Località (qv)

Riserva wine, usually from a better year and/or selection of grapes, aged longer than normal; minimum ageing time controlled by wine law and differs from wine to wine; applicable to some denominations only

Rosato rosé

Salumeria shop selling salumi (qv)

Salumi cured meats; salami, prosciutto etc occasionally fish (salt cod, anchovies and the like)

Salumificio shop preparing and maybe selling salumi (qv)

Sopraelevata long, fast overpass cutting through central Genoa

Sori south-facing vineyard (Piedmontese dialect)

Spalliera training system; vine's trunk kept short, from which one or two canes trained horizontally to provide the fruiting shoots of the next year's growth. One of those shoots then becomes the following year's cane

Spumante sparkling (for wine)

Statale state road, its number prefaced by SS for *strada statale* (eg SS26) and indicated by blue road signs

Stoccafisso dried cod, speciality of Liguria; salt cod is *baccàla*

Strada Provinciale road maintained by the province rather than the state; numbering system depends on province

Superstrada fast, toll-free, dual carriageway road

Tajarin tiny tagliatelle, made with very thin egg pasta (sometimes yolk, sometimes entire egg); Piedmontese speciality

Talento newish, semi-generic term for high quality sparkling wine, replacing the little-used *Classese* (qv)

Terme spa

Terroir French term adopted throughout the winemaking world; the combination of soil, microclimate and other natural factors that give the wines of any distinct location their particular individual characteristics

Torrente stream, subject to large rushes of water when in spate

Vintage harvest; the year a wine is made

Vivace alternative term for frizzante (qv) (for wine)

INDEX

149

GAZETTEER

ACKNOWLEDGEMENTS

Producing a book is not only impossible without the aid of experts on the ground and friendly help along the way, it remains lifeless. Those who gave time and effort to help this tome along not only provided invaluable assistance but were the personalities around which all others impressions flowed. As such their contributions have helped lift and shape the pages as much as anyone's and I could do no less than publicly and permanently acknowledge them here.

First and foremost there is **Chris** -"shall we just run through that again"-**tine** whose determination to beat received wisdom and find an even better, prettier and more winey route through was even stronger than mine, and who kept gloom at bay; **Elio Archimede**, without whom quite simply there would have been no tour and **Chiara Castino** without whom there would have been all sorts of gaps – I hope they appreciate just how significant were their contributions – and the manner in which they made them; **The Villano of Vigliano**, with his infinity of good nature, attentiveness, patience and restraint and **Sonia Beretta**, a magnificent foil; **Paola Corrado De Ferrari**, who let me discover the true Genoa – and the true Genoese; **Maria-Giulia e Giovannella Fugazza**, for the friendliest of hospitality and invaluable advice on the Oltrepò; **Delfina Quattrocolo**, wonderfully hospitable and kindly; **Mario from Asti**, another expert in the art of relaxed hospitality; **Luigi Ferrando**, for taking the cover off Carema and the Canavese; **Gianni Cacciabue**, who survived my onslaught to put Alessandria into perspective; **Anna del Conte** – for superfino rice advice; **Mauro Feola**, so willing, so amenable, yet beaten by the clock; **Roberto Bava**, regional delegate, Movimento del Turismo del Vino, a galvanising force; **Guido Zublena**, for a memorable morning; **Renato** – is there any tome on Italy that hasn't benefited from his imput? **Ann and Roberto from Alitalia**, for easing the ways to and fro; **Liz**, a life-line at the end of the phone; **Mum**, who dropped everything to help out on one unforgettable day; **All the Gamberi and Arcigolosi** who, unknowingly pointed me in the right directions for good food and places to eat it; **Lucy**, an invaluable, calming influence; and finally **Christine**, the essential aid. The agency has been informed.

PICTURE CREDITS

Front Jacket: Cephas/Mick Rock
Back Jacket: Scope/Jacques Guillard
Maureen Ashley 24, 33, 36, 37, 39 bottom, 55, 88, 92, 95 top right, 99 top, 103 bottom, 108, 119, 121, 130, 131, 135, 137 top right. **Anthony Blake Photo Library** 84, /**Maureen Ashley** 86, /**John Sims** 78 /79, 80, 140 top, 143 top right. **Cephas Picture Library** /**Franck Auberson** 109 bottom, /**Andy Christodolo** 18 /19 top, 28, /**John Heinrich** 101 right, 104, 105, /**TOP/Pierre Hussenot** 20 /21 bottom, /**Mick Rock** 5 top, 5 top centre, 8 /9, 10 /11, 14 /15, 16 /17 top, 22 /23 top, 27 top, 29, 45 right, 46 /47, 57 left, 58 /59, 60 right, 62, 64, 65, 68 right, 69, 71, 74, 75, 77, 89, 90 /91, 102 /103, 106 /107 bottom, 109 top, 112, 114 /115, 118, 120, 122, 123 top, 124, 126 /127, 129, 132 /133, 134, 136 /137, 140 bottom, /**StockFood** 20 /21 top, 22 bottom, /**Wine Magazine** 52 right. **Patrick Eagar** 85 bottom, 87. **Armin Faber** 76 left. **Robert Harding Picture Library** /**Jan Baldwin** 97, /**Duncan Maxwell** 40, 41 left, 42 /43, /**Mike Newton** 5 bottom, 16 bottom, 45 left, 67 top right. **Mitchell Beazley** /**Alan Williams** 26 /27, 50 /51 top, 66 /67 top, 76 right, 100 /101, 110 /111, 142 /143 top. **Scope /Jean Charles Gesquiere** 98, /**Michel Gotin** 30, 31, 34, 39 top, /**Jacques Guillard** 3, 6, 7, 12/13, 18 /19 bottom, 32, 41 right, 44 /45, 49, 50 top left, 67 bottom, 68 left, 70, 72, 94 /95, 99 bottom, 103 right, 106 top, 111, 141, 144, 145, /**Sara Matthews** 5 bottom centre, 9 top centre, 21 bottom right, 47 right, 52 left, 53, 56, 57 right, 60 left, 61, 73, 93, 123 bottom, 125, 128. **Alan Williams** 81, 82, 85 top, 116 /117, 138.